THE PRIVATE WORLD
OF HIGH SOCIETY

THE PRIVATE WORLD
OF HIGH SOCIETY

By Lucy Kavaler

DAVID McKAY COMPANY, INC.
NEW YORK

For Arthur

Acknowledgments

I SHOULD like to thank all those who have helped me in doing the research for this book. Prominent among them are the many society men and women and debutantes who spoke openly with me. I also wish to express my gratitude to the members of invitations committees for debutante balls and subdebutante parties, private school principals and teachers, social secretaries, press agents, charity organization officials, and social and country-club officers who furnished me with much of the information I needed. Acknowledgment should be made of the fine cooperation accorded me by the officials of the Association of Junior Leagues of America. Geri Major, associate editor of *Ebony* magazine, was of great assistance in compiling the material for the chapter on Negro society. I must give a word of thanks to Robert R. Endicott and Lawrence C. Goldsmith of the New York *Herald Tribune,* who started me off on the debutante trail. I should like to tell my parents how much their encouragement has meant to me. And above all, I want to thank my husband who came through for me every time I needed help most.

Contents

Introduction

SOCIETY is having a revival. In cities, small towns, and suburbs all over the country Americans are returning to a class system that seemed doomed a generation ago. They are following all the traditions developed by the Old Guard of an earlier era.

But there is a difference. The top rung of the social ladder is now the goal of the many rather than the few. Social position can be earned, whereas, formerly, it could be achieved only by birth.

That is why the old-line families are claiming that "Society is dead." And they may be right when they think of society as their grandmothers knew it. But a new society is springing up that bears the closest resemblance to the old.

It is bigger; many newcomers have reached the heights. But they have not killed society, even in its original sense. The prestige of the old inner circle has never been higher. Acceptance by this Old Guard is the criterion by which newcomers gauge their success.

Almost all the recent arrivals in the world of high society are rich. But they are not satisfied with wealth in itself. In the prosperity that followed World War II many Americans began to earn large incomes. The result is that the possession of money no longer guarantees prestige. And so a position in society has become a status goal.

The comeback of society is, of course, a side reaction to the comeback of money. But why? At a casual glance it might seem that traditional society is an anachronism in this era of space satellites, jet planes, and universal education. However, careful study reveals that there has never been a time more perfectly suited to the renascence.

This is not the heyday of the individual. Conformity is the dominant emotion of the age. Many people want the sense of security gained by belonging to an established group. High society insists upon adherence to a set of rules and rituals. A way of life is evolved that differentiates this class from all others. Members are active in prestige charities. They belong to the top-ranking social and athletic clubs. The children are sent to the "right" schools. They also attend the correct dancing classes and subdebutante parties. Then the girls are presented at a recognized debutante ball or have a debut party arranged to meet exact specifications. The style of life in terms of address, home, dress, vacation, and use of leisure must fit within the given standards. The social leaders are in the happy position of being viewed as individuals, without running the slightest risk of being considered "different."

A renewed emphasis on social standing is a seldom-recognized effect of the rise of the large organization. For one thing, acceptance by society improves a man's chances for success within a corporation. Even more important is the fact that organization life deprives a man of a feeling of individual importance. Today, the executives of the leading industrial concerns have no separate identities. Inventions are known by the name of the manufacturing companies, not by the name of the inventor. To compensate, men look for satisfactions outside of business. They want the recognition of the community. Far from scorning their wives' efforts to rise socially, husbands second them energetically.

The revival of society parallels the rise of the suburbs. This is not mere coincidence. The pattern of suburban living encourages the development of traditional society. There is a popular misconception that the suburb is just one big happy family and that class lines are forgotten there. This view stems from early studies of suburbia made shortly after World War II. It was no doubt true at that time, but it is now out of date. Sociologists observe that stratification appears after the first few years.

The country club—and practically every suburb has one—provides a nucleus around which the top social group is formed. Its membership gives a ready-made list of the local elite, to be used by service leagues, community charities, dancing classes for children, debutante cotillions, and subscription dances for grownups. The country clubs resemble the inner circle's city clubs in many ways. Admittance depends upon recommendations from members, manners and personal appearance, background, and style of living.

The growth of the suburbs has brought about a change in the position of women that is of great significance to the rebirth of society. The typical suburban wife today is a homemaker, not a career woman. She has to be. Most communities are located far from the city where the best job opportunities exist. The shortage of competent help ties the mother to the household. Her home and children and her position in the community become her major interests. She makes every effort to advance her family socially. And so, naturally, she is interested in the development of a local high society. She can become a member of it herself—with the right kind of husband behind her. Her daughter can become a debutante.

The population shift to the suburbs has brought about a change in urban areas as well. Most cities now are left to the very rich and the very poor. This encourages a return to the old-time class structure, with an inner circle group on top.

In addition to these major factors, a number of lesser influences combine in producing a social climate favorable to the development of high society.

Literature both reflects and encourages such interest. The works of F. Scott Fitzgerald have been revived and read by large numbers of Americans. And although much has been said about Fitzgerald's fascination with the "different" world of the rich, it was not money alone that he exalted. It was rather the inborn sense of superiority known by those who are accepted as society. The novels of John O'Hara and the late John P. Marquand have made the best-seller lists time after time. The key characters in these books are either members of the upper crust or are doing their best to achieve that rank. The memoirs of society women have also been particularly popular during the last ten years.

Advertising's siren song has been heard by Americans in all walks of life. The advertisements play upon the longing for status. Schweppes' bearded Commander Whitehead and the monocled gentleman in the Hathaway shirt are stock society figures. They sell the product and the society way of life, too. The campaign for the

Rolls-Royce stresses the social advantages of owning the car. And even products that could not, by the wildest stretch of the imagination, be called fashionable are displayed with background scenes that connote wealth and social position.

The public relations industry discovered society, and has shared its findings with the world. Millions who have never tasted caviar follow the doings of society matrons down to the ordering of the guinea hen, selection of the Balenciaga gown, and vacation at Hobe Sound. Mass-circulation newspapers run society columns. Society news is no longer limited to that page. Press agents have succeeded in getting it into almost any section of the newspapers, into magazines, and on radio and television as well. The "number-one" debutante has become a national symbol of glamour, causing parents to wonder why their own Nancy or Sally should not have a chance, too. The blaze of publicity that surrounds the careers of those who have risen out of comparative obscurity to dazzling social position makes others feel that they could do it, too.

In the last few years there has been a growing awareness of the comeback of society. In city and suburb alike the expansion or development of a top social group has been observed. Members of the inner circle view high society as their own private world, and keep information about it to themselves. As a result, very little is generally known about what goes on beneath the surface. Social historians have concentrated on the *why* of the social revival, rather than the *what* and the *how*. In this book I shall try to fill this gap for the many Americans whose lives are being touched in some way by the changing social structure. My aim is to provide a complete picture of high society today—its ways and its workings.

THE PRIVATE WORLD
OF HIGH SOCIETY

CHAPTER I

What Has Happened to the Social Register?

MY first brush with the *Social Register* took place when I was five years old. My mother took me marketing with her, and in the butcher shop I became fascinated by an eccentric, imperious old lady who was selecting a steak. She made the butcher bring out one piece of meat after another until she found one that looked tender enough to suit her.

"It's not for me, it's for my dog," she explained haughtily to the waiting women in the shop who were beginning to be impatient.

"That dog's going to make the *Social Register* yet!" the butcher declared to an appreciative audience when she had left.

For some time after that, I believed that the *Register* was an exclusive listing of dogs—and it came as quite a shock to me when I discovered the truth.

I was reminded of that incident for the first time in years when I was told one of society's legendary stories about the Massachusetts family that had gotten its Pekingese, Rose, listed in the *Register*. The dog's name had been slipped in along with the children.

Most people assumed that the family involved had planned this as a practical joke, but remembering my odd, old lady of the past, I sometimes wondered.

Whatever the motives in that particular case, I have found very few people prepared to laugh at the *Social Register*. In today's social climate, it has come to occupy a unique position.

I was struck by this one afternoon when I was walking down New York's Fifth Avenue and noticed heads turning to watch a small, thin woman in a flawlessly tailored gray Chanel suit. Her face has been familiar to newspaper readers for twenty-five years.

"I always walk on Fifth Avenue in my lunch hour," a young girl just in front of me said to her companion. "I like to watch society people go by."

"Why, *she* isn't society—not real society," her escort replied superciliously.

"Well, then, who is?"

"Real society is made up of the people in the *Social Register*" was the glib answer.

Now I know that this response would be viewed as naïve by members of the inner circle who never tire of telling me that the *Social Register* stands for nothing at all.

"It's just a glorified telephone directory" is the right thing to say about it in that set.

And yet the *Social Register* simply cannot be ignored. It is the only listing of America's first families. And this is a country where people like to see things in black and white. Witness the continuing interest in *Who's Who, Celebrity Register,* Ten Best-Dressed Women, Ten Richest Men, and so forth. In this atmosphere, the *Register* offers documentary evidence of arrival in society.

It serves as the chief reference book for invitations committees of major balls, for social secretaries planning high society parties, charity organizations arranging benefits, mothers of debutantes making up debut party lists, society-page editors deciding how much space to give an engagement or wedding announcement, dancing-class teachers, and even many private schools. And though they try to dismiss the *Register,* those in the Old Guard rely on it, too.

When I was first planning this book, I went to call on a well-known society matron who lives on Park Avenue in the Seventies. I happened to ask her if she knew a woman whose name often appears on the society pages of the newspapers.

"No," she replied, looking faintly troubled. It is the thing for inner circle members to maintain that they all know one another.

Although she had spent some time assuring me of the unimportance of the *Register,* she picked up the current edition—by chance, it was lying on the coffee table—and leafed through it.

"Well, you see, that woman isn't even in the *Register!*" she exclaimed triumphantly.

Observing the faint smile I was trying to hide, the socialite added: "Being in the *Register* doesn't count for anything. But being left out can be disastrous."

Despite my smile, I understood what this woman was trying to convey. The *Social Register* is too big. New York's edition contains more than 30,000 names, Boston's over 8,000, and Chicago's tops 3,000. This is a drastic change from the 881 names selected for the first New York *Register* in 1887. And many in the set dominated by Mrs. William Astor, the social arbiter of the day, considered that too big. In fact, just five years later, Mrs. Astor and socially prominent Ward McAllister made up what they considered a real society list of four hundred.

The idea of a small elite group is old, but it is by no means out-of-date. New York society members concede that the original circle has expanded through marriages and births to say 1,600 . . . but certainly not to 30,000.

It is clear that many newcomers have worked their way into the *Register.* I know some of them myself—and they have told me how they did it. Their stories are a basic part of this book.

But the very fact that these people are in the *Register* and are accepted by all, except two or three thousand individuals in the entire country, as members of high society is an indication of something that has happened to the social world. In the years since the end of World War II, more Americans than ever before have been engaged in a struggle for status. Society is having a revival. A social system that seemed out-of-date a generation ago is in style again. The rigid code of traditional society is followed by thousands—and thousands more would follow it if they could.

Many an average American believes that he—or at any rate, his children—will someday join the Astors and Rockefellers on the receiving line at the debutante cotillion. And that is not just a Walter Mitty dream of glory. A large number of people are actively working toward that goal.

Several years ago as a reporter, I attended an important business meeting of a major industrial concern. Matters of policy were being discussed heatedly. Tempers flared, as opposing views were presented. All at once one of the executives was called to the telephone. Although he had been heading one of the most vocal factions, he did not return to the meeting at all. Was it a sudden emergency on the production line, I wondered, or news of serious illness at home?

Some time later, I ran into his wife and learned what had happened to him on that fateful day. The couple, not yet accepted in the world of society, had been trying to get their daughter into one of the prestige private schools. A personal interview with the headmistress had been scheduled for that morning. Unsure of herself, it had occurred to the wife that the charming manner that had helped her husband to win a high position in industry was needed to give the final push. And so she had called him out of conference. The husband had balked, claiming that his presence was badly needed at the meeting.

"It's not as important as this!" she had told him.

"And I was right," she added softly, as she finished telling the story. "Allison did get into that school, and she's going to make her debut next year."

The base of society has broadened to the point where it alarms those who see in it the dissolution of a gracious way of life.

I had long wondered why one of New York's most experienced society editors devotes so much space to descriptions of social history. One of his friends volunteered an explanation:

"He writes about the past because he can't stand to see what society has become."

In the days he likes to remember, when society was in flower—some seventy years ago—it was made up of an inner circle of a few hundred people and outer circles of several hundred more. If life was more gracious then, I think it was so for only a few. Today thousands of Americans are accepted members of the inner circle, and thousands more are on the outskirts, eager to make their way in.

There are several levels of high society. One of these is closed to newcomers. To be perfectly accurate, I would have to amend this to "almost closed" All of the others are possible for outsiders to enter.

Who is at the top of the top level, the group that is in, but considers itself above the *Social Register?*

"This inner-inner circle of society was formed generations ago," a man who bears one of New York's oldest names explained to me. "A real social register would have to be compiled from the membership lists of the hereditary organizations."

These include such national and international groups as the Order of the Founders and Patriots of America, Society of Mayflower Descendants, Sons and Daughters of the American Revolution, Sons of the Cincinnati, Daughters of the Cincinnati, National Society of Colonial Dames, Sons and Daughters of Colonial Wars, Sons and Daughters of 1812, St. Nicholas Society, Children of the Confederacy, Magna Charta Dames, Huguenot Society of America, Descendants of Knights of the Garter and Lords of the Manor.

All of these have the most rigorous membership requirements, my informant continued. The Order of the Founders and Patriots of America, for example, is composed of direct male descendants of those settlers of the United States who came here during the first fifty years after the Jamestown colony was founded in 1607. Membership in the Sons of the Cincinnati is limited to direct descendants of Continental Army officers in the American Revolution. The St. Nicholas Society is composed of those who can trace a New York heritage back to 1800 or earlier.

There are also city clubs that base membership on inheritance rather than financial or professional achievement. Prominent among these are Charleston's Society of St. Cecilia, New Orleans' Mystick Krewe of Comus, Atlanta's Piedmont Driving Club, and Houston's Eagle Lake Club.

Those who belong to this Old Guard try to keep themselves apart. They entertain one another or attend private subscription dances from which all outsiders are barred.

One Philadelphian returned to that city after an absence of thirty years and went to a subscription dance. She looked around the floor and exclaimed in satisfaction: "Why, it hasn't changed at all! The people are just the same, and look the same—except that they've gone a bit gray."

The committee of patronesses for one of New York's most exclusive subscription dances has not changed in the last ten years. The membership has been virtually frozen for much longer than that.

"How can anyone break into that level of society?" my friend concluded. "Its members have been born to it. A name cannot be artificially aged. Like old wine, it must mellow. If Grandfather was a grocer or a railroad conductor, no amount of effort will transform him into a Biddle or a Van Beuren."

The logic seems indisputable. And yet close investigation of the inner circle and its hereditary organizations reveals a small but significant number of exceptions.

"There is a crack in the wall around the inner circle. It leaves just enough room for a man with valuable business connections to slip through," says a lawyer, who has done just that.

There is a group of impoverished aristocrats within the inner circle. Those in it are most popular, as they provide living proof of the adage: Money does not count in society; only family background is important. But these well-born individuals cannot live on name alone. They must find jobs, and keep those who hire them happy. And so it sometimes comes to pass that the employers are taken into the social group of the employees. These employers, of course, must have the manners to "pass" as society. Otherwise, they remain outsiders—cowboys in Indian country.

Even the hereditary organizations are not always as hereditary as all that. Last year, for example, I met an influential businessman who casually dropped the fact in conversation that he had just become a member of one of the organizations limited to descendants of the old established American and British families. As he spoke with a clearly recognizable foreign accent, it was clear that the basic requirement had been waived. The fact is that this man's good will in business was so important to several members of the group that they engineered his acceptance. I also know of a number of cases in which the organization member is the last of his line. He may then select his closest relative to fill his place, and the family tie is sometimes as distant as a nephew by marriage. And on occasion membership has been passed to a good friend.

"But you haven't mentioned the biggest crack in the wall around the inner circle," the lawyer's wife chimed in. "I mean marriage, of course."

Marriage does not always provide the entering wedge. Marrying in haste is prevalent in the leisure class. Third, fifth, or, in extreme cases, ninth wives are given short shrift. But in general, if a junior member of the Old Guard marries a "nice" girl or boy, he or she will be seized to the dowager bosoms of the group. And even such exigencies of life as divorce may not throw the newcomer and his children back to the level of society from which they came. In one much-publicized case the socialite's wife, a former model, was actually involved in a murder trial. And yet she never lost the position in high society her marriage had brought her.

Just outside the old inner circle is a set that can be described only as a "new" inner-circle group. This is made up of the grandchildren and great-grandchildren of those who earned vast fortunes at least two generations ago. The old families, playing their favorite game of family trees, know that these people were unknown fifty or so years ago. But they have been taken in, nonetheless. In the case of the Rockefellers, acceptance has been complete. Others in this group include such quickly recognized names as Vanderbilt, Morgan, and Stotesbury.

There has been time for the past to be forgotten. Few today can remember that the late Edward T. Stotesbury started out as a six-dollar-a-week clerk or that J. P. Morgan the elder in his day was considered *nouveau riche* by the De Peysters, Van Beurens, Van Rensselaers, Morrises, Livingstons, and Astors.

Coming down the social scale just a little bit, one finds the names of those who have amassed fortunes forty, thirty, and, in some cases, as recently as twenty years ago. The Du Ponts, Chryslers, Fords, Dodges, and Woolworths have by now gained a niche in society for their less sensational members anyway. They are still "new" society. But individuals among them have already been accepted, and others are working on it. Crystal ball gazers can see that in another generation most of this group will be joining the Aldriches, Woodwards, Blairs, Lowells, Cadwaladers (with one "l," of course), and their fellows in society's stratosphere.

At this point one comes to an area of constant change, a sort of social no-man's land. Newcomers can break into it. They may never be invited to sit at Mrs. Biddle's side at an informal dinner for twelve; they may never be asked to join the Mystick Krewe of Comus, but they can do practically everything else. And they can certainly get into the *Social Register*. They are viewed as members of society and have the status accorded those in the top economic and social class. Their lives follow the pattern set by members of the inner circle. If anything, they observe the rigid forms of traditional society with more vigor than those born to it, displaying the fanaticism of converts.

Many will go to all lengths to gain and protect a position in society. In a fashionable suburb in the Midwest, everyone in the inner circle belongs to the country club. Last year a socialite discovered that she was no longer welcome there. No one told her the reason in so many words, but she knew. Her membership had been dependent on her husband's position in the community, and she had divorced him.

There was only one thing to do. She would have to figure out some way of having the divorce declared illegal. It was unfortunate that this would cause her former husband no end of trouble, as he had remarried. And she bore him no ill will. After all, she had lived very well since the divorce on the generous settlement he had made her. But she felt she had no choice. Her position in society was threatened.

The socialite did succeed in having a local judge declare the divorce invalid on a technicality. Her husband's life was disrupted. His second wife was no longer a wife at all. But presumably the first wife's club privileges were restored.

And then there is the case of the Boston man who refused to give his wife, an Old Guard socialite, a divorce. He insisted on continuing a joyless marriage, because he was afraid that he would be cut out of the *Register* if they broke up.

The surprising thing about these incidents is that they caused so little stir in the world of society. To thousands who value social position above all else such actions are completely understandable.

What lies behind the rush to the *Register*? If I had to give a one-word answer to that question, it would be "money." The prosperity that followed World War II is largely responsible for the revival of interest in traditional society.

So many people have high incomes that money and possessions in themselves no longer provide status.

"Our television repairman drives a Chrysler; he's too sophisticated for a Cadillac," one of my friends commented recently. "And the mechanic in the garage was telling me the other day that he's putting a swimming pool behind his home."

But the repairman or the mechanic does *not* send his son to the Knickerbocker Greys or have his daughter presented at the Cotillion. He is not on the committee for the Ball of Roses; he is not a member of the Union Club, and he most certainly is not listed in the *Social Register*. And so these have become today's symbols of status.

Even cities gain in prestige from having *Register* editions. Those which have them claim to be more truly social than cities that must make do with *Social Lists*. There are eleven editions of the *Register:* New York, Buffalo, Philadelphia-Wilmington, Pittsburgh, Boston, Washington, Baltimore, Cleveland-Cincinnati-Dayton, Chicago, St. Louis, and San Francisco.

The New York edition is by far the most difficult to get into. I know of one New Yorker who moved his business and entire family to St. Louis, as he had heard it was easier to get into that edition. His information was quite correct, and he did in time gain a listing in the St. Louis *Register*. Thereupon he returned to New York, assuming that he would simply be transferred to the New York *Register*. That proved to be a miscalculation. He was transferred, but it was not simple. It took him and his family ten years of effort.

Those outside of society's secret world assume that listing in the *Register* somehow just comes to those who deserve it. A man goes to bed a nobody and wakes up a fellow of the Whitneys and Lodges. That is not quite the way it works.

People who want to be listed in the *Register* must apply for it, just as they would put in for a club. No one is placed in the book against his will, although listening to members of the Old Guard leaves one with quite the opposite impression. I have heard of only two men who have refused to be listed: John Hay Whitney and Alfred Gwynne Vanderbilt, Jr. Mr. Whitney insisted that his name be dropped from the book in 1946, asserting that the *Register*'s criteria represented a "travesty on democracy." But other members of society carefully supply the *Register* with information about changed addresses, marriages, club affiliations, and births, while pretending to throw the forms into the wastebasket.

Getting into the *Register* follows a cut-and-dried pattern, or so it sounds when explained by a member of the Social Register Association. The first step for the person who wishes to be listed is to find a friend who is in the *Register* and is willing to make a recommendation to the Advisory Board. The friend must send a detailed letter, giving considerable information about the background of the applicant and his family, and indicating why they should be included in the *Register*.

After getting this, the Advisory Board may—or may not—send the applicant a form letter asking for four or five additional letters from people who are listed in the *Register*. These people must know the applicant well, or appear to, and must be prepared to say flatly that they believe he ought to be in the book.

I know of one Philadelphian who actually checks every business contact he makes through the *Register*. Those who are in get more favorable terms than those who are not. The reward he expects from them is a recommendation to the *Register*. I sometimes wonder what those who administer the Robinson-Patman Act, the law which bans business discrimination, could make of this form of favoritism.

If the letters pass the Board's scrutiny, the applicant will be sent a form on which he is to fill in the information needed for his listing. No one is notified of failure to make the book, or of being dropped. An applicant hears only when he is accepted.

The *Register* lists the names, addresses, clubs, colleges, deaths, and marriages in the families. The abbreviations used make the listings read like a secret code, but I know many socialites who can read through them as if the *Register* were a first-grade primer, without so much as a glance at the key. "Un., Ln., B., Pg., Myf., H.," is quickly translated as "Union Club, Links Club, Brook Club, The Pilgrims, Society of Mayflower Descendants, and Harvard."

Children (called "juniors") are listed under the name of the current head of the family, even when their names are different as a result of divorce, or death, and remarriage. "Misses" have the junior listing between the ages of twelve and seventeen; "masters" between fourteen and twenty. A separate section, entitled "Married Maidens," helps those who have trouble keeping track of the marriages and remarriages of this group. Each woman is listed under her maiden name, with her married name alongside.

The annual edition comes out each November, with pamphlets sent out in December and January containing recent changes—mostly marriages, deaths, and new addresses. These are somewhat coyly named *Dilatory Domiciles*. In June a single summer edition is put out, which gives the rural and foreign addresses of people listed in all the *Registers*. A summer version of *Dilatory Domiciles* is sent out in July, containing information received after May 20.

In addition to the regular edition, a volume called the *Locater* is published annually. This is a compilation of the names of all the people listed in all the *Registers* and tells where each one can be found.

I have discovered that a good many people do not know that anyone can buy the *Register* if he puts down his money. They assume that even readers are selected. Of course, to say that one is going to "buy" the *Register* is a dead giveaway of social position. The proper term is "subscribe to." A subscription to the New York edition costs $12.00; adding the summer volume brings it to $14.00; with the *Locater,* it is $16.00. Subscriptions to the Washington, Philadelphia, Chicago, and Boston editions, including the summer volume and the *Locater,* come to $10.00; in all other cities the charge is $9.00. Single copies of the *Locater* are priced at $5.00. A complete set of *Registers* for all the cities that have editions can be purchased for $55.00. This includes the *Locater*.

The *Register* enhances its prestige by remaining completely shrouded in mystery. I telephoned the Social Register Association at its office at 381 Fourth Avenue, New York, just to see what response a simple request for information would get.

"No information at all is given out about the *Register*—except the cost of subscription," I was told.

"Then how is it that so much is said about the book?" I ventured timidly.

"It's all conjecture" came the firm answer.

This close-mouthed attitude is particularly surprising when compared to traditionally secretive England. There everyone who cares to can find out that the British social registers, *Burke's Peerage* and *Burke's Landed Gentry,* are edited by Leslie Pine, whose address is 42 Bramney Hill, South Croydon, Surrey, England. This common knowledge does not make Mr. Pine's life any easier.

"It's unbelievable the things people will do to get listed," he said in an interview recently. "I'm offered bribes. I'm invited to bring my wife and children to their estates for as long as we wish to stay. I'm even threatened."

I daresay that Americans might go just as far if they knew whom on the *Register* to bribe or threaten. Very few people here know that this book, which influences top-drawer society, was run for many years by the daughter of a train conductor, who began her career as a secretary. The *Register* was started in New York in 1887 by a man named Louis Keller, as a commercial venture. He soon branched out to other cities. In the early 1900's Mr. Keller hired a secretary, Bertha Eastmond, whose reputation has long since surpassed that of her employer.

The two of them ran the *Register* together until Mr. Keller died in 1922. After that Miss Eastmond, aided by Mr. Keller's heirs, continued to control the listings. A secret advisory committee helped her with her selections. At present there are five stockholders of the Social Register Association. Miss Eastmond, who became Mrs. Edwin C. Barry, is now in her eighties but is still extremely influential.

No one has yet figured out how listing in the *Register* comes about. Every year when I look over the new edition I am reminded of a rule for determining social caste that was developed by a friend of mine who is an interior decorator for the very rich. She maintains that she can differentiate members of real society from newcomers within five minutes.

"If I find myself looking down to check if my stocking seams are straight, they are real society," she declares.

This sounds absurd. But, like many simple rules of thumb, it works. Social climbers, no matter how successful, simply cannot develop that manner. It takes generations.

For all anyone knows, the Register Association may be using some similar method.

The arbitrary nature of certain *Register* listings and exclusions, in my opinion, adds immeasurably to the reputation of the book. It guarantees publicity—front page of the afternoon newspapers, at least. And it increases readership. People leaf through the *Register* avidly, looking for new names or old ones that have been touched by scandal.

Society editors check over each issue with excitement, sure of finding a story. Why, a man or woman can be listed, while the sons and daughters are excluded. They sigh with relief to see that Stephen Rockefeller's Cinderella bride, the former Anne Marie Rasmussen, is in. They single out such notable exclusions as Gloria Vanderbilt, her mother, and her aunt, Thelma, Lady Furness; Doris Duke; Mrs. William Randolph Hearst; Mr. and Mrs. William Paley; Cornelius Vanderbilt, Jr.; Winston Guest; Winthrop Rockefeller; Tommy Manville; the Topping brothers; and Barbara Hutton.

Scandal or unfavorable publicity will usually cause a name to be removed from the book, but not always. One socialite bride-to-be was kidnapped by a rival suitor. This produced reams of publicity in the tabloids. Nonetheless, when she returned and married her proper fiancé, she retained her listing in the *Register*.

At one time divorce took a name out of the book automatically. Now, sometimes it does, but more often it does not. Brenda Frazier, the all-time debutante symbol, is in, despite a divorce and some unfavorable publicity. And in cases of divorce there is never any certainty as to which member of a couple will be dropped. When Cornelius Vanderbilt Whitney, long in the *Register,* and the former Eleanor Searle broke up their marriage, he was cut out and she was left in, although she became listed only after her marriage to him.

Americans living abroad are not supposed to be listed, but quite a number of foreign addresses can be found. The best known of these belongs to Lady Astor, whose legal residence is in England. To make it more confusing, Robert G. Shaw, III, her son by her first marriage, is listed; the Astor sons are not. The Duchess of Windsor is not included; neither is Princess Grace of Monaco.

In theory, no one on the stage is in the *Register*. Social historians point out that Dorothy Benjamin was dropped when she married Enrico Caruso and Ellin Mackay when she married Irving Berlin. Somewhat more recently Elliot Roosevelt was removed from the book when he married Faye Emerson and Anthony A. Bliss when Jo Ann Sayers became his bride. But Cornelia Otis Skinner (Mrs. Alden S. Blodget) and Jane Wyatt (Mrs. Edgar B. Ward) are listed, as is Mrs. Stanley M. Rumbough (Dina Merrill).

I believe that the Association encourages the air of pure whim. And as I look over *Registers* for the last few years, I note that the "bread-and-butter" listings are constant. By this I mean the solid socialites—old or fairly new—who lead quiet lives, unnoted by the society columnists.

Some slight consolation is offered those who do not make the *Register* by a number of lesser social listings. Even cities with *Social Register* editions often have social lists as well.

A friend tells of going to call on a socialite she knew well and finding her in tears.

"What's the matter?" she asked in concern.

"Oh, I just found out I made the *Social List* and not the *Register*," the woman replied.

"Well, that's wonderful, too," said my friend.

"Oh, it's almost worse than getting nothing at all. It's like winning the consolation prize in the donkey game at children's parties. Even when the present is nice, you don't really enjoy it."

Appearance on the lists is not always greeted with such gloom. The status of the social lists varies considerably. In cities without *Register* editions they have great prestige. The "Blue Book" is the most common name for these directories, although many are simply called the "Social List." To be included in the *Blue Book of Brooklyn,* which is typical, an applicant must be sponsored by two families who are listed. Directories of this sort are found in such cities as Dallas, Houston, Denver, Indianapolis, Kansas City (Missouri), Minneapolis, New Orleans, Palm Beach, Portland (Oregon), and Seattle.

The social lists and the *Register* have never been so influential as they are today. One reason for this is the passing of the social leader. This is the woman who determines who is in society and who is not.

When I ask socialites or society editors in most cities who is the social leader, I almost always get a historical answer. It is the late—all of these are "the late"—Mrs. Sarah Drexel Fell Van Rensselaer and Mrs. Edward T. Stotesbury in Philadelphia. Washingtonians speak of Mrs. Truxton Beale, Bostonians of Mrs. John Lowell (Mrs. Jack) Gardner or Mrs. Fiske Warren. In Chicago, the name of Mrs. Potter Palmer is promptly pulled out for my benefit. And in New York I am taken back to the days of Mrs. William Astor and then of Mrs. Cornelius Vanderbilt. These women all ruled as absolute monarchs.

In contrast, the leading society matrons of today are not social leaders in the sense of controlling a group with an iron hand. In New York the names of Mrs. William Woodward, Sr., Mrs. T. Markoe Robertson (the former Cordelia Drexel Biddle), Mrs. August Belmont, and Mrs. Lytle Hull (the former Mrs. Vincent Astor) carry great weight and influence. And the group that counts itself their friends claims to be "in." But none of these ladies runs the lives of those around her in the style of the social leader of old. Many of them are retiring and lend their names to few causes. The younger society matrons enjoy entertaining and being on committees, but they do not govern the social world. A popular saying over the Rock Cornish game hen and wild rice is that the most prominent member of the New York younger set does not run society today; it runs her.

A few years ago the Chicago *Daily News* held a poll asking people listed in the *Social Register* to pick the queen of Chicago society. Mrs. Chauncey McCormick won it hands down. But she is not the social leader of bygone days. A shy woman, I understand that she burst into tears when she heard the news.

Another prominent socialite in Chicago is Mrs. Howard Linn. But she, too, does not dominate her group. Mrs. Reginald Bird, Mrs. Richard E. Danielson, Mrs. Henry Coffin Everett, and Mrs. Russell Howell are all big names in Boston, but none is synonymous with society in the way of a Cabot or Lodge in an earlier era.

There is no longer one woman in a city who serves as social arbiter. And so those interested in finding out who is society turn to the *Register,* even if they look down on it.

"Nowadays it takes an expert to work his way through the *Social*

Register, sifting the old names from the new," a member of the Old Guard said to me ruefully.

I reported that statement to a woman who asserts that she will be in the 1965 *Social Register*—or else!

"That's what I'm banking on," she replied, with a smile. "All the people who are in the *Register* object to the way it is growing. But as for me, I say that if society is to stop changing, let it be after I have made the *Social Register.*"

CHAPTER II

Living the High Society Way

WHEN I started to interview women in society to gather information for this book, I was struck by an odd fact: they all had the same hair. (The style was bouffant—arranged in a puffed-out circle; the color was blond—corn silk tinged with gold.)

After several days of observing identical heads I stopped to take stock. How did it happen? And then it became clear to me. They must all use the same hairdresser. Judicious questioning revealed that my guess was right. Even in a city the size of New York the names of the same three or four hairdressers are given me repeatedly; in smaller cities, all the society trade goes to the same man.

Take New York's Claude (it is particularly easy for me to take Claude, as his press agent buttonholed me once for the better part of an hour; actually his neighbor, Carita, or Antoine's at Saks Fifth Avenue are equally acceptable), his clientele is drawn from the Old Guard plus the international set. Mrs. Winston Guest, Mrs. John Hay Whitney, Mrs. Bedford ("Peggy") Bancroft, Mrs. Munn Baker, Tina Livanos (Onassis), the Duchess of Windsor, and Mrs. Nicholas Goulandris all hang their minks in the cloakroom of Claude's salon. The Duchess pulls rank and has her hair set in a private room separated from the rest by a yellow bead curtain. When on vacation at Fisher's Island, Mrs. Whitney has Claude flown to her. Mrs. Henry Ford II calls him to Grosse Pointe when she wants her hair done the society way; in fact, Claude did the coiffures of the ladies in the Ford family for Charlotte's fabulous 1959 debut.

19

Loyalty to the accepted hairdresser knows no bounds. When California's socialites come to New York for the April in Paris Ball, they naturally are accompanied by George Masters, their hair stylist. He sets up shop at Antoine's for the duration.

Now this brings me to something I have observed about the inner circle. The fact of the identical hair-dos is not just an unaccountable coincidence. It is simply one example out of hundreds that display the character of the high society way of life. The performance of dance music reveals the same phenomenon.

The socialite at a New York ball could close her eyes and dream that she is dancing in Philadelphia, Wilmington, Washington, or Boston. It is not that the music is similar; it is precisely the same. So is the name on the bandstand. It is most often Meyer Davis or Lester Lanin. This trick is not performed with mirrors. Meyer Davis maintains fifty bands, all required to play the same arrangements of the same music in the same style. During the December and June social seasons he ups the number to eighty. Lester Lanin has twenty-five bands.

"By the time either Davis or Lanin sends out a fourth or fifth band, you have to look at the name on the bandstand to see whose it is," says Emmett Davis, press agent, who has publicized both. "They draw musicians out of the same pool, so it's often just chance who gets which ones."

But the socialite who hires the band feels secure, knowing that the music at her party will meet society's rigid standards.

By its very nature, society must be conformist. Members follow a way of life that is almost ritualistic. It is such rituals as the debut that set them off from others. This is not the heyday of the individual. Conformity is the dominant emotion of the age. And so this era is particularly suited to the revival of traditional society we are witnessing.

Society's world is really one world. The place names are different ... the pattern of life is the same. In some cities the inner circle accepts newcomers; in others, it does not. But in all, the society group leads the same kind of life. Top-drawer socialites can move from city to city and feel at home in any one.

Aspiring socialites must do as high society does in order to gain acceptance. The style of life is more important than ever before. Who can be sure of the family background of the big-corporation executive who is moved to a new community by his firm? And even more significant, who can possibly keep track of the millions of Americans moving to the suburbs? People are likely to be judged on the basis of their homes, cars, and dress, rather than their family trees.

Today's pattern of movement from city to suburb and from one city to another favors the thousands of Americans who want to make the move from one social group to the next. The first step into the charmed circle is taken by those who know how to live the high society way—or who learn it.

Society is not tolerant of individualists. Address? There are only three or four possible locations. Style of home? It can vary within narrow limits. Decoration? Interiors should be based on the work of a few big-name designers. Vacations? There are barely a handful of places to go.

Socialites do not realize this. They deny it vigorously when questioned. But they are unaware of people who do not live as they do. "Where did you say you lived? The Bronx? Oh, yes, my maid's family lives up there."

In New York those belonging to the inner circle congregate on the East Side of Manhattan (below Ninety-sixth Street, of course) or in such suburbs as Oyster Bay and Cold Spring Harbor on Long Island, Bronxville and Tuxedo Park in New York, Darien and Greenwich in Connecticut, St. George and Dongan Hills in Staten Island, and Far Hills and Montclair in New Jersey. Hardly any of this set lives in Brooklyn, which was once fashionable. The social members of the Remsen, Pratt, Schermerhorn, Suydam, Bedford, or Pierrepont families have moved away.

The Philadelphia socialites I know have abandoned the Main Line, although the words remain synonymous with wealth and social standing. Most members of society have moved out of the city into the fox-hunting country around Radnor, or to Bryn Mawr, Wynnewood, and Bala-Cynwyd.

Bostonians are still found on Beacon Hill or in semi-suburban Brookline and Chestnut Hill. But many are going farther out to

Dedham, Andover, Concord, Framingham, Wellesley, Westwood, and other suburbs.

Georgetown with its narrow old houses and cobblestone streets is viewed as the "only place to live" by many Washingtonians. A good number of the original "cave dwellers" are gone, though, and their houses taken over by government officials. Connecticut Avenue is also an excellent address in the city proper. Chevy Chase is the suburb Washington society likes best.

And so it goes around the country. Those learning how to live the high society way simply check the addresses given in the local *Social Register,* if there is one, or the marriage and debut announcements on the society pages. These serve as a directory of fashionable city addresses and socially favored suburbs.

Not only the location but also the type of house or apartment affects the position in society. It is quite possible for the impoverished aristocrat to live in a broken-down brownstone in a neighborhood that time has forgotten and fashion has passed by. This will not affect his social standing in the least. As a matter of fact, it may even help. Society is sentimental about its own.

I remember one of the most talked-of debuts last year was a tea given by a grand old lady of society in the shabby parlor of her run-down home. The biggest social leaders rushed to attend. As for the granddaughter who was presented, she was welcomed to the Assemblies, a living testimonial to the oft-made boast: "The Assembly and/or Cotillion cannot be bought."

Last year an instructor at Sophie Newcomb College in New Orleans wrote to me, telling how he had wandered by chance into an antique shop on a dark side street. On a dressmaker's dummy in the back he noticed a beautiful old ball gown, with the lace yellowed and the silk organza of the skirt eaten away by time. The owner of the shop came over then, his worn shoes and frayed shirt collar revealing his poverty. He stroked the gown fondly, and said that it had belonged to his grandmother, who had worn it when she was queen of one of the Mardi Gras balls.

He excused himself for a moment to go upstairs to the rooms over the shop where his family lived. When he came down, he was carrying an incredibly beautiful dress. This one, he said, had been worn by his mother when *she* had been queen of the same Mardi Gras ball. He was hoping, he admitted, that his daughter would receive the same honor. Any student of the ways of society could be almost certain that he was not just hoping in vain.

The newcomer trying to break into the upper stratum can hardly get away with living over a store. He literally has to keep up with the Vanderbilts in terms of housing. The address and type of home are of tremendous importance in meeting the right people, entertaining them, being accepted at their clubs and on their committees. This takes money—great amounts of it. In these groups the $30,000-a-year man might just as well be on relief.

It is the thing for people in the inner circle to view themselves as poor. Taxes leave them utterly impoverished, they assert.

"Why, if you had to be rich to do the society thing, Edwin and I simply couldn't do it," one matron told me recently.

This conversation was interrupted several times by the maid's bringing fresh cigarettes, the older daughter stopping in to change her clothes to go horseback riding, the baby's nurse coming in with her charge to say good afternoon, and a frantic appeal from the cook who reported that the butcher had sent only twelve guinea hens instead of the fifteen that had been ordered.

The fact that society women periodically go on economy drives when they serve spaghetti and meat balls and buy skirts in Ohrbach's—or its local equivalent—cannot be taken too seriously. The economies seldom reach the point of dropping membership in the yacht club or withdrawing the daughters from the subdebutante dancing group.

The style of life taken for granted costs so much that it should not be attempted without a very high income. Society on a budget just cannot be done.

I was at a fashion-show luncheon one day when the conversation turned to apartments. One woman at my table said sadly: "We need a bigger apartment, but it's impossible to find anything decent for $600 a month."

I am afraid I was the only one who laughed, and I quickly realized that it was no laughing matter. The woman's rent budget was not high enough to get her a large apartment in the few blocks viewed as suitable. Why, I know one family that pays $825 a month for a seven-room apartment. And when a luxurious apartment building on Fifth Avenue was converted in 1959, cutting fifty-four apartments out of the original eighteen, rents for the eight-room apartments were pegged at from $1,040 to $1,340 a *month!* A particularly lovely seven-room unit rents for $1,415.

Many prefer to buy cooperatives. Most selling prices run somewhere between $30,000 and $150,000. The maintenance starts at about $300 a month and goes to $800.

Town houses are also favorites of the wealthy city dwellers. These afford even greater opportunity for striking interior decoration than do apartments. In terms of maintenance and taxes, they are much costlier than a cooperative. Purchase prices are often comparable, in the $100,000-up bracket.

In the suburbs the home gives a clear indication of family social position. The market for estates and luxury houses has become so great that one New Jersey real-estate broker recently established a separate department with this specialty.

What is the difference between the two? It certainly is not one of price. Both are in the $90,000-and-up range. After sounding out real-estate brokers, I have come to the conclusion that the chief difference is one of seclusion. A luxury home can front on the street; the estate usually has a private road.

"You wouldn't know that there are neighbors within hundreds of miles" is the correct thing for an estate owner to say.

One impoverished gentleman, now working for a large corporation, recently asked his employer, a more fortunate son of society, for a raise. He complained that some new houses had been built and he could see them from his land. He wanted the extra money to finance the creation of a hill to shield his home—an estate beyond question—from theirs. His employer, apparently feeling that he was paying the man as much as he was worth, refused the increase, but he paid for the raising of the hill himself. He understood that this was really important.

An estate should have some supplementary cottages. Not long ago I went to congratulate a friend who had just given birth to a baby. The nurse came in to show off the new arrival and stayed to regale us with tales of her previous jobs, as is the way with baby nurses. She had just come, I learned with interest, from the Long Island estate of a prominent television executive who is fast becoming a society figure. He maintains a separate house on the grounds for his children, a maid, and a nurse.

But in general estates are not what they used to be. The increasing difficulty of getting enough servants for the house, and gardeners and handymen for the grounds discourages many from buying estates, no matter how great their wealth. And so it is getting to be quite all right to purchase a luxury home instead.

In many of these I note that the kitchen is well equipped and is planned for use by the lady of the house. But then it is hard to find a modern counterpart of the matron who was once known in social circles for having been in her kitchen only once in twenty-five years and having had a kitchenmaid for seven years without seeing her.

Around New York, Washington, Philadelphia, and other big cities the possession of a farm is a real prestige builder. I heard a number of comments by socialites on the obituary of R. W. Woolworth, a nephew of the founder of the chain of stores that bears his name. The headline of the New York *Times* story ran:

R. W. Woolworth
Raised Guernseys

The farming is usually done with a paid professional on the spot, just in case.

The last farm advertisement I studied listed a price of $160,000.

Among the elite, house or estate hunting by individuals is frowned upon. For one thing, the sellers are often reluctant to open their houses to any but people who are really planning to buy. And buyers like to think that they are either too busy or too well known to shop around. And so agents or real-estate brokers do much of the preliminary screening for them.

The purchase of the house or the renting of the apartment is only the first step. Today the interior is taken more seriously than the outside. A well-decorated home can be a tremendous social asset.

This was true in the case of a woman who moved from Alabama

to a Connecticut suburb. For the first year she was ignored by local society. Then word got around that her home was most beautifully decorated. A member of the Ladies' Aid Society of a nearby church asked her if she would allow her house to be included on a benefit home tour. (In nearly every city and suburb it has become the thing for socialites to allow visitors to go through their homes or apartments, paying a fee that goes to a charity.) The newcomer's house was the talk of the suburb for weeks thereafter. And so when the hospital, the prestige charity of the community, planned a home tour, she was again asked to be a hostess. When I last heard from her, she had just been accepted in the country club and was becoming known in local society.

"Do it yourself" is not necessary in the top social set. The services of a decorator can—and usually are—called upon. One couple, fast rising in society, allotted a furnishings budget of $100,000 to their decorator. When I phoned the office of this professional a short time ago, I was informed that he had set off for Italy in search of the perfect Venetian mirrors for the foyer.

Newcomers are often at a loss as to how to find an approved interior decorator.

"You certainly can't admit your ignorance to your friends," one woman told me ruefully.

And so I asked a friend who is a decorator how a professional can be found.

"The associations are the best source," she replied.

The American Institute of Decorators, which is the prestige group in this industry, will send the names of five decorators in response to a query. The National Society of Interior Decorators will also give assistance. And going on home tours is a way of getting the needed information, as the name of the decorator used is always given. It is easy to discover that Melanie Kahane and Michael Greer are current pets of the society set. Solid inner-circle support is given to such great names in the field as William Pahlmann, Ellen Lehman McCluskey, and Dorothy Draper. Mary Dunn (successor to the late Nancy McClelland, socialite-decorator) is also doing many noted houses.

The same style of decoration can be found in the homes of

socialites all over the country. And the reason again is that a handful of decorators gets all the society trade. Most of these designers, as they like to be called, live in New York, but wealthy clients do not hesitate to fly an approved decorator to Houston, Cleveland, or Los Angeles. When in New York to attend a charity ball, a homeowner will often call on the professional herself, bearing blueprints and photographs.

The designer may turn a home into a showplace, but for this result, the client's bankbook must be wide open. It is true that some do not charge separately for their services. They make a commission by buying furnishings wholesale and reselling them to clients at retail prices. But many demand a fee as well. A charge of $25.00 an hour for the decorator's time is not at all uncommon. And most will ask an average of $250 a room for redesigning the layout.

But the chief expense in using a decorator is that of paying for the furnishings he encourages the client to select. One woman, a new arrival to the ranks of the rich, decided to have her apartment decorated by the man who is "doing" society's homes this year. He appeared with an entourage and completely captivated her with his charm. She was dazzled by the slides he showed of other apartments he had decorated. Her furniture budget had originally been $25,000, but her views changed quickly. A few months later she confided in me that the dining room and a part of the living room had been furnished at a cost of $30,000.

The size of this figure did not surprise me, as I have found that many decorators view a sum of $5,000 as barely adequate for wallpaper. A designer such as Inez Croom, who has her own wallpaper factory, will show the client the outline of designs to be used. The colors are then specifically blended to be an exact match with the furnishings.

The home tours I have gone on during the last few years reveal the current style of decorating to be a particularly costly one. Oriental rugs or patterned ones woven in the mountains of Spain and Portugal are extremely popular, for example, and add thousands of dollars to the furnishings budget.

I was amused to notice the hostess at a home tour last winter running swiftly to put plastic covers over her Portuguese rugs before they could be touched and possibly marked by the Delman-shod feet of her visitors. She never did attain the casual air that is expected of the homeowner on these tours.

In general, I have noted a swing away from modern back to old-fashioned furnishings. The two styles are frequently combined. The established decorators are so confident of the absolute rightness of their taste that they do not shy away from such expensive oddities as a small oriental rug placed on top of wall-to-wall broadloom. And modern vinyl flooring (usually in black and white) is to be found in many entrance halls, which also boast old-fashioned Venetian mirrors and wallpaper copied from that used in Versailles.

Antiques are viewed as essential in any truly modern home. These are seldom of the type picked up on "antiquing" trips in New England. They are predominantly European. In the home of one society matron, for example, I was told that the dining-room chairs were brought from poet Robert Browning's Italian villa. The Directoire style of decorating is very popular, too, possibly a result of Mr. Greer's fondness for the period. And eighteenth-century English furniture is to be seen in many society homes.

Many rooms are decorated "around" works of art. In almost any home, not only those of collectors, I have spotted at least one or two big-name paintings—by Matisse, Chagall, Picasso, Georgia O'Keeffe, or even an old master such as Goya. Chinese vases, French silver tureens, and small bronze statues are also part of the current decorating scheme.

In the bedrooms it is the fashion for the walls, beds, and chairs to be covered with the same fabric, a style associated with designer McCluskey. At the moment, in nine homes out of ten, the fabric is pale yellow silk covered with hand-painted flowers.

I found the extreme impracticality of fabric both fascinating and alarming. Sofas and armchairs are upholstered in white shantung, creamy yellow satin, or soft sea-green silk.

"How are they kept clean?" women frequently wonder.

When I have dropped in on some of these homes when they were not on view, I discovered one way—slip covers. Endless care is the other.

The late Mrs. Byron C. Foy, whose fabulous collection of art works and furnishings was auctioned after her death for nearly two million dollars, used to have her chairs cleaned or re-covered "after they were used a few times."

Kitchens in city apartments are frequently a disappointment. Most of the ones I have seen are old-fashioned in terms of design and appliances. In a number of the smartest homes they are actually rather dirty. I can only assume that despite the much-discussed servant problem, the lady of the house seldom sets foot in the kitchen. The reverse is true in the suburbs, where the kitchen is often the nicest room in the house.

Along with the home goes the car, or cars, as the case may be, and usually is. By now everyone knows that the Cadillac is *nouveau riche.* As a result, both the old and newly rich are forced to turn to the Chrysler, Lincoln, or even Buick. And it is preferable for these cars to be old and beat up.

In addition, there is a foreign car in many of society's garages. The British Rolls-Royce and Bentley are popular as a main family car. These, too, gain in status when they are old. This was brought home to me last year when a friend in the advertising field told me that a single advertisement for a 1935 Rolls-Royce at $4,860 had drawn one hundred inquiries.

Other foreign cars occupy second- or third-car position in the garage. The German Mercedes-Benz and the French Facel-Vega are often used. The latter has a Chrysler engine, and is frequently described as a compromise between American engineering and French styling. Of the Italian cars, Lancia's Flamina, a five-seater that features windshield wipers for the rear windows, pleases those who want something a little different. As for sports cars, the British Jaguar is almost commonplace; the Italian Alfa Romeo and the British Austin-Healey are also well liked. Those looking for something offbeat turn to the Italian fun car. This is a small open car built to look like a motorboat with the engine in the rear.

But the right address, the right type of home, and the right car combine to make up only one aspect of high society life. The mode of dress, speech, and behavior is every bit as important.

Dressing the part is essential, because socialites in common with women everywhere notice and remember what everyone wore when.

The eager young stenographer selecting her spring wardrobe out of designer Henry Rosenfeld's latest moderate-priced line often worries that she may meet many of her friends at a party in the same dress. If only she had money, she thinks, she could be sure of being different.

That is certainly not the case with the moneyed social set.

"It is more important to be dressed correctly than to look different," advises a social secretary.

As a result, at several top balls each season at least two ladies appear in the same gown. A fashion editor who attended the Paris openings last season told me that six women in the elegant audience at Chanel's showing were wearing the identical light-gray suit trimmed in navy. When *Life* magazine published a photograph of eleven young society leaders of New York, four of them appeared in gowns by Mainbocher.

The rule for correct society dressing is simplicity by day and elegance at night. Sports clothes must not look new.

"I just buy a few good things. I've had the suit I'm wearing for eight years" is the correct society gambit in a conversation on clothes. It may not hurt to slip in the fact that the suit was an original Dior.

Evening gowns should be creations, and the socialite's wardrobe includes at least a few Paris or Rome originals fresh from the drawing boards of St. Laurent, Crahay, Mainbocher, or Simonetta. Custom-made gowns, dresses, and suits from Bergdorf's, Saks, Bendel's, or Milgrim's are almost commonplace. Casuals are from such stores as the Woman's Haberdasher.

For the benefit of those who cannot quite go the expense of this type of wardrobe an interesting business has developed in the last few years. Designer dresses that have been slightly worn are purchased from their original owners and resold. The society woman who passes along her clothes gets a percentage of the sale price, and the buyer gets a creation cut rate.

The Encore Resale Dress Shop on New York's Madison Avenue is the best known of these. Many real society women favor, at least for their daughters, the Two-Time Shop on East Seventy-eighth Street. This shop is noted for its ball gowns; many of them come from international society figures. There is a persistent rumor that the Duchess of Windsor uses this shop to dispose of some of her fabulous wardrobe. For small children, a number of matrons patronize the Second Act Resale Children's Apparel Shop on Madison Avenue.

But clothes—new or used—do not make the socialite. What does? Speech is the clearest indication of origin. Graduates of private schools have a way of speaking that can be recognized a mile away (both figuratively and literally). People disagree as to whether this can be imitated. Alan S. C. Ross, well-known philologist at the University of Birmingham (England), maintains that an adult can never attain complete success at changing his speech. That is probably true, and yet I have observed an odd fact about the upper crust. In middle-class groups, affected pronunciation is considered something to joke about. An honest Bronx accent is preferable. But society, curiously enough, will accept affectation in speech.

And so a multitude of schools and classes to teach correct speech and good manners has sprung up. Even Philadelphia social secretary, Mrs. Edward J. MacMullan, at one time taught classes in charm. Washington's social arbiter, Carolyn Hagner Shaw, writes a column on good manners for the Washington *Star*. And a former reporter on the Richmond *News Leader* tells me that the society editor receives frequent phone calls asking for advice on etiquette.

The teacher of a speech class comments: "It is no harder to learn to use the society style of speaking than to learn which fork to use. All it takes is observation and mimicry. It doesn't take long to stop saying, 'It's a good party,' and to start saying, 'It's a fun ball.'"

Not only speech but a whole way of life is involved. It is essential for the society woman to learn to be a skillful hostess. Quite a number of newcomers have gained social recognition by being good party-givers.

"In the last ten years the number of big parties has increased 25 per cent by a conservative estimate, and possibly as much as 33⅓ per cent," says Meyer Davis, the band leader, who is in a position to know.

It is helpful, though it is not essential, for a woman to give huge parties. But anyone in society must be able to handle a small dinner correctly.

Consider menus. In middle-class homes hostesses frequently rack their brains to find new dishes to serve guests. Many would never dream of repeating themselves or serving the same menu they were offered at friends' homes. The same is not true of high society. The house may be different; the city may be different; the company may be different...the menu is the same. One is expected to groan about the number of times he has been served Rock Cornish game hen. Wits like to estimate the number of hens they have eaten in a five-year period. Peggy Bancroft, for example, admitted in an interview that for her first two years as hostess she served the hen at every dinner. Since then she has changed. She serves it only every other time. Her alternate main course is chicken Kiev.

A guest at the Southampton buffet suppers given each year by Old Guard socialite Mrs. T. Markoe Robertson reports that she "always" serves roast beef, cold lobster mayonnaise, green peas, mashed potatoes, vanilla ice cream, and apple pie.

Although bridge and party games are quite permissible after dinner, the art of conversation is highly prized. As a result there are many who follow the advice of famed party-giver Elsa Maxwell: "Cultivate a memory for anecdote....Never try to extemporize. Do as any good actress does, rehearse the bit in private before you try it on an audience."

In the high society set the nights are usually filled with parties, the days with sports. Even the hard-working executive is expected to devote a great number of hours to athletics. And for many of society's favored children sports are virtually a life's work. The aspiring socialite can, therefore, ride, play, or shoot his way into the inner circle.

In certain groups the horse is the thing. Some of the inner circle's biggest names are involved in racing. Owners of horses spend a good part of the year moving from Maryland's famed Laurel Race Course to New York's Belmont, to Warrenton for the Virginia Gold Cup, to Kentucky for the Derby, and on.

One New Yorker tells that he was involved in an automobile accident with a Long Island socialite. A day or two later he received a telephone call from her housekeeper. She wanted to know if he would defer making his insurance claim.

"Madam has gone to Saratoga for the races. She owns a stable, you know."

And what does it cost to own a race horse? The most conservative estimate given me is that it would come to $4,380 a year for feed, shelter, and training. Veterinary bills, shoeing, vanning and other expenses must be added to that.

Breeding is taken so seriously that at the Middleburg, Virginia, Hunt Dinner one year a stud fee to the stallion Skyscraper was raffled off as the prize of the night.

Hunting is the major interest of many socialites all over the country. I have heard many times that Taylor Hardin of the old Virginia family wrote his thesis at Harvard on fox hunting. There are now ninety-two recognized hunts in the United States. Eighteen of them are in Virginia, which is "hunt country." These include the famed Piedmont, Orange County, Middleburg, Warrenton, Farmington, Deep Run, Rappahannock, Loudon, and Blue Ridge hunts.

In Maryland members of society ride with the Green Spring Valley Hunt Club and the Elkridge Harford Hunt Club. In Chicago it is the Mill Creek Hunt, the Du Page Hunt, and the Fox River Valley Hunt. And in the New York area Long Island's Meadow Brook Hunt, started in 1881, is viewed as the most exclusive.

Every major hunt touches off a series of parties. Hunt breakfasts last from noon until midnight in an American version of Merrie England. In Virginia the banquet tables groan with everything from onion soup to creamed oysters, suckling pig, turkey, roast beef, Virginia ham, and southern spoon bread. A folk singer with a guitar is favored as the entertainer at these affairs. Hunt balls, like Virginia's famed Golden Horseshow Ball, are exclusive in the extreme.

Horse shows are still society shows the country over. Of the ninety-three box holders at New York's National Horse Show, thirty-three are in the *Social Register*. The ability to ride well enough to compete successfully is one of the less conventional ways to break into the inner circle. The time to show what one can do is when very young, in the junior events in such major horse shows as the Upperville Colt and Horse Show in Virginia, the Pin Oak Charity Horse Show near Houston, and the Devon Horse Show in that suburb of Philadelphia. Socialites attend horse shows all over the United States, but many are not content with the American competitions. They fly over to Ireland for the Dublin Horse Show, too.

The well-to-do like to say that polo is no longer a rich man's sport. They point to the fact that some polo clubs are sponsored by business firms. This is true, and polo may no longer be exclusively for the rich. But a lot of big-name socialites can still be found on the polo fields. A polo-playing friend advises me that the Meadow-brook and Blind Brook clubs on Long Island, the Squadron A Indoor Polo Club in New York, the Washington Polo Club, Washington, D.C., the Ivory Polo Club in Detroit, the Broadmoor Club at Colorado Springs, and the Pima Country Club in Tucson are all well known.

Dogs are society's best friends. One socialite spent $75,000 in his efforts to make "best-of-show" at New York's top-ranking Westminster Dog Show. He traveled to Europe with his handlers to buy up blooded stock. When last heard from, he had not won yet but was still trying.

Competition in dog shows is not limited to members of society, but many of the Old Guard are among the proud exhibitors at the shows given by such leading clubs as Chicago's International, Washington's National Capital, and Long Island's Ladies' Kennel Association of America. Some go on to Bermuda for the Bermuda Kennel Club Dog Show.

As socialites cannot be separated from their dogs, a popular resort such as the Homestead at Hot Springs, Virginia, actually invites dogs weighing under forty-five pounds for a charge of only $1.00 a day. A dog can accompany his master on a Caribbean cruise for $36.00. One socialite travels to Europe by ship several times a year, accompanied by his four beagles. He is happy to pay the $50.00 per dog that it costs.

"I've never met any people on board I like half as well," is his misanthropic comment.

Another member of society flies to Europe with his dog by the simple expedient of paying the excess-baggage rate. The last time he went, this amounted to $64.39 plus the cost of a kennel (the dog weighed forty-seven pounds; the trip was from New York to Frankfurt, Germany).

The boating craze has swept the nation, but yachts are still for those who do not need to ask how much it costs, to paraphrase J. P. Morgan.

"And when they talk of the yacht club in Grosse Pointe," says a resident, "they really mean yachts. They don't mean outboard motorboats."

Those who do not care to take their boats when they go resorting can charter them. At the Mill Reef Club at Antigua, British West Indies, members can charter yachts for fees ranging from $28.00 a day to $2,500 a week. The yachts vary in size from 36 to 134 feet, with accommodations for from two to twelve in private cabins.

Although many Americans think shooting is done by television cowboys only, guns are to be found in the non-calloused hands of socialite sportsmen. Most start shooting as boys in prep school. The problem of whether to allow a young boy to have a gun is frequently discussed by members of society—and is a very correct subject to bring up when social conversation gets around to children.

When high society says: "Tennis, anyone?" it is not just plain old-fashioned tennis. For those who really wish to be "in," there is court tennis—a game that remains in inner-circle hands only. It is played mostly at private courts or clubs in such fashionable spots as Tuxedo Park, Newport, or Aiken, Colorado. This is a game that cannot be picked up on a two-weeks annual vacation. I once saw a statement by New York *Times* sports writer Allison Danzig to the effect that court tennis has the "most complicated rules of any game played by man."

Those who like to live dangerously go in for sports-car racing, using a Ferrari, Maserati, O.S.C.A., Lotus, Lister-Jaguar, or Porsche. This is a most costly sport. Any of these cars costs about $12,000, and there is no prize money. The winner just gets glory and a cup. Some have cars specially built for them. Lance Reventlow, Barbara Hutton's son, for example, has his car designed and built by his own company, Scarabs. Popular races are held at Bridgehampton, Long Island; Lime Rock, Connecticut; Danville, Connecticut; Vineland, New Jersey; Watkins Glen, New York; Elkhart Lake, Indiana; and Sebring, Florida. Nassau speed week in early December also draws many of the socialite drivers. I have had that "week" described to me as "three days of racing and ten days of cocktail parties."

But not all members of society devote their leisure to sports and high living. The pursuit and support of the arts are favored by a large group that includes the easily recognized names of Rockefeller, Mellon, Chrysler, Widener, Kress, Lehman, and Harriman. The curator of a museum has commented to me that he credits the current tax structure for bringing art collecting into fashion among the social and rich. A work of art bought as a donation for a museum is tax deductible. The purchaser can keep it in his home all his life.

Music gets great support, particularly from women. In Philadelphia, society matrons traditionally go to the Philharmonic Orchestra Concert in the Academy of Music every Friday afternoon. Such a well-known socialite as Mrs. Lytle Hull is credited with starting the women's committee of the New York Philharmonic. And symphony orchestras in other cities have received similar aid. Members of the Opera Guild are usually of *Social Register* rank. In New York, society's night at the Metropolitan Opera is now the first Monday after the opening. The first night is no longer the "right" one.

In the last few years, jazz has become a society thing, too. This has produced some interesting side effects.

"Since the upper crust took up jazz, I've had to be very careful when combing the *Social Register* for names of people whose patronage I want to encourage," says the press agent for one of New York's top night clubs. "The jazz enthusiasts will drag just about anyone in with them."

Many members of the Old Guard vigorously object to the jazz furor.

"It's too bad it started at Newport," one of them told me. "Until that Festival, Newport still seemed to me to be the last place where people lived as they used to. And it was a way of life I loved."

Resort going is, of course, essential for this group. And every student of Cleveland Amory knows the Newport-Hobe Sound-Fishers Island-Bar Harbor circuit. These older resorts are right, simply because of their age, though some, such as Newport, have lost much of their earlier luster.

Florida's Hobe Sound, for example, in season attracts socialites from Detroit, Cleveland, Chicago, Philadelphia, New York, and most other cities. I know several young executives who have dropped everything in the midst of a busy season to accept invitations to Hobe Sound.

At any of the inner circle's resorts studied simplicity is the rule. Homes must be called "cottages," even if they are mansions.

"*Nobody* dresses for dinner here," says a member of the Chicago Club at Charlevoix, Michigan, favored by the society sets of Chicago and Detroit.

As the clientele includes such notables as Mrs. Howard Linn, it is clear that this is not because they could not produce a Dior or Balenciaga creation every night.

At the Harbor Point Association at nearby Harbor Springs, which is also typical of society's resorts, simplicity is carried to the point of banning automobiles. Residents like to point out that the eighty-two cottage owners from Chicago, Detroit, St. Louis, and Cincinnati include four Ford families. Even they have to "get a horse" at Harbor Point. Although life is theoretically austere, entertaining is so constant that hardly anyone attempts to get by with fewer than three in help.

But the highest status goes to those who lead a rough, primitive life when on vacation.

"We go up to the Bay of Fundy every summer," says one New York society matron. "It's absolutely unspoiled. There isn't even any hot water."

This is the right thing to do. And the approval it wins is not affected in the least by Easter trips to Bermuda, winter jaunts to St. Moritz, and occasional hops to Nassau or Jamaica.

Some resorts cater to this back-to-nature urge. San Francisco society, for example, goes native at Lake Tahoe. One group owns Secret Harbor there. Each family has its own camp site and does its own work. There is a central clubhouse where members may take shelter when it rains. Chicagoans who insist on roughing it go to Desbarats in Ontario, Canada, where blue jeans are worn, even at parties.

When not vacationing at these primitive hideaways, socialites can just relax and act rich at the newer, more glamorous spots.

In Dallas, as might be expected, the simple life has never really caught on. Vacationers favor such American resorts as Coronado Beach, Palm Springs, and Palm Beach. A large contingent can be found on the beach at Southampton. The moneyed set journeys anywhere from Venice to Tahiti. Some maintain homes in Italy. There is a group now building a luxury resort at Tryal in Jamaica, consisting of a polo club, golf course, and yacht basin.

The tax structure has had considerable effect on resort habits. A system has been evolved making it possible to enjoy resort life for practically nothing. This is the way it works: A group of friends buys shares in a hotel. As part of the deal, each participant reserves the right to build a cottage right on the hotel grounds. If the hotel loses money, it can be charged off income tax as a business loss. If it is a success, the shareholders make money—even if that income tax does take most of it. Husband and wife become directors of the corporation and so can deduct one round trip a year as a legitimate business expense. To make it even more profitable, the cottage can be rented—I know of at least one that commands $150 a day—during those seasons of the year when the owner is on Madison Avenue or the ski slopes of St. Moritz. The cottage then becomes a source of income, and maintenance and improvements can be counted as business expenses.

Round Hill, on a beautiful bay northwest of Montego Bay in Jamaica, is the best known of such resorts. I understand that the original twenty-five members chipped in $30,000 apiece.

Similar resorts can be found in Nassau, where the outer islands, such as Hog, Andros, or Eleuthera, are "in."

Hawaii is viewed as quite the place for the well-to-do to keep an extra house. Kahala Avenue on the outskirts of Honolulu has been called "Millionaires' Row" ever since Doris Duke built "Shangri La" there.

Although those who "know" drive twenty-five miles north to Hobe Sound, the climate at Palm Beach is so good that it cannot go the way of other old resorts. Every winter society columnists follow the sun and the subjects of their columns to Florida's lush Palm Beach. The Everglades Club is the center of social life. The Coral Beach Club and the Bath and Tennis Club are also meeting places for socialites. The season starts on December 31 and goes on for three months—a continuous whirl of Thursday-night dinners, Saturday-night dinner dances, and charity affairs.

"I always bring the children along," one sun worshiper told me. "The schools are quite accustomed to transfer students."

I also note that Mrs. William de Rham, who runs New York's top-society dancing classes, moves down to the Bath and Tennis Club at the height of the season to hold her classes there.

There is always a group who really wants to be different, and can afford to attempt some out-of-the-way trip like an African safari. This requires wealth, daring, and athletic prowess—all of which are qualities highly regarded by society. Africa has become so popular in the last few years that a friend who works for a foreign-language record company reports a small boom in sales of records teaching Swahili.

I understand that a big-name white hunter gets $750 for his services. But this is only a fraction of the costs of a safari. Bearers, supplies, gas, trucks, food, and liquor bring expenses up to an average of $3,550 per person, exclusive of the fare to Africa and back. When socialites are roughing it, a chef is likely to be taken along. While they may not dress for dinner, they certainly expect a good, really dry martini. When I last asked, a Kenya major hunting license good for twelve months, covering up to seventy-six animals, and excluding elephants and rhinoceros, came to $140. To kill rhinoceros required an additional license costing $56.00 and extra elephant licenses at $210 for a first elephant and $280 for a second were also needed.

Now all of the activities that have been described up to this point can be followed by anyone with money, information, and inclination. But there is yet one aspect of the high society life that cannot be bought so easily. That is membership in the social clubs. I mean by that clubs of the caliber of the Philadelphia Club for men and the Acorn Club for women in Philadelphia, the Somerset Club for men and the Chilton Club for women in Boston, the Pacific Union Club for men in San Francisco and the Detroit Club for men in Detroit.

"At one time it would have been impossible for a newcomer to be accepted in any of these clubs, but that is no longer true," a member of New York's top-ranking Union Club tells me. "When I joined the Union, twenty years ago, you had to be related to a member or belong to an old and distinguished family. Nowadays lots of people get in just by being friends of members."

The Brook Club and the Knickerbocker also enjoy considerable prestige in New York. The Brook is usually described as the club for the "fabulously rich." I am told that members do not even sign checks. A servant keeps track of their expenditures for them. Backgammon for enormous stakes is a popular afternoon's activity. The Knickerbocker was started in 1871 by a group who disapproved of the Union Club's liberality in accepting men without New York ancestry. Then there is the Century Club, known as the club for men of accomplishment in the arts and other creative fields. The Union League, the Manhattan, the Metropolitan, and the Jewish Harmonie are also tops among the influential men's clubs in New York.

"Not one of these clubs is as hard to get into as it used to be," a Union Leaguer admits. "Most of them are actually hungry for members. The day of the clubman is over. Time was when everyone belonged to half a dozen. Today, lots of men don't even belong to one."

The decline can be attributed to the rise of the country club and to the change in men's thinking. They no longer flee to the clubs to escape their wives. When home becomes unendurable, they get a divorce. And so most of the clubs are actually admitting ladies.

"The children and I sometimes join Bill at the Metropolitan Club for dinner. I think it's very dull," is the unkind comment of the wife of a member.

The women's clubs also have great social prestige. Many of them are harder on applicants than are the men's clubs. This is true of New York's Colony Club. And membership in that club is generally viewed as a sign of being accepted by the inner circle. Newcomers can and have made it—after untold years of struggle, of course.

As the Colony is typical of the country's top-ranking social clubs, I asked a member to spell out for me its requirements. A woman needs to have a proposer, seconder, and letters of recommendation. She also needs to meet with the chairman of the Board of Admissions and her three assistants and talk with them at some length. If admitted, she will get a letter informing her of this and a bill for the initiation fee and dues. If blackballed, she will never hear at all.

"You really need to know a lot of people in the club to be accepted," my friend told me. "It's hard to do it with just the few people technically needed for letters of recommendation."

But even if one is accepted, it takes about three years to become an active member. There has to be an opening in the club; a member must either leave or die.

This practice keeps the age level high. A typical new member is likely to be in her fifties. At tea, on a comfortable old sofa in one of the drawing rooms, I noticed that most of the ladies I met were in their seventies or eighties. The atmosphere is quiet and genteel. Members are checked in and out unobtrusively, so that guests or messages can be directed to them quickly.

The unfortunate coincidence of one of New York's most fashionable restaurants having the same name has led to considerable embarrassment.

As one woman puts it: "If a friend says she'll meet you at the Colony for lunch, it's inexcusable to ask if it's the club or the restaurant. You're supposed to *know*."

The second-ranking club for women is the Cosmopolitan, founded in 1911, eight years after the Colony was started. This club is intended for women active in the arts or professions, but many who are active in society only are members. Although highly regarded, this club is also very short on youth.

"It's the sort of place your aunt takes you to dinner," is the way a debutante described it to me.

The cult of togetherness has led to the rise of a number of family clubs of high social standing. The River and the Regency are among the best known of these.

The top athletic clubs are really just social clubs, too. One of the most noted is the New York Yacht Club, the oldest of its type in the country. The Racquet and Tennis Club is one of the centers for the strictly society games of court tennis and towie, a three-handed form of bridge. There is also the Links Club, founded in 1921, for golfers. The membership list has on it such notables as President Dwight D. Eisenhower, Henry Ford II, and Henry Luce. Then there is the Leash Club, started in 1926, for dog lovers.

The gradual easing of membership requirements at all of these clubs works to the advantage of newcomers. Membership is no longer limited to the inner circle. And yet, belonging to a club remains an Old Guard criterion for distinguishing the "ins" from the "outs."

"I managed to get into a club, even though my family never was in society. But I worked on it for years," one woman told me frankly. "The problem is one of making contacts with the right people."

"How did you do it?" I asked.

"Through charity," she replied.

CHAPTER III

Ah, Sweet Charity!

"IF A WOMAN comes to a strange city where she knows nobody, and wants to become a member of society quickly, all she needs to do is head for the nearest hospital and work like hell."

I could not even count how many times that statement has been made to me by members of society, public-relations men, social secretaries, and the paid officials of charitable organizations.

The number of charities aided by almost any socialite today is truly staggering.

"What does my brother-in-law do?" a society matron exclaimed in answer to a question. "Why, he doesn't do anything of a business nature, if that's what you mean. But he's the busiest man I know. He's president of the boys' club, chairman of the board of the museum, director of the settlement house, and, of course, he's active in raising funds for our hospital and for the alcoholism association."

At first glance one might almost assume that the capitalistic system has broken down, and that the rich are in Robin Hood fashion robbing themselves to give to the poor. But a second look will show that it does not quite work that way.

"I dread to think what would happen to us if they ever amended the income-tax law," the director of a leading charity told me privately.

Contributions of up to 30 per cent of annual income are tax deductible. This means that anyone who takes in half a million dollars a year—not unusual in the society and almost-society sets—

can give away $150,000 of it, most of which he could not have kept anyway.

Many socialites are, to be sure, truly dedicated people, donating both money and time to worthy causes. They feel a sense of obligation to the poor.

"It is unreasonable to suppose that because a man is rich he is also useless," the late Vincent Astor once said wistfully.

The chief way that the rich make themselves useful nowadays is by organizing and attending charity balls. In the last few years these have become the most conspicuous aspect of society life. Attendance is compulsory. Each socialite has his own pet charity. In order to get the support of his friends for his benefit, he must attend theirs.

"This is wonderful for all the charities. The only problem is wear and tear on the people who go," one young woman said to me wearily. "One of these days I'll break down."

She would certainly have cause. In checking through the newspapers, I discovered that in a six-week November–December period, fifteen major benefit balls were held in New York, and thirty others in Washington, D.C., Chicago, and San Francisco combined. There were also countless lesser affairs. Sources in Washington tell me that in six years sixteen new big balls have been added to the charity social calendar.

The frantic society matron calling a hotel manager and pleading desperately: "Give me a charity quick; I've got a ball organized!" has become a cliché joke comparable to "Who was that lady I saw you with?" Runner up is "Name a disease and there's a ball for it."

As a result, those in the ball set now look down their noses at the benefits they attend. It is correct table conversation to complain that there are too many of them, that they are too big and too flamboyant.

The classic example of bigness is New York's annual April in Paris Ball, which literally overwhelms the mind of anyone economically inclined. One year Cecil Beaton, topflight scenic designer, transformed the ballroom of the Waldorf-Astoria into a Paris circus of the eighteenth century. Marlene Dietrich acted as ringmaster, introducing acts from the circuses of American John Ringling North and Frenchman Jean Amar. And just in case the circus motif might not appeal to some of the 1,000 guests—some years there are more—scenes were presented from a current Broadway hit. There was also a fashion show of creations by big-name French designers. Ten French wines and champagnes were served at dinner. Guests danced until dawn to the music of two orchestras, and those who were still strong enough stayed for breakfast. The air was scented with perfumes costing $25.00 an ounce. In the course of the night an estimated $10,000 worth was sprayed out.

But all of this extravagance did not take a single penny away from the beneficiaries. Commercial sponsors paid for the lavish display. The entire $150 per person charge (tax deductible, of course) went to charity.

Most of these big balls actually do a tremendous amount of good. Balls raising $30,000 for the beneficiary are almost commonplace, and some do even better than that. One annual ball nets more than $200,000.

Despite their objections, it is hard for socialites to find any other really effective way to help the less fortunate. Very few are equipped to do social work, or even to manage an office, type, or file. And so the basic function they can serve is that of financiers—providing the money that makes it possible for the charity to hire trained workers and office personnel, to buy equipment and supplies, maintain or build new hospitals and homes.

The Old Guard complaint about charity balls is quite sincere. This group really prefers home entertaining. But members are afraid of being labeled ostentatious (a society curse word). A huge party costing between $20,000 and $100,000 can be justified—among the rich, anyway—if it is for a debut or a wedding. But there are, unfortunately, only a limited number of either in any given family. And so charity affairs have begun to enter the home. This is a growing trend in suburban areas.

"A private party in a private home, completely underwritten," is the way one socialite in Philadelphia's suburb of Radnor describes a dance given at her home. The beneficiary was this woman's favorite charity, a health foundation, and the commercial sponsor was a large Philadelphia department store.

Those in society do not limit their benefit-going to the evening hours. The charity luncheon is also a fixture on today's social scene. Some women attend these daily, reducing the size of their bankbook totals (which does not trouble them too much) and increasing the size of their figures (which does).

The luncheons today are criticized by many serious-minded socialites. They know they must go—again it is essential to support the activities of friends. But I have become aware of a growing feeling that these luncheons do not really benefit the charities enough.

"The problem is that hotel costs are so high," one active committee member revealed to me. "At many luncheons costing $7.50 a plate, the charity gets only 50 cents per person.

"I favor the luncheons anyway," she added. "They bring the charities to the attention of many women with money to contribute. And that's very important in the long run."

Although daytime and evening benefits are the most publicized aspect of society's contribution to charity today, they are the end, not the beginning, of a life at least partly devoted to philanthropy.

"If you want to go to the parties, you've got to do the work first," says the chairman of one of Chicago's big charity balls.

This may not be true for a McCormick, Armour, Van Beuren, Lodge, Belmont, or Rockefeller. Directors of charities will go to any lengths to entice a big name onto a committee.

And as most organizations have one paid secretary who does the basic jobs anyway, they are able to use the standard approach: "You don't have to do anything; just let us use your name."

But for the rest of struggling, rich humanity it is work, work, work.

Most think it well worth the effort.

"Charity's importance to the budding socialite has become measurably greater during the last two years—largely because of the increasing number of benefits," a leading society press agent reports.

The charity road to social advancement is often tried nowadays, and is frequently successful. Valuable contacts can be made along the way. Anyone who is really willing to work hard becomes essential to a charity and wins her way into the hearts of the society people supporting it.

And so through the years this realization has attracted a number of would-be socialites to philanthropic organizations. The charities are well aware of the fact that some of their most ardent workers do every chore with not-so-selfless devotion. But they do not care. If anything, they encourage these aspirations. The work is done, anyway—and it is good work.

The social aspect helps the charities to tap the pocketbooks of even that group described by the irrepressible Lady Astor: "I find that so many people don't love their neighbors."

Selecting the right charity is a basic problem for newcomers. An organization or auxiliary must have prestige and yet be open to people without old-line antecedents. In a small town or suburb little choice is offered. There is usually only one major hospital, one art museum, one symphony orchestra, or one old-age home. In some areas only a United Fund, Community Chest or Heart, Cancer or Arthritis Foundation has an active fund-raising committee. But in the bigger cities the number is so great that it bewilders the un-initiated. Often the prestige charities are the least publicized. The benefits given for them are apt to be unpretentious (I mean com-paratively, of course). They may have guest lists of only 300 to 600 people, instead of the 1,000, 1,400, and even 3,000 men and women at some of the balls which have no real society standing.

The social position of a given charity is very hard for the new-comer to discover. A study of the names on the committees is singularly unrewarding. Keen-eyed social aspirants from time to time triumphantly spot important names on relatively new charity committees. But the mere fact that these women are listed is in itself of little significance. In some cases the committees are virtually closed to outsiders. Or the woman may be there in name only.

"Many socialites let their names be used for charities with which they have no real connection," says Emmett Davis, society public-relations man. "Sometimes one woman will even be listed on com-mittees for three or more benefit luncheons to be held on the same day. She may not attend any of them."

The newcomers must attempt to find out who really holds

positions of responsibility in a given charity. For example, Mrs. Lytle Hull works hard for the Musicians' Emergency Fund. Mrs. Augustus G. Paine, II, whose mother is the former Consuelo Vanderbilt, gives her time and energy to the Boys' Club in and out of ball season. Mrs. August Belmont, who founded the Metropolitan Opera Guild, remains active in that group. Mrs. T. Markoe Robertson devotes herself to Boys Harbor and the International Rescue Committee.

The charities which get this type of valid society support have the highest ranking. These are the ones which are apt to give outsiders the cold shoulder, but they are always worth a try.

I have observed that the auxiliary of one major hospital that benefited from a debutante ball is made up of women whose names are *not* listed in the *Social Register*. And so the mother who wishes to make her daughter a debutante can easily see that she has a better chance for that ball than for, say, the Grosvenor Ball given for the Old Guard Grosvenor Neighborhood House. On the other hand, recognition by such a charity does not mean so much in terms of social standing as does acceptance by the more conservative one.

And newcomers sometimes do get in to the prestige groups. I have a friend, not of the world of society, who became interested in the work being done by a philanthropic organization and offered her services as a volunteer. She was accepted without question. When she began to work, she found herself surrounded by members of New York's inner circle.

"How do you get along with them?" I asked.

"Oh, they're delighted to have me," she replied. "I'm the only volunteer who knows how to type and write good business letters. The problem is one of conversation. They mostly talk about their daughters' debuts. I never know what to say. But lately a couple of them have warmed up to me and have hinted that they might consider recommending my little girl to the cotillion committee when she gets older. I haven't had the nerve to ask which cotillion that might be."

This sounds like the kind of blind luck that strikes only those who do not want it. But actually the same sort of thing has happened to many with real social ambitions.

A list of the most conservative—and, therefore, most prestige-laden—charities in New York would have to include the Yorkville Community Association, Sheltering Arms Children's Service, Boys' Club of New York, Roosevelt Hospital, Judson Health Center, and Musicians' Emergency Fund. All of these are supported by some of the biggest names in the city's social roster. The annual midwinter dinner dance of the Yorkville Community Association is a must for old-line society. This group is so exclusive that it shuns publicity. Two of the recent chairmen for the tea dance given for the Sheltering Arms are descended from families associated with that charity for a century. That is typical of this group.

Many of the neighborhood settlement houses have a high society aura. These were the classic charities for the rich of an earlier era. And so descendants of old and wealthy families often inherit a settlement-house connection. In a number of cases the philanthropic group becomes so well organized that it lives on long after the neighborhood's need for aid has ended. For some years New York society members were troubled by snide comments about the maintenance of a settlement house for what had become a nice residential section. Someone finally got the idea of merging it with an underendowed center in a slum district—and so everyone was happy.

Most society press agents advise clients to concentrate on likelier prospects. They suggest such philanthropies as the New York Foundling Hospital, Kips Bay Boys' Club, Lenox Hill Neighborhood Association, the Lighthouse for the Blind, and the associations that deal with cancer, heart disease, and other illnesses. Most of these have considerable support from the old-line families, too, so they have prestige. But they are ready to consider newcomers who are willing to work hard and contribute money.

I know of one charity that has been eating its old society cake and having its new society money, too. It has been giving two balls a year—one exclusive and one not so exclusive. At the second one generous newcomers are accepted on the key committees. Even the chairman sometimes bears a name never heard in these circles before 1940. In recent years the second ball has become so successful that there is talk of merging the two.

As is the way in the one world of society, the philanthropic setup is similar in almost every city. What are some of the nation's key charities?

In Boston the older families support the Massachusetts General Hospital. The board of trustees is of *Social Register* rank. The affiliated Vincent Memorial Hospital is aided by the Vincent Club, which is "the" club for young women socialites.

"It's so exclusive that it looks down on the Junior League," a League executive, just returned from Boston, revealed to me.

The Red Cross also receives the assistance of the social set. This is true in most other cities as well, by the way. Inner-circle families traditionally like to find a place for a son or brother as an official of the Red Cross.

Philadelphia society supports Emergency Aid and almost any local hospital I might name. Moving west to San Francisco, I find the Children's Hospital of the East Bay a most fashionable charity. The fact that it benefits from the East Bay Debutante Ball does not hurt it at all. The San Francisco Symphony has the support of music-loving socialites. The annual Symphony Ball is one of those balls to end all balls—it is held simultaneously in four of the city's leading hotels, and shuttle busses carry the 3,000 guests from one to the other. Down in Los Angeles the Children's Hospital is aided by many of the city's oldest families. It is the beneficiary of a prestige debutante ball, the Las Madrinas.

There is a lot of money in Texas, and many people benefit from it. The late Hugh Roy Cullen, the oilman, contributed $100,000,000 to the University of Houston. The story goes that he once threw in an extra $2,250,000 when the football team beat Baylor. Hospitals, such as the Methodist, are also favored charities. In Dallas, the Dallas Symphony Orchestra and the Dallas School of Blind Children are just two examples out of the many, many beneficiaries of society's largesse. Both receive the proceeds from huge annual balls.

"In Cleveland, charity balls have never gained a real foothold," a member of one of that city's oldest families tells me. "Socialites work instead for the annual Christmas Mart, held for the benefit of Maternal Health."

Chicago society is sometimes unkindly called the "hospital aristocracy," a reference to the fact that charity has been used by many to achieve social advancement. Presbyterian-St. Luke's Hospital is supported by inner circle families. Most of the Chicagoans to whom I have spoken rate it as the number-one charity.

"Newcomers have hard going," one of them added.

The Passavant Hospital's Women's Board is under constant siege by ladies with daughters, as it is the beneficiary of the Passavant Cotillion, Chicago's top-ranking debutante ball. It, too, does not encourage recent arrivals to society. The Boys' Club, which is the city's third major charity, is more likely to extend a welcoming hand to outsiders.

The charity ball setup is highly developed in Washington, D.C. As the make-up of society there changes at least partly with every election, few of the charities limit participation by newcomers. The International Ball, given for the Children's Convalescent Home, and the Symphony Ball for the National Symphony are two of the most important events on Washington's social calendar.

In all cities newcomers face the same problems. And many of them have admitted to me privately that they have no idea of how to get into a charity and gain acceptance by the key members of the committees.

In general, those charities that give huge benefit balls—and most of them do nowadays—offer the best opportunities. But attending these affairs is one of the least effective ways of being noticed by the socialites in the sponsoring organization.

A newcomer can attend ten balls and never meet anyone who will help her social career. Society is a closed circle. Members tend to view anyone they do not know already as unworthy of acquaintance. A woman may be ever so beautiful and smartly dressed. A man might be a model of charm and good manners. Both can go through an evening ignored. "Who are you and why are you here?" is the question they will read in the eyes of those around them.

And so the approach must be made long before the benefit ball. It is best if an introduction can be obtained to someone who works for the charity. Press agents, of course, provide this service—for a fee.

"I found that a woman I know only casually through church was ready—more than that, was eager—to bring me into her charity," one brand-new socialite told me. "I guess she figured I'd contribute heavily, and money is what they all want."

Most charities are also hungry for volunteers willing to take over the many tedious jobs connected with fund raising or running an organization. Business friends and fellow members of private school Parent-Teachers Associations are also often willing to perform introductions.

When a contact cannot be found, the direct approach must be tried. A letter should be sent or a telephone call made to the headquarters of the organization. Interest in the aims of the charity and a willingness to do hard work should be stated. I have known this simple method to succeed many times, despite the doubts often expressed about it.

I sometimes think, however, of one woman who was not able to get anywhere with the old-line charities she had set her heart on. As she had plenty of money, she tried a completely new approach: She started a charitable organization of her own. The first year most of the people who worked with her were newcomers themselves. The cause she was aiding was, and is, a very worthy one and had widespread appeal. And so by the second year she began to attract a few members of inner-circle families. When I looked over the committees for her most recent benefit, I could see a balance between old and new names. This woman will probably soon be welcomed by those very charities that were cool to her only a short time ago.

This is an extreme case, however. Most eager volunteers can find a charity ready to accept their money and energies.

As is true of all aspects of society life, the earlier a person applies, the better. Junior volunteers—from private schools and good colleges, of course—are welcomed with open arms. Many of the prestige charities actually have requests for volunteers posted on the bulletin boards of the socially favored private schools. I have seen them there myself. The youngsters help out in settlement houses or children's hospital wards after school, or in camps for the needy in the summer. I even detect the beginning of a trend toward subdebutante balls. The annual Gold and Silver Ball, for example, for the Girls' Service League (to aid girls with emotional problems), is arranged by teen-agers. Debutantes and postdebutantes can usually find places on the junior or debutante committees for many of the ranking benefit balls. And a good number of charity organizations have junior auxiliaries. As the juniors become seniors—marriage does it, as well as the passage of time—they naturally move on to the regular women's auxiliaries and positions on the policy-making committees.

There are, of course, countless volunteer activities for people of all ages. Workers can type fund-raising business letters, or read to the blind, or help in a children's playroom in a hospital, or organize activities in a settlement house, or assist in the library of an old-age home, or catalog pictures for a museum, or organize concert or lecture series, etc., etc. These are the basic volunteer jobs, and most people know about them.

But very little is known about the aspect of charity work that is most important for the rising socialite—the newcomer's role in organizing a benefit.

Here are some of the possibilities: Volunteers always have the opportunity to raise money for a benefit. In fact, they are required to do so. And those who are successful on the financial end are apt to be successful on the social end, too. Almost every ball chairman is dreaming of a commercial sponsor. A woman whose husband will underwrite the affair is nearly "in" already. That is why so many of the most recent arrivals in society are wives of presidents or chairmen of the boards of major companies. Today a number of women head businesses themselves. One female president has her firm sponsor one major ball each year and underwrites a part of the expenses for at least one more.

If the volunteer cannot sponsor the ball herself (individually or through her husband), it is nearly as good for her to bring in the firm that will do so.

"It was easier than I thought it would be," I was told by a woman who has done this. "I made appointments with executives of several corporations. Naturally, I picked those who do business with the firm my husband is associated with. The third one I asked was interested. After all, underwriting a ball is a comparatively inexpensive way of getting a great deal of publicity and advertising."

But those without big-league industrial connections have many other opportunities to make the benefit a success. Selling tickets is vital. And so buying (or getting friends to buy) huge blocks of tickets, costing from $25.00 to $150 apiece, may bring a volunteer sudden popularity.

"This is so overt that it works best for a quiet woman with charm," an official at one of the charities commented to me. "Others are apt to be called 'pushing.' "

Another way of buying in is by getting advertisements for the ball program, or by having gifts donated for door prizes or raffles. This is the method most often tried by those who do not have unlimited funds themselves. By aggressive selling a woman can bring in a huge number of advertisements or gifts.

"I always ask for the ad first, and if they won't give me one, I ask for a gift," one volunteer explains.

In cities where there are a lot of charity balls and luncheons, the tradespeople get hardened to such requests, however. The owner of one of New York's most fashionable pastry shops told me that he gets as many as thirty requests a day during the height of the benefit season. He turns almost all of them down. Hairdressers, who were once likely customers, have gotten tough, too.

"I used to let them offer permanents as gifts," one Fifty-seventh Street hairdresser remembered, waving a hand in despair. "But now I only give a shampoo and set, and even that is just for my very best customers."

The volunteer with money can get around this reluctance easily. She simply donates the gifts, be they diamond clips, cars, or cases of scotch, herself.

Sometimes volunteers arrange for the entertainment. I know of women who have provided fashion shows through connections in the industry, and others who have used contacts in advertising and television to get entertainers to donate their services.

One woman with no previous social background decided two

years in advance that she wanted her daughter to be presented as a debutante at a cotillion given for a hospital charity. The first year she brought in a tremendous amount of advertising for the program. As a result, the second year her daughter was asked to be on the junior committee selling books of chances for the gifts raffled off at the ball. The girl was charming and had the opportunity to use her charm on committee members. The mother did not let up anyway. She brought in even more advertisements that year. And the following season the daughter was presented at the ball.

If the pressure is great enough, the preparation time can be shorter. One family decided almost at the last minute that they wanted their daughter to come out at one of the mass balls. The grandfather, owner of a large local firm, promptly offered a big advertisement for the program, to be given if the girl was accepted. At the same time he had a number of his business contacts with social background write letters recommending his grandchild. The pressure was such that the invitations committee gave way and asked the mother and daughter to come in for an interview. They managed to pass with flying colors, and the young lady became a debutante.

This reminds me of a scene I observed one day when I was in the office of a charitable organization. Applicants for the debutante ball were being discussed. And I found that the daughters of women who had devoted both time and money to the charity had suddenly become as acceptable debutantes as any Vanderbilt or Whitney.

One seemingly eligible girl, however, was turned down. A committee member gave the reason succinctly: "Her family is just too stingy."

This simply goes to show that there is no substitute for prolonged expenditure of money and hard work.

"I do so many jobs that they can't get along without me," one woman reveals.

Such a volunteer can eventually become a member of the key committees. She may be made a member of the invitations committee to a debutante ball. In time she might come to be the chairman of a charity ball. And this position is recognized even by the Old Guard as a symbol of belonging.

I was recently introduced to a woman who had just become chairman of a prestige benefit ball. She had no compunction about admitting ("but don't mention my name") that this was the end result of a long and calculated plan.

"A number of my friends plugged away at the old-line charities right from the start. They figured that in time they would work their way up. And some of them have done it, too," she told me. "But that was never my system. I began with charities where I would have a chance to shine. And gradually I moved to others with higher standing. I was always careful to pick those which set up committees containing a mixture of old society names and those of people I knew were fairly new. If another newcomer had made it, I figured I could, too."

She paused and thought for a moment. "I guess that right at this minute there are people looking over the committees for this ball. They're spotting my name and saying to themselves: 'Why, if she made it, so can I!'"

CHAPTER IV

Society's Backstage Wife

THE modest title of social secretary conceals some of the most powerful women in society today. Considering their influence, I find that surprisingly little is known about them. They are not secretaries at all. They actually run social bureaus. But no one calls them by any other name. The same term is used—just to add to the confusion—for those who handle correspondence for socialites. Members of the inner circle know intuitively which type is being mentioned. But even they are apt to dismiss social secretaries as mere party-givers, to be called in to arrange a daughter's wedding reception, a debut supper dance, or a business cocktail party.

In theory, that is all a social secretary does. In practice, she becomes a social arbiter and can make or break a newcomer. The source of her power lies in her lists of subdebutantes, debutantes, escorts, and society people. These lists are never published, never publicized, and are seen only by the social secretary's clients, but they determine to a considerable extent who will or will not be invited to the major events of the season. It can be almost as important to get on the list of one of the big social secretaries as to make the *Social Register*.

Most names on the lists are old line, but I have observed that there are also a good many newcomers with money. As these are the lists that are checked and rechecked by society people giving parties, being included can make all the difference to an aspiring socialite's future. A position on the key lists cannot be bought in an obvious way. To buy in, the newcomer must be prepared to give lavish parties, handled for her, of course, by the secretary.

To become recognized as socialites, a family must be able to give a party that is successful in society's own terms. It is not enough for people to have a good time. The question that is always implied is "which people"? In other words, a debut is not just a party for an eighteen-year-old girl. If it were, any girl could be a debutante. The word "debut" has come to mean that a girl is presented to society. Socially prominent people must attend her party if it is to count. Similarly any party can be a society party, or just a party, depending on the guest list. And that list can be gilded by the social secretary. Her real society clients do not need her help in this aspect of party-giving. For newcomers, it is essential.

A woman whose name appears in the 1960 *Social Register* for the first time told me that she owes her present position in society to the efforts of one of New York's leading secretaries.

"I came to New York from Chicago fifteen years ago. My husband owned his own business and was making a lot of money, but we weren't society people. For a couple of years I must admit that we just floundered. I knew that we needed outside help. I had heard of one of the social secretaries, so I went to call on her. I was planning to give a big cocktail party, and I thought I could use that as my excuse for sounding her out. But I found her very understanding. She knew just what I was driving at."

Her first concrete suggestions concerned that original party. She naturally took over all the arrangements—the catering, flowers, decorations, and music. That is social-secretary standard operating procedure. But then she began to give that little extra push at which these women excel. She helped the hostess to expand her guest list by suggesting socialites with whom some connection could be found—mostly through the husband's business and through the church the family attended.

But seeing the party as just the first step in a long-range plan, the secretary had a number of other suggestions to make. Most of them concerned the children. She urged that the son be transferred to prep school, the little daughter entered in society's favorite dancing class.

And she implemented the suggestions with facts about how to apply and whom to approach for necessary recommendations.

The mother kept in touch with her from then on, and found her particularly helpful in getting the daughter presented. She explained the whole subdebutante setup and helped to get letters of recommendation. When debut time drew near, the secretary actually picked the mass presentation ball where the girl stood the best chance of acceptance.

"What surprised me most," the woman continued, "was the way this whole society thing snowballs. Within a few years my husband and I were being invited to some fairly high-level parties. We got into the clubs we wanted to. Last year we were asked to join a subscription dance group at the Sheraton-East. And as for the children...they go absolutely everywhere. My daughter was invited to nine debut parties in the Christmas vacation of the year she came out. And my son, of course, can go partying every night he's home from college."

The power to achieve such results is concentrated in the hands of a very few women. In New York they are Mrs. William H. Tew of Tappin & Tew, Mrs. Chester Burden of Burden Littell Entertainment Bureau, and Katherine Palmer of Chapin & Palmer. All three are socialites themselves, with *Social Register* listing. And all of them emanate an air of absolute confidence.

Small, trim, well-groomed Mrs. Tew started in business in 1930 in partnership with the late Mrs. Huntington Tappin. Her bureau has tremendous social prestige. A number of members of well-established families declare that they swear by her list of debutantes. And yet Mrs. Tew has said to me that every year more girls who are not of the old-line families are making debuts.

Mrs. Burden opened her bureau in Saks Fifth Avenue in 1929, together with Mrs. Robert Littell, who has since retired. The office was taken from Saks a long time ago and moved to the fashionable East Sixties. In addition to the private parties, which are the specialty of all these secretaries, Burden Littell handles many theater benefits. As far as parties go, everyone I know who has used her services has reported that Mrs. Burden is a perfectionist, giving meticulous attention to the smallest detail.

"Katherine Palmer's rise can only be described as meteoric," an Old Guard society matron asserts. "In just a few years she has gotten both the bulk and the cream of the business."

And yet, running a social bureau is the second career of her life, and New York is the second city. The first career was singing and the first city was Philadelphia. In her younger days Miss Palmer augmented her income by addressing invitations for a Philadelphia stationer. Her handwriting is beautiful—an old-fashioned skill still highly regarded by social bureaus.

She started her own business in 1950 in the Hotel Carlyle, but soon moved it to her old-fashioned, comfortable apartment on East Seventy-second Street. Despite the use of the name, the partnership with Mrs. L. H. Paul Chapin lasted a brief six months. To bring in the fashionable Long Island social crowd, Miss Palmer approached Mrs. Roger Tuckerman, a socialite with excellent Long Island contacts. Mrs. Tuckerman is still a staff member, handling parties for her own clients.

The influence of these three ranking secretaries extends to the most distant suburbs.

"Easthampton and Southampton are our happy hunting grounds," one of them reported to me cheerfully.

They handle parties for former New Yorkers in Virginia, Massachusetts, and Rhode Island. And their contacts are excellent—at least throughout the eastern seaboard.

I was in Miss Palmer's office one day when a prospective client telephoned from Princeton, New Jersey. Without an instant's preparation, Miss Palmer was able to respond: "Your daughter is marrying a Whiting (name fictitious)? I wonder if he's related to Beatrice Sanders Whiting of Philadelphia? She's his mother? Well, I know Mrs. Whiting and her sister, who is Mrs. Thomas Bainwright, and I handled the debut party for—"

It is these little things that separate the women from the girls in society's exclusive circle.

The social secretaries in other cities possess the same power.

"About two thirds of the big parties in Philadelphia are arranged by social secretaries," Meyer Davis, society's best-known orchestra leader, informed me. "That's about the same proportion as in New York. In Detroit I'd say about one third."

I asked Mr. Davis, who is booked by these women, to select for me the top social secretaries in key cities. He named Philadelphia's Mrs. Edward J. MacMullan, Mrs. Wirt L. Thompson, and Mrs. S. Powell Griffits; Washington's Mrs. Kurt Hetzel and Mary-Stuart Montague Price; Wilmington's Secretariat, Ltd. (Mary R. Hynson, Kathryn A. Buchan); and Detroit's Gertrude Engel and Frances E. Brossy.

All of these women maintain the local lists of those who are in the inner circle, or are moving there as fast as they can go.

I asked Miss Palmer how people get on her list.

"My first source is the *Social Register,*" she answered. "I go through it with a fine-tooth comb, picking out people who have sons and daughters and would be likely to give parties."

Registers for other cities are consulted as well. This is done mostly to expand the list of boys, as names of available escorts are an absolute requirement in getting and holding debut business. And boys will come to New York parties from Boston, Philadelphia, or even Detroit if the hostess has a famous society name or is a former native of those cities. So will girls, but nobody needs girls, unfortunately, at least as party guests. There are too many of them already.

Miss Palmer gets additional names from the society pages of the newspapers, from friends, and from the guest lists of the parties she gives.

"I add to my lists every day," she went on. "By now I'd say that about one third of the names are not in the *Social Register.*"

Parents frequently call up and ask that a child be put on the list. This simple method sometimes works, Miss Palmer intimated, particularly in the case of a boy. The youngster is not put on the list just like that. The secretary checks around and if the child goes to a good school and is known to some other client, she may add him (and in rare instances, her) to the list.

I looked over the cabinets that contain the filing cards with the names that make up the famous "list." They are divided in this manner: a "baby" file on girls from ten to seventeen and a half, current debutantes, postdebutantes, prep-school boys, men aged from seventeen to twenty, and men over twenty. Girls and boys over seventeen are considered as being in the "party" file. Girls stay there three or four years, boys indefinitely. Only marriage removes them from the list.

"On a boy's wedding day I tear up his card," Miss Palmer declared dramatically, adding a moment later: "Of course I expect him back on file in eleven or twelve years as the father of a future debutante."

As Miss Palmer specializes in weddings and debuts, she is more drastic in this regard than are many of the other secretaries, who go in more heavily for grown-up parties.

The lists of current debutantes and eligible boys, all the secretaries agree, are the ones most frequently consulted. It is a commentary on today's social scene to realize that Miss Palmer maintains a list of 300 debutantes, similar numbers of sub and postdebutantes, and 2,500 boys ("Or is it 2,800 now?" she mused).

The lists are studied by anyone giving a party. The hostess—somehow it hardly ever is the host—goes to the secretary's office to make up the invitation list. When completed, it includes the party-giver's close friends, *plus* a group culled from the secretary's list.

I do not mean by this that complete strangers are invited on the say so of the secretary. But by studying the facts about each girl or boy listed, the debutante and her parents can frequently find some connection—through school, business, church, charity, or mutual friends. The debutantes and boys do not insist on knowing the hostess well, anyway. If the word gets around that "everyone is going" to a party, they will go. And when a top social secretary is handling the affair, that word gets around.

Even members of the old-line families consult the lists, particularly for debuts. Many young girls feel it essential that *every* debutante and desirable escort of the season be invited to their private debut parties, and they are likely to miss a few, without the reminder of the names on file.

A Philadelphia debutante who came out at the Assembly and might be expected to know "everyone" told me that she and her mother spent three hours at Mrs. MacMullan's apartment in the

Rittenhouse Plaza, consulting the lists before sending out invitations to her private debut party.

"The way Mrs. MacMullan works it is to have every deb blue-pencil her initials on the card of each girl or boy she decides to invite," the debutante explained. "Whenever I saw a card with a lot of initials put down by other girls, I added mine. And then Mrs. MacMullan suggests people she thinks would help make it a good party."

This is no doubt the reason why a friend without *Mayflower* background once commented to me: "If you want to get ahead in Philadelphia society, it would be hard to find a more valuable ally than Mrs. MacMullan."

To make insurance doubly sure, many of the leading secretaries hold dances of their own, or take over the arrangements for leading society balls. Mrs. MacMullan, for example, handles Philadelphia's noted Charity Ball, an annual benefit for six hospitals. About one thousand Philadelphians attend the ball. But the society set can be found among the three hundred guests specially invited to a pre-ball dinner. As is the way at these affairs, positions on the debutantes' committee are particularly high in prestige.

"I don't know why I was asked to be on that committee," a little debutante confessed to me ingenuously. "My family moved to Dallas when I was little and we only came back to Philadelphia the year before my debut." I understand that Mrs. MacMullan arranged the girl's lavish private debut party.

Mrs. MacMullan's influence with the younger married set is enhanced by her handling of the Piccadilly Dinner Dances, one of Philadelphia's many private subscription dances. She has been running these affairs since 1941.

In Washington, D.C., the Debutante Cotillion and Thanksgiving Ball was started and is still run by Miss Price. A debutante in her day, she was presented at Baltimore's top society Bachelors' Cotillon. She sees to it that subdebutantes are invited to her ball. It is the first major event they attend.

In New York a number of the ranking subdebutante affairs are in the capable hands of the social secretaries. The sought-after Colony Dance is handled by Mrs. Gertrude L. Earl, who is one of the grand old ladies in the field. At the age of eighty she has given up the frenzied work of debuts and weddings, but she still serves as secretary-treasurer of the Junior Assemblies. Invitations to the exclusive Junior Dinner Dance are handled by Mrs. Sidney Mc-Call of Tappin & Tew. The Metropolitan Dances are run by Mrs. Burden.

"The Bureau handles the mechanics only," Mrs. Burden was careful to make clear to me. "Invitations are up to the policy committee of eight ladies."

But she did concede that applications often come straight to her from mothers of subdebutantes, who are well aware of what a social secretary can do for them.

In assessing the power wielded by the social secretary one might well consider the inside story of the Versailles Debutante Ball. I heard the beginning of it from Stuart Whitmarsh, former publisher of the *Debutante Register,* who originated the ball, and the rest of it from Mrs. Tew.

When Queen Elizabeth banned debutante presentations at Buckingham Palace, it became obvious to a number of entrepreneurs that a substitute could hardly fail to be a great success. And although members of society are apt to gloss over this fact, many major functions are started purely as commercial ventures. The best idea to come up was that of holding a ball at Versailles and having French royalty in attendance.

Setting up such an event was not too difficult. The French Government was assured that the ball would be a benefit for the restoration of Versailles. A French committee, headed by the Duchesse de Maille and the Duc de Brissac, was quickly formed to provide the required aura of royalty. But to produce the essential debutantes, the group planning the presentation knew they had to approach a leading American social secretary. Miss Price did the job the first year. The following year Mrs. MacMullan took over. The committee believed that by adding her contacts to those already brought in by Miss Price, they could make the affair a social landmark.

Then shortly before the ball trouble came. The French committee decided that it had become too commercial, in terms of tie-ins with tours and American sponsors. Mrs. MacMullan resigned. Almost everyone connected with the ball felt that with her action, the affair would have to be called off. The group of debutantes she had selected had no choice but to follow the lead of Philadelphia's social arbiter and withdraw.

At this critical juncture an American committee member thought of Mrs. Tew. And she did not let him down. Her contacts both in New York and other cities were solid enough to produce a group of thirty-three American debutantes almost immediately, and the ball went on as planned.

The following year, the ball was held without the assistance of Mrs. Tew. The net result: six debutantes from the United States.

What a social secretary can do for a major ball is as nothing compared to what she can do for the individual. Her ability to help her clients is increased by the fact that she knows of virtually every single party that is given in both city and suburbs. She is literally forced to be a record-keeper.

There are only about forty days of the year that are suitable for debutante parties—the Thanksgiving and Christmas holidays and the so-called "little seasons" of June and September. The secretaries maintain date books in which they list all debut parties being given, by others as well as themselves, so as to prevent conflicts. As the same debutantes and men go to most of the parties, having two big affairs on the same night could prove disastrous to both sets of hosts. Weddings, charity balls, visits by royalty, and sports events can be equally devastating in their effect on private parties. And so records of these are kept, too. The fear of getting caught is such that even the deadliest enemies exchange information on who is giving what party when.

A couple of years ago a leading social secretary refused to clear dates with her chief rival. Her silence lasted until she discovered she had arranged a debut party in Westchester for the same night that the other secretary had one scheduled on Long Island. As Long Island's "Gold Coast" area of Cold Springs Harbor, Syosset, and Locust Valley outranks Westchester in high society terms, it was a ghastly error. The following day she telephoned to compare all future dates.

The need for a record of social events is so great that a date-book system is in operation in almost every city. And as a rule the person who keeps it becomes influential in the society setup. In Philadelphia the dates are checked by George W. Rehfuss of J. E. Caldwell & Co., jeweler and stationer. And Mr. Rehfuss is regularly described to me by friends in Philadelphia as "our social arbiter." In Boston mothers of debutantes register with M. T. Bird & Co., stationers. In Dallas it is Party Service. In many suburbs a local matron keeps the book and is listed in the community association yearbook.

Even in communities in which socialites claim "there is no social secretary here," closer investigation has led me every time to one woman, usually the mother of several girls, who is keeping an informal date book.

"I don't do it as a business," one of them told me, "I just do it for fun. I like to know what's going on in town."

And I observed that everyone called her as a matter of course before scheduling a party. Even though her gain was not financial, she did profit from her work. She literally acted as her own social secretary. Her entire family was invited to everything. It never even occurred to socialites to exclude her children from the sub-debutante parties. Without any old-line connections she had become a key member of local society.

The degree of power possessed by these date-book keepers was brought home to me recently when a young executive I know was transferred to Norfolk, Virginia. Remembering that one of my friends was a native of the town, a Junior Leaguer and a debutante, I suggested that he ask her how to get to know people there. She promptly gave him the name of the woman who keeps the informal date book.

"She knows everybody and everything that's going on. She can get you invited to any of the really good parties."

In some cities the society editor of the newspaper does the job. As she has to keep a date book for her own information anyway, she is a natural source for local hostesses. Most editors—at least for a time—try to stay off all other social secretary work. But it is a constant struggle. The person who keeps society's date book by that very fact is in a position to create debutantes and socialites.

A former society reporter on the Richmond *News Leader* informed me that Mrs. Adelaide Goolsby, the society editor, keeps the Richmond date book and is constantly besieged by would-be socialites. She receives a steady stream of phone calls requesting information on how to act when invited to a formal tea or which fork to use.

When the record-keeper is a social secretary as well, her power is truly formidable. All of the ranking secretaries have grown accustomed to giving newcomers that needed push.

As I have always heard that using a social secretary to arrange the way into society requires almost unlimited funds, I asked several of the most prominent women in this field just how much it does cost.

"I don't charge at all for advice," Mrs. Burden told me.

Social secretaries may not put a price tag on guidance, but they naturally expect to do a party at some point. And the party—or parties—of course, is where the cost lies.

"The absolute minimum for a dinner dance in New York is $5,000," said Miss Palmer. "A supper dance for 375 to 400 guests would start at about $10,000."

Those figures are the rock-bottom minimum. New York socialites have reported to me that usually a supper dance runs from $25,000 on up. In some parts of the country the cost is lower. In Boston, for example, lavish expenditures for parties are considered in poor taste. But in Philadelphia and Wilmington, not to mention Texas or southern California, costs are similar to New York.

The social secretary is paid, either directly or indirectly, for the party. Some charge a percentage of the cost of the affair. Others get commissions from the caterer, florist, decorator, dance band, photographer, ballroom manager, and anyone else whose services they use.

Most of the secretaries I spoke with favored this method. They contend that it means that the client really is not paying for the service at all.

"It's the same thing as buying furniture through an interior decorator," one of them pointed out. "You pay the standard retail price, and yet you get the decorator's services thrown in. The caterer

or florist charges you the same amount whether you go to him by
yourself or through me."

This logic is indisputable. But in practice, hostesses insist, parties
handled by social secretaries have a way of moving out of the four-
figure price bracket and into the five. This is particularly true in
cases where the secretary has guided the family's social career "free
of charge."

Some secretaries prefer to charge a flat rate for their services.

"It often works better that way in the suburbs," Madeleine Torrens,
a top social secretary in the fashionable New Jersey suburbs, told
me. "When you charge a commission, you really have to deal with
the few firms with which you have a business arrangement. When
you are on a fee basis, you are free to deal with anyone. And in
many communities there is likely to be a small local florist or caterer
who knows your client and will make an extra effort to please her."

All the secretaries do charge a fee for use of the lists and addressing (by hand, of course) and mailing invitations. This fee is
moderate.

For non-party activities, such as arranging theater benefits, social
secretaries charge a flat rate. This is apt to be in the $500 range.

Jessie Fanshawe was the specialist in this field for many years.
The business was taken over upon her retirement in 1960 by her able
assistant, Mrs. Gillette Boland.

Weddings and debuts form the bulk of the work of the social
secretaries. As a result, although they are ready to steer clients of
all ages through the social protocol of a community, their best
efforts are reserved for families with daughters. They all feel that
a successful debut party this year all but guarantees a big wedding
reception in another year or two.

It is customary for the mother of the would-be debutante to get
in touch with the secretary two or three years in advance. She does
not need to do this if her name appears in the *Social Register*. In
that case, the secretary will call her, or send a card. The leading
social secretaries make it their business to know when a *Register*
child is ten or eleven. But the newcomer must make the approach
herself if she is to obtain the needed help in getting her child onto

the subdebutante party lists and in obtaining a good date in the brief season when debutantes flower.

"My daughter's debut party was scheduled three full years in advance," I learned from a woman who has almost overcome a garment-district background. "The secretary I used suggested that we give it at the very beginning of the 'little season' in June. That way it would be one of the first parties of the year, and debutantes and boys would come—even if they didn't know us very well— because they hadn't been to many debuts yet. Later on they go only to the big-name parties. It worked very well for us. My daughter had a tremendous debut year. She got invited back to the parties the other girls gave later.

"Since then," she added, with a gleam in her eye, "I've noticed that the first tremendous debut party of the season is given for a girl who is being handled by either a top social secretary or a press agent."

Advice on scheduling of other social functions, such as weddings, is equally sound, particularly when newcomers are involved. The bride and groom become almost incidental in the planning. The mother of a bride says that the secretary would not hear of the wedding being held on a Saturday.

"She insisted that men do not like to attend parties on Saturday in the summer. It interferes with golfing and sailing. On Friday you're much more likely to get a big crowd."

It seems that men are the essential ingredient, even for parties for grownups.

Every one of the secretaries is a noted party-giver. That is the talent that makes it possible for them to attract clients from the old-line families. The patronage of the inner circle in turn puts them in a position to give aspiring socialites a hand up.

Mrs. MacMullan says that she started out her career simply by writing notes to parents of debutantes and offering to relieve them of party worries. The response was staggering. In her first twenty-five years in business she arranged 5,200 balls, dinner dances, and teas.

Miss Palmer informed me that in the course of a typical year she handles forty debuts and fifty weddings. Every year before the "little season" in June her office sends out some 17,000 invitations. She suggested helpfully that I glance through her current date book for that season. As I riffled through the pages I noticed a steady stream of notations:

June 11—A wedding in Princeton, New Jersey; a dinner dance on Long Island. (Most of the dances at this season are debuts.)

June 13—A dinner dance and two supper dances—in Long Island and New Jersey.

June 14—One tea dance in Greenwich, Connecticut; another in Katonah, New York.

June 15—A supper dance, preceded by a dinner dance, on Long Island; a dinner dance in New Canaan, Connecticut.

June 16—A supper dance on Long Island.

June 17—A supper dance, preceded by a dinner dance, on Long Island.

June 18—A supper dance on Long Island; another in Bedford, New York.

June 19—A supper dance in Red Bank, New Jersey; a wedding in Princeton, New Jersey.

June 20—Three weddings—two in Connecticut, one in Southampton, Long Island.

And so on.

Guest lists for the dinner dances averaged 150 to 200 people. The supper dances were bigger, averaging 375 to 400, and there were even a couple with 750 guests. The wedding receptions were attended by a minimum of 250 guests, and at some 600 people went down the receiving line.

Parties in the suburbs, Miss Palmer pointed out, are usually larger than those in the city, possibly because of the space. On a suburban estate the party can be kept out of the house altogether. Marquees, which are huge gaily decorated tents, are set up on the grounds. If the kitchen is inaccessible, a separate service tent is set up, and the caterers even bring their own stoves. Carpets are laid underneath a tree for the receiving line. Rain does not frighten social secretaries. The marquees have clear plastic sides that can be used in such emergencies.

A large plot of flat land is most desirable for the marquee. A typical tent stands on an area of 60 by 120 feet. One Locust Valley hostess, worrying about how to have a marquee big enough to accommodate her 600 guests, phoned Miss Palmer with the solution:

"Tell your men to disregard all the trees on my land, except for the two Scotch pines. I'll have the rest of them taken up before the party."

The phrase "your men" is an accurate one. Miss Palmer claims to be the only secretary in the business who furnishes her own marquees. This is one of her great selling points, as the tents look spectacular. She likes to use canvas, the same color inside and out, in soft shades of pale pink or light blue, or in stripes of brilliant red and gold. One of her current favorites is cream colored on the outside, with cloth of gold appliquéd in stripes on the inside.

The secretaries vie with one another in creating party masterpieces. Philadelphians have described to me a debut arranged by Mrs. Thompson with a North Pole theme. A snowstorm with imitation snow, an aurora borealis, and an igloo set the scene. At another party she brought in white doves. She tried peacocks, but admitted that she found them too skittish. Mrs. MacMullan, not to be outdone, had the replica of a roadside diner built just off the ballroom of the Bellevue Stratford Hotel. Chefs served up hot dogs, hamburgers, and soft drinks to the debutantes. At yet another affair for the daughter of a noted racing family she produced a 200-foot replica of the Hialeah race course, complete with a life-sized horse and jockey in the colors of the family stables.

Producing celebrities is a social secretary's ace in the hole. Mrs. Tew, for example, got Ethel Merman for one party and Victor Borge for another. But in general celebrities go over better at adults-only parties. Debutantes and their escorts want to dance, drink, and talk. They don't want to sit and listen.

Food is taken very seriously by all these women.

"At debuts it is vital," one of them stated sagely. "It's the only thing that can keep the boys away from the bar. If they're not eating, they're drinking. And the affair can easily deteriorate into a drunken brawl."

In addition to running the party, secretaries can provide one other essential service: they can get it publicity. Most of them do not act as press agents, but the prestige of their names is such that most society editors will run photographs and news stories sent to them by these powerful women.

"Which papers do you want the story in?" I heard one secretary ask a debutante's mother. "And be sure you send me a picture. They'll want to run it."

When the client seemed a bit dubious about whether the newspapers would feature her daughter's picture, the secretary raised her eyebrows and commented in surprise: "But *of course* they'll use it."

The success of the social secretaries—and their clients—is due in large measure to their absolute dedication to their work. There is no facet of social life too trivial to receive hours of their time, thought, and energy.

I asked Miss Palmer how she has been able to equal (or even outdistance) her formidable rivals in the field so quickly.

She thought for a moment, then answered: "I'm the only one of the three who has never married. This is my whole life."

CHAPTER V

The Private Facts about Publicity

ONE OF THE writers for a national news magazine was recently assigned to do an article on some little-known aspect of society. He decided to uncover the role played by publicity. As is the way on this magazine, he went straight to the top for his information. He interviewed Count Lanfranco Rasponi, the biggest name in the field of society public relations today. That afternoon he returned to his office baffled.

"I *still* don't know what these press agents do!" he exclaimed in despair to his researcher. "I couldn't even find out if Rasponi handles a single one of the big society women. And some of them get so much publicity that there must be something to the rumors that he works for them."

I can quite understand the writer's plight. His experience reminds me of a conversation I once had with one of the nine account executives who surround Count Rasponi's titled head. "Society accounts make up only a small percentage of our annual business," I was informed blandly.

Oddly enough, this statement is not quite so flagrantly inaccurate as it sounds, although I did not realize that at the time. A great deal of society publicity is done indirectly. The press agent's clients are most often huge industrial concerns, or hotels, charity organizations or groups arranging benefit balls, rather than individuals.

Part of the public-relations campaign for a business consists of building up the social prestige of the executives and their wives.

When a professional is called in to publicize a benefit ball, he again may devote much of his time to making socialites of the top-level personnel of the commercial sponsor of the affair. If the hotel is the client, social events held in the ballrooms and individuals living there fall under the press agent's scrutiny. Committees for charity balls, theater benefits, and the like meet at the hotel, and both inner and outer circle members are blessed with considerable publicity. When a charity, museum, or art gallery hires a public-relations man, he is often asked to handle a benefit. In such a case he may actually help to form the committees.

And so the press agent may work for an individual but be paid by an industrial firm, philanthropic organization, or hotel. Both may be telling the truth when they insist that there is no business arrangement between them. (And then, again, they may not. This is a hush-hush, top-secret operation.)

The public-relations man may also be paid by an individual and by a charity or business concern at the same time, and do a good job for both clients. And this is the type of situation where I can easily find tie-ins between the great society figures of today and the top-notch press agents.

Last year, for example, a most prominent young matron was chairman of a major benefit ball. Upon investigation, I learned that one of the best-known public-relations men in the city was handling that very affair. He naturally placed articles about the lady in news-papers and magazines for months preceding and following the event. Now any relatively successful press agent handles many charity affairs the same year and any popular socialite must serve on innumerable committees. And so it is not surprising to find the two names linked again a short time later.

In some cases the public-relations man may have placed his society client on a benefit committee. If she possesses a great family name and a fortune, he is performing a valuable service for his charity client.

But what about the lady? Would not society-page editors run stories about her as a matter of course? Why does she need a press agent? The amount of publicity she gets as a ball chairman is good, but it is not enough. It takes a long-range campaign to lift her above the throng of other well-born women and to make her a symbol of "young society" today.

It is much harder—and costlier—for a newcomer to achieve the same results.

"The really good public-relations firms are out of reach for most individuals," a friend in the field has explained to me. "Some people have spent up to $3,000 or $4,000 a month for a major campaign. And building up a newcomer socially is a long-drawn-out procedure. It takes five or six years. In order to get an income-tax deduction, an individual would have to prove that this type of publicity is a business expense. That is very hard to do. And so most individuals deal with us through their businesses. It is understood that we will give the executives a society build-up."

When I pressed her further, however, she admitted that there are many, many exceptions.

"Officially, publicizing of individual socialites does not exist. I say this so many times that I get to believe it myself," she confided. "But in practice, of course, it does."

There are people quite ready to pay anything at all to break into society, whether it is $150,000 or $250,000 or more. And not all press agents are so high priced. The cost varies with the man used and with the difficulty of the job. I understand that $800 a month is a fairly typical price for handling an individual, and the charge can go as "low" as $400 a month. Parents of debutantes are likely to hire a press agent just for the debut year.

Even with "bargain" prices, public relations remains one of the costliest ways of advancing into society. But many people try it, because it works so often. Publicity has become the great leveler that makes it possible for a Miss Jones to wrest the title of Number-one debutante away from an Astor, and for a Mrs. Smith to become a leading society matron.

Socialites tend to deny the power of the press agent. I could hardly count the number of times the point has been made to me that the Rockefellers avoid society publicity as much as possible. Yet they are welcomed on the oldest of the old-line charity committees and invited to everything from the Junior Assemblies on down. That is true today—as a result of public relations in the past.

Few inner-circle members remember that John D. Rockefeller, founder of the family's fortune, hired Ivy Lee, the greatest public-relations man of his era. And Mr. Lee carefully created an image of Mr. Rockefeller that made it possible for his children and grand-children to become acceptable to society.

The uninformed believe that all the modern press agent does is to plant items in the syndicated society columns of Cholly Knicker-bocker and Charles Ventura. This is true as far as it goes, but it applies only to café society. Yetta Golove, publicity woman for the Harwyn Club, and Gary Stevens of the Eden Roc (New York), for example, build up the names of those who patronize these supper clubs.

"People sometimes call me up and ask about individual publicity," Miss Golove told me. "Of course I don't handle individuals as such. But I tell them that if they come on down to the Club regu-larly, I'll see what I can do for them. I can certainly get them into the society columns."

The publicity firms specializing in theatrical folk and celebrities often apply the same huckstering tactics to clients who care about society. Arthur P. Jacobs Co., Inc., handles mostly theatrical per-sonalities, but it also has the principality of Monaco as an account, and sees to it that reports of Princess Grace's doings are placed in all the columns.

Members of the inner circle, however, do not take the creations of night club press agents seriously.

As one society matron puts it: "Café society is nowhere at all. These people are not really welcome on the prestige charity com-mittees."

It is not hard to see why. One day last fall I met with the press agents for two of New York's top night clubs. I handed them a list of names that appeared regularly in the society columns, and asked for information about the background of each one. Many of these prominent café society women were, as I had expected, former actresses. Theater-society marriages are quite frequent. After that came erstwhile models; these included five of the best-known women on my list. Then there was one matron who had once upon a time been a hat-check girl in a night club, my informants continued, and another who had been a manicurist. The two remaining on my list had started out as a receptionist and a waitress, respectively. Not only press agents are aware of these origins; I find that members of the Old Guard know about them, too. And the café-society label, therefore, is a strike against the person with inner-circle aspirations.

Those with real society ambitions need a completely different type of public relations. They must find a publicity man who will keep them out of the society column and get them on the society page.

At the very top of this profession is a small group of men and women, known only to the initiated, who can actually *make* socialites. They have both society and newspaper contacts, and do not hesitate to use the former on behalf of their clients.

But tracking down a society press agent requires the talents of a Sherlock Holmes. Friends—even friends who use one—will not admit that fact to anyone.

To listen to people in society nowadays, one fact becomes clear: Everyone else uses a press agent. The person speaking does not employ one, never did, and would not dream of doing so:

"It's somebody else, not me."

Upon investigation, I found that although many press agents will take on an occasional individual socialite account, there are few real specialists. The best known of these are to be found in New York City.

I have already mentioned Count Rasponi. Although his name is quickly recognized, most people know very little about him. He has risen to the top of his field very quickly, having gone into business in the late 1940's.

A friend of his assures me: "He knows the jet set, the Capri crowd, Elsa Maxwell's set, the Windsors' set, the New York international set, the Southampton set, and the Newport set."

Although close-mouthed about individuals, Count Rasponi's firm is happy to say that it handles such accounts as Elizabeth Arden, Hattie Carnegie, Ferragamo Shoes, Carlton House, Brazilian Real Airlines, a number of art galleries, some big-name opera stars such as Mario del Monaco, decorator Valerian Rybar, many theater benefits, and about six benefit balls a year, including the Heart Ball and the Spoleto Festival Ball.

Igor Cassini, who is Cholly Knickerbocker, wears another hat as Martial & Co., Inc. His firm, too, has many large industrial accounts. And Mr. Cassini is also one of the handful of press agents who can "make" a socialite. He has been largely instrumental in starting the Knickerbocker Ball Foundation for the benefit of the Sister Kenny Foundation and Universal Symphony Orchestra and Music Institute. Mr. and Mrs. Cassini serve as chairmen of the annual ball. And control of a major ball is a great asset to a press agent—and to his clients.

Alexandre Tarsaidze also handles many of the city's big benefit balls. His clients are the charity organizations involved, he tells me. Mr. Tarsaidze specializes in those with international connections—exiled Russians and the like. In New York, by the way, the Russians —White Russians, of course—are particularly popular. An aura of romance still clings to the Russian aristocracy. And the international set plus members of real society give their support to such Tarsaidze-handled affairs as the Mi-Carême Ball, which benefits officers of the former Imperial Russian Cavalry and Horse Artillery.

Then there is Marianne Strong, who represents the Stork Club, orchestra leader Meyer Davis, and many individual society people. A member of the Junior Assemblies in her day, she, too, is able to bring out a debutante or create a socialite.

Ted Howard is still active in the field. He is best known for the job he did in publicizing the late Joanne Connolly. His clients include society women and debutantes, and he also does publicity for the Bath and Tennis Club of Westhampton and the Eden Roc Hotel in Miami.

Emmett Davis, who handles the Mardi Gras Ball for the Junior League, L'Aiglon Restaurant, and the Drake Hotel, also publicizes individual socialites.

The press agents are the Pygmalions of today. And no one is more aware of it than they are themselves. They see themselves in the role of Professor Higgins in the George Bernard Shaw play, *Pygmalion*. The newly created socialite is Eliza, the Cockney flower girl.

"She didn't know anything," they are apt to say privately about a client, when given the least encouragement. "I showed her how to dress and entertain, where to dine. I got her interested in the arts and music."

There is, to be sure, a certain amount of truth in this. In the front office of a society press agent, for example, I noticed some photographs mounted prominently on the wall. One showed him taking a client to a leading hairdresser; in another, the two were shown at Henri Bendel, and he was approving her choice of a dress.

No matter how much of this I see and hear, I tend to be a bit suspicious of the idea that the poised, glittering society matron was a hopeless, uncouth slob just a few short years ago. I feel the same way about movies when the heroine comes on with straight hair and glasses. I know that she really is not a mess. She will take off her glasses and curl her hair, and it will turn out that she was Elizabeth Taylor all the time. Similarly, I believe that the women who have risen successfully in society had what it takes from the start. The guiding hand of the public relations man gave them that little push they needed.

Society rules by conformity. The press agent can and frequently does direct his client to the "right" hairdressers, dress shops, restaurants, and caterers. This is invaluable assistance, but it is the least important part of the job done by the titans of the industry in creating a social figure. The aspects of the public relations campaign that really count are those that provide the client with Old Guard contacts and at least partial acceptance.

How is it done?

"The classic way is to get the client on important committees of the right charities, the good balls, the theater benefits," Lee Bond of Rasponi Associates tells me.

She asks the would-be socialite: "What are you interested in?"

The client racks her brains and comes up with an answer: "I like babies."

Mrs. Bond then considers "baby" charities with which Rasponi Associates has solid connections. This is likely to be one with an important theater benefit, as the firm handles many such affairs.

The client is then sent to see an official who is personally known to the press agent. She is first briefed as to what is expected of her: She must be ready to make a contribution; she should offer to do some work. When there is a benefit, she is expected to take tickets by the score, stuff envelopes, call her friends.

"I figure that if she does all this, she can get on a committee by the following year," Mrs. Bond informs me. "In two or three years she may get to be head of it. People active in the chic charities are well on the way to being accepted socially."

The woman going the charity road to social advancement alone must be careful to select a charity that looks kindly on newcomers with money. Many will not even consider an unknown. A press agent can open doors at those old-line charities through his own contacts.

This is arranged in a number of ways. Clients who want rapid results (and are prepared to pay for them) can be placed directly on some charity committees. A public-relations firm is frequently hired to handle a theater or luncheon benefit for a charity, museum, or art gallery. The press agent is right on hand when the committee is being selected, so he can easily suggest the addition of one or two names. In fact, the charity involved usually wants him to do so. The press agent has, after all, been called in to help the benefit earn more money. And no one connected with the charity is unaware that the public-relations man will bring in people who are prepared to contribute heavily. In addition, most of them have important contacts they will be urged to approach. With the guidance of the press agent, they will sell huge blocks of tickets.

An individual client's presence on a benefit committee for another client produces a lot of publicity for both. The press agent has the greatest possible incentive to place photographs and news items about committee meetings and about the affair itself.

"In taking committee-meeting photographs for the newspapers, I usually try to get one pretty woman and one woman with an old society name together," one press agent told me. "The editors use pictures of attractive people whenever possible. But by the time most women have the leisure to devote to charity work they are dowagers, and look it. If I have to choose between the two, it's the old society name every time."

The newcomer handled by the press agent is, of course, carefully posed in the photographs with the Old Guard members of the committee.

But as one woman who has risen socially with the aid of a public-relations man confides: "The publicity is the least important part of it. What really matters is getting to know the people on the committee. The press agent may arrange to put you on, but you've got to use that opportunity to become someone of importance to the charity."

A number of professionals do not limit themselves to placing clients on committees. They create benefits in which the men and women they represent can play key roles. I know of more than one case in which the public-relations man approached a worth-while charity and offered to organize a benefit luncheon. The beneficiary was, naturally, delighted.

For this system to work, the press agent must have society contacts of his own. He must have some inner circle friends who can be induced to serve on the committee being formed. The appeal to them is both friendship and the opportunity to help in a good cause. With a few big names to mention, the press agent can call other important people and ask them to join, too. The client is made a prominent member of the committee. Her name is linked with many well-known society figures, and she has the chance to get to know them.

This kind of publicity work commands very high prices. The charge for getting a newcomer named chairman of a ranking charity ball is even higher. This position is generally taken as an indication that a man or woman is accepted by society. And I find that even the sophisticated are quite unaware of how often a public-relations man has gotten his client that spot. It can be managed only by the biggest names in the field. The press agent must have great influence both with the beneficiary and with the socialities who are interested in it. His role is usually that of middle man. He arranges for the client to make a huge contribution to the charity in return for the position of chairman.

One of New York's top society public-relations men has told me privately that his charge for such a service is between $15,000 and $20,000. This does not include the contribution to the charity.

When the client is an industrial concern, rather than an individual, the approach is slightly different. The press agent gets in touch with a charity giving a benefit and suggests that the firm underwrite the expenses. All he asks is that one of the executives of the company—or his wife—be named chairman of the ball. Many charity organizations are quite willing to give away that position to attract a commercial sponsor. The same situation applies when the charity is the client. The public-relations man can offer to bring in an industrial firm (usually another client) to pay the bills, with the understanding that the president or his wife be named chairman.

Not many clients get to be chairmen, but most get on the key committees for the balls. That is standard procedure for a society build-up, and is usually included in the regular monthly charge. In addition, the publicity man will see to it that his clients are seated with people who are worth-while contacts. Press agents are often asked to make seating arrangements at the tables, putting out the place cards. They are sometimes foiled. One woman operating without professional help confides gleefully that she once got the better of the press agent handling the ball. She got there early and switched the cards around herself so as to get at a table with people she wanted to meet. When I asked a press-agent friend about this, he said that it has happened more than once, and that he carefully guards the tables where he places important clients.

Nowadays a public-relations man is expected to get his industrial clients on the key committees of any ball he handles, too. I recently went over the names on the committees listed for a major ball, handled by a public-relations man whom I know. Every important position was filled by either the president or vice-president of his business accounts. They neatly balanced the society names needed to maintain the benefit's prestige.

Sometimes the commercial sponsors of a ball are not clients at all, but still demand—and get—a society build-up by the top-flight public-relations man hired by the beneficiary. The press agents are dismayed by this "free riding" but are quite unable to control it.

I have observed this in action at one ball given each year for an Old Guard charity. The affair is publicized by one of the leading society publicity firms. The wife of the president of the commercial sponsor quickly realized that she could use this position as her entree first into the charity and then into real society. She asked to be placed on the key committees controlled by the old-line families, and expected to be photographed with them.

When I first heard of this demand, the public-relations man involved was complaining bitterly. The firm was not a client, and the woman was not paying him either. In addition, it is difficult and risky for a press agent to use his newspaper contacts too often to obtain publicity for people who are not in society. He needs to save the favors he can get for his individual big clients. But he was really in no position to refuse to help the executive's wife. If the ball was to be a success, it had to be underwritten; the sponsor could not be antagonized.

I have followed the social career of this woman for several years and she has advanced steadily. She no longer serves only on the committee for the ball sponsored by her husband's firm; she is active in many other charities as well. I find her activities mentioned on the society pages regularly. She has not yet won acceptance by the inner circle, but she is working on it.

I asked the press agent if she had become a client.

"Not that one!" he said bitterly as he slipped a photograph of a committee on which she was serving into an envelope and sent it off to an afternoon paper.

In contrast to this sort of thing, I was somewhat touched recently by a complaint I heard from another press-agent friend: "I've got a real problem," she said. "Several of my clients are sincerely interested in non-social charities, like the Girl Scouts or the U.S.O. They refuse to change to one of the old-line charities such as Judson Health Center or the Boys' Club. And it's almost impossible to get the others into the newspapers."

Charity is most often used by newcomers guided by publicity people, but it is by no means the only way to enter society.

"In today's resurgence of religion the churches are more important to the rising socialite than ever before," comments press agent Marianne Strong, "and clients are usually advised to become active in theirs."

The only note I must add to her advice is that it presupposes membership in the "right" faith. North, south, east, west, members of the Episcopal Church are best—in terms of social ranking. Next come the Presbyterians, Congregationalists, Unitarians, Methodists, Lutherans, and Baptists in just about that order. In Philadelphia, of course, the Friends' influence is strong. The Roman Catholic Church is extremely fashionable in some cities, discriminated against in others (particularly in those where there is a large Italian-American population).

In New York public-relations firms guide their clients to such top-ranking churches as St. James Protestant Episcopal Church, St. Thomas Protestant Episcopal Church, St. Bartholomew's Church (Episcopal), Holy Trinity Church (Episcopal), Brick Presbyterian Church, Madison Avenue Presbyterian Church, and Central Presbyterian Church (not so widely known as the others, but extremely fashionable).

One woman used the coffee hour held in the parish house after church as an opportunity to meet the highly social members. On the advice of her press agent she joined the women's auxiliary and became one of the hardest workers in it. Her church held an annual Christmas fair, and she was invaluable in rounding up merchandise for it. She was also one of the best saleswomen at the fair.

"She isn't a very subtle woman, and most of us have had the feeling that she uses the church to advance herself socially," one society matron commented. "But she does so much good that we have put her on the committees anyway."

No press agent will allow a client to overlook the arts. They have provided a springboard to social success for many. The publicity man tells the world about his client's collection of paintings, patronage of museums, and support of orchestras and theaters. Such ventures are eminently respectable, as they are the traditional activities of old-line society. And so they give the press agent a good basis for refined publicity.

The patronage of the arts is carried on in a way that staggers the mind of anyone living on a salary. I asked one press agent if she could think of any examples of people who had worked their way up in society via the arts.

"But of course," she replied. "Don't you remember that heiress from the Middle West who contributed $3,000,000 to be used for an arts center? And what about the one who invested $1,500,000 in building a repertory theater in her native town?

"Music and the arts work best when there is some municipal tie-in—some tremendous gift to a city," she continued.

A benefaction to a city does not need to be in the million-dollar class, however. The wife of a well-known industrial tycoon recently sponsored the visit of a famous opera company to her Middle Western city for four performances. I was hardly surprised to note that the publicity she received for this action was nationwide. Others have brought symphony orchestras to their home towns. Concert series are put on, underwritten at least partly by an individual.

Not all music support must be long haired. Hardly anyone in America can have missed the jazz-festival furor. At least one social career, press agents tell me, has been considerably aided by the most widely publicized of these.

Collecting art provides both publicity and a certain amount of social entree. The world of art collectors is very small and closely knit, and the person who buys on a big scale can get to know and entertain the others in that set. The openings of the art galleries are attended mostly by members of the international set, public-relations men observe. To be effective with the Old Guard, some connection with a museum should be made. Most of them have boards of trustees or affiliated groups supported by old-line families. The collector can place his works of art on loan, or, better yet, he can endow a wing.

In an earlier generation, it was the thing for the great collectors to build museums bearing their names to house the impressive works of art they had brought together. This proved to be successful in raising the social levels of their families. As a result, a modern press agent with a collector client usually has a museum gleam in his eye.

I understand that one family with a fortune earned all too recently has been guided by a publicity firm for some years. One of its members is an art collector. And I was interested to note that there is now a museum bearing his name. This is clearly a key factor in the social rise of his family.

It is not necessary to be a millionaire patron of the arts, press agents are quick to point out. I once met a woman whose place in society is based on her support of a small art gallery. At the suggestion of her public-relations man, a contest bearing her name has been held for a number of years. And art contests get a good deal of high-level publicity. The first prize in the contest is $500, and the winner is allowed to put on a one-man show in the gallery. If the sponsor considers the winner particularly talented, she gives him a fellowship to study abroad for a year. When he returns, he exhibits his work at the gallery and so helps to build up its reputation.

Sometimes the art gambit costs the individual nothing at all. His business firm sponsors the art contest—sometimes it is music—or art gallery or concert series. The industrial public-relations firm does the publicity for the event as a part of its over-all job. This is one of the indirect ways in which public relations is used by individuals advancing socially. They are then able to say quite honestly that they do not have a press agent.

Those who do hire public-relations men are given countless other suggestions of ways in which to seek the bluebird of social happiness.

"Don't forget horses!" exclaims one of New York's leading press agents. "When I have a client who wants to work into the horsy set, I suggest that he start by getting a box at the National Horse Show and inviting some powerful businessmen to join him there. I also urge him to take an advertisement in the program."

As society takes parties seriously, many press agents help women to build up their reputations as hostesses. This is a system that works better in a city such as Washington than it does in say San Francisco, Boston, or even New York. In Washington, where society is based largely on politics, everyone will go to parties attended by government officials, no matter who is the hostess. And politicians know better than to play hard-to-get. But in other cities members of society will not go to the home of an unknown.

"Becoming recognized as a hostess is the last step in the build-up," a press agent tells me. "The client must already have worked her way up via charity, church, art, or what have you before inner circle members will accept invitations."

This is true only for those seeking Old Guard acceptance. One woman with slightly lower social aspirations gives parties for singers, actors, and other well-known figures. She attracts a reasonably social crowd, which finds the lure of a big name irresistible. Her press agent locates the willing celebrity for her. Many are quite ready to come—possibly for public relations motives of their own. And their presence guarantees newspaper coverage for them and the lady giving the party.

Some press agents go a step further. They introduce a client by giving a party themselves for a prominent personality (usually another client, of course). Members of society come to meet the celebrity and are introduced to the newcomer at the same time.

Even using all these methods, the top press agents admit that it is very difficult to turn a contractor or self-made businessman into a member of society. But making the daughter into a debutante is far less of a challenge.

This was true in the case of a family which was trying to advance socially without professional aid. For the daughter's debut year, however, they hired press agent Ted Howard, and he helped the girl become one of the best-known debutantes of the season. I remember seeing some of the newspaper and magazine stories about her, although at the time I was unaware of the role played by Mr. Howard. The debutante was presented as the all-around society girl—on horseback, in a canoe, and so forth. And she succeeded in getting an invitation to a major debutante ball, despite a background that was anything but old line. In fact, the story on the grapevine is that her father once owned a fish store—and not even one on Madison Avenue—it was actually on the west side of Manhattan.

Debutante publicity is of value to the father and mother, too. The parents of a girl who is properly presented to society gain status themselves.

Creating a debutante is often a part of the long-range build-up of an entire family. One business executive and his wife had been working with one of New York's leading press agents—Cassini, rumor has it—for five years before their daughter reached debut age. I began to watch the newspapers for her name as she approached her eighteenth birthday. And sure enough, her private debut party was one of the first of the season, and was the most conspicuous. The girl not only made the newspaper debutante lists—standard operating procedure for a press agent—but her photograph was featured with the ranking debutantes of the season above one of the major lists. And I was interested but not astonished to observe that she was presented at two of the most important debutante balls.

As this young woman's family had been moving into society for several years, it is quite likely that they already had good enough contacts to get these ball invitations by themselves. But in many cases not only has a press agent got a girl publicity, he has actually made her into a debutante. The small group of top-level public-relations men can arrange to have a girl presented at one of the leading mass debutante balls.

They use their society contacts on her behalf. This is an American version of a system that has operated in England for years. Impoverished gentlewomen have sponsored not-so-well-born debutantes. Through their own friends they have arranged to have the girls presented at court (until this was discontinued) and at the top debutante functions. In America, press agents fill the same function —usually for a much higher price. The family involved not only has to pay the public relations man, but must also make a big donation to the charity benefited by the ball. The press agent handles the contribution.

Several of New York's leading publicity people have told me that they like to have a two-year head start to bring out a girl through their own efforts. It can be done in one year if necessary, they add.

"I was approached by three mothers last year, each asking me to arrange a debut at any of the mass presentation balls," Mrs. Strong reported to me. "I had to refuse one of them. The girl was nice, but she could not have passed committee inspection. The other two became ranking debutantes of the season."

As one press agent put it bluntly: "Most of the balls are for charity. So if you know some members of the invitations committee and the girl is acceptable and the family wants to make a big contribution, how can they say no?

"It's even easier when a ball is run as a commercial venture," she added. "The person in charge simply wants to make money—and often is amenable to an approach."

In addition to the ball invitation, these girls are made into society, rather than "glamour," debutantes. Press agents do this in much the same way that they create society matrons. The transformation is achieved more easily, because most eighteen-year-old girls are pretty, public-relations man Emmett Davis concedes with a smile. Photographs of them are relatively simple to place in newspapers and magazines. One press agent actually got a picture of his debutante client on the cover of a national news magazine.

In keeping with tried and true techniques, the young ladies are urged to join junior charity or theater benefit committees. In photographs, their lovely faces appear together with those of girls bearing old society names. This pleases the conservative editor.

The society public relations men who are in the swim have countless additional opportunities for getting publicity for their junior clients.

I was in Mr. Davis' office one day when he got a telephone call from a man who is a favorite with both the international set and society columnists. He had been approached by a lipstick manufacturer eager for a publicity tie-in. The firm was introducing a new shade, to be called "Continental," and it wanted the gentleman to be named "our favorite Continental" by a group of debutantes. They could then all be photographed together at a society hotel. Although this sounds pretty obvious, pictures of this type do appear regularly in the afternoon newspapers. Mr. Davis, of course, was expected to produce the debutantes—getting publicity in his turn for his clients or their daughters.

Not all debutantes, though, are society girls. This is the one aspect of society life in which café society plays a major role. Today's "glamour" debutantes are flowers of the night clubs.

One of the most persistent rumors in society and out is that the press agent for El Morocco, the Stork Club, or the Harwyn has literally "created" the Number-one debutante of the season from Gloria "Mimi" Baker to Brenda Frazier to Cobina Wright on down to such debutantes as Cary Latimer and Natalie Trundy.

Since these professionals discovered that debutantes attract customers, they are all eager to build up likely girls. The glamour debutante may not even have to hire her own press agent. A promising girl can get a free ride from those connected with the big-name night spots.

"The Number-one deb doesn't need to have a recognized society name. She doesn't need to have a lot of money. She can become a debutante by association," Mrs. Strong emphasizes.

It is, of course, necessary for the girl to go to a private school and to dancing classes as well, so that she starts to move in a social set that includes debutantes. To become a ranking debutante without benefit of a personal press agent, a girl must be popular enough to be taken out to the clubs night after night by a succession of boys. She must be pretty, so as to catch the eye of the press agent for a café. In time she will be mentioned in the columns as being seen with this playboy or that actor or that noted man about town. If she has the little spark that attracts publicity, that may be all she needs. As time passes, the news-hungry columnists themselves will begin to look for stories about her.

I know of one girl, a budding actress, whose family induced her to abandon the stage and to enter the arena of society. They were not even on the fringes of society themselves but were eager to be. The talents that might have advanced the young woman's career were equally suited to the café society whirl. She was beautiful, charming, spoke with a lovely accent, and was attractive to boys. Any reader of the society columns would recognize her name, as she became one of the best-known debutantes of her season.

"In recent years the trend has been for the top glamour debs to come from unknown families with comparatively little money," says Mr. Davis.

It may seem surprising that few of the recent crop are daughters of the big-name families. After all, those girls come out, too. But they are usually not so eager for publicity and not so cooperative as the newcomers.

Last year the society columnist of one of the big daily newspapers decided to write a profile of a debutante. She admitted to a friend that she had to settle for a girl who was being built up by two night-club press agents. None of the real society girls she approached was willing to be the subject of an article.

The daughters of the old-line families may not haunt the cafés at all, spending the school term in boarding school and the vacations in travel.

If a debutante from a recognized family does want publicity, she has it made. All the press agents will rush to give her a hand, anxious to have that famous name associated with their club or restaurant.

This was certainly true in the case of Gamble Benedict. When she was seventeen, two night-club press agents selected her for me as a top debutante of the coming season. She was in the *Social Register,* they pointed out, and was, in addition, cute and lively and fond of going out. Even they, however, did not foresee that she would explode into the headlines of all the tabloids following her debut-year elopement with a chauffeur.

On the café-society level, the featured girls need not be debutantes in any true sense of the word. One of the glamour debutantes of a year or two ago never had a real debut. Others come out at quite second-rate balls or are presented at private debut parties that are not attended by society.

"But a debut like that doesn't count for anything!" one society matron exclaimed to me. "Why, if my son were to start going with a girl who'd come out at a second-string ball I'd make it my business to find out about her."

I do not think that would do much good. If a girl gets on the debutante-party circuit and attracts the son of one of the oldest families, he is not likely to drop her just because his mother tells him to do so. And the café-society debutantes do meet real society boys who like to go night clubbing. One of the most highly publicized debutantes of the late 1950's—a girl of unknown family—met and married the heir to a $45,000,000 fortune before the end of her debut year. How do I know that figure? Her press agent told me, of course.

Marriage is the surest way of all to advance socially, and many a night-club debutante does win inner-circle acceptance. The press agent cannot take full credit for this, but he does, nonetheless, deserve some of it.

Although public-relations men like to stress their success stories, most will admit that the degree of acceptance achieved is variable. Things that seem trifling can make all the difference. This can be seen by considering the difference in the social positions achieved by two women, handled by the same press agent for about the same length of time.

One of them is so well established in her role as society matron that even the purists do not remember to ask: "Who was her father, anyway?" She is active in several old-line charities and is a regular chairman or co-chairman of ranking benefit balls. Her spare time is devoted to riding and hunting. Her son is at a leading prep school and her daughter is a noted debutante. Recently she and her husband were admitted to one of the most exclusive clubs.

The other lady is frequently mentioned on the society pages, too. Her daughter had a huge, well-publicized debut. But somehow she has the new-society label and has not succeeded in breaking into the inner circle. The chief reason, her press agent believes, is that she devoted too much of her time to activities favored by the international set and not enough to the less showy charities of the old-line families.

But even when a public-relations campaign is not a complete success, it can take a would-be socialite a long way on the road to the inner circle. And many enjoy getting publicity. The desire to see one's name in the newspapers is a characteristic ambition of today, and is shared by both newcomers and members of the Old Guard.

The society pages are taken seriously in small towns and big cities alike. People will go to great lengths to be mentioned in the sections edited by Russell Edwards of the New York *Times*, Katharine Dunlap of the Philadelphia *Inquirer*, Lucille E. Green of the Charleston *News and Courier*, Madison Calvert of the Baltimore *American*, Alison Arnold of the Boston *Herald*, Athlyn Deshais

Faulkner of the Chicago *Daily News,* Bete Gillespie of the Detroit *Free Press,* Sara Tyler of the Dallas *Times Herald,* Lynn Spencer of the Los Angeles *Examiner,* Frances Moffatt of the San Francisco *Examiner,* and their sister and brother editors throughout the country.

Even in society's inner circle very few pay more than lip service to the still much-quoted cliché: "A lady's name should appear in the newspapers three times—when she is born, when she is married, and when she dies."

Many of them secretly agree with the woman who told me openly: "I just contributed $10,000 to charity. And I think people should know about it."

CHAPTER VI

Society Goes to School

I ASKED the mother of a current debutante just how much she had spent on launching her daughter, exclusive of the expenses of the private debut party. Taking out pencil and paper, she calculated briskly for about fifteen minutes and then came up with the staggering total: "$45,000."

I stared at her in amazement, trying to figure out how she had arrived at that amount. Dancing classes, club dues, riding and tennis lessons, clothes, subdebutante parties are not likely to make up such a sum. Could she have been adding in a heavy contribution to the charity that benefited from the cotillion or the services of a press agent, I wondered? But it turned out that she had used neither of these. What she had added in was the cost of eight years at one of the city's leading day schools and four years at boarding school.

"That wasn't what I had in mind," I explained. "I don't think that school can be counted as a debut expense."

"But school is the most important of all!" she replied. "That's the basic thing. You can leave out some of the others, so long as you send the child to the right school. It's worth every cent you pay."

Everybody knows that sending a child to private school costs money, but few people realize just how much. Prices have been mounting steadily during the last few years. One mother entered her child in a New York school with a comparatively moderate rate, only to discover that the tuition was to be increased by 40 per

cent. I have checked catalogs of more than 130 leading schools.
And I learned that nearly all of them have raised their prices substantially in the last year or two. In many cases new rate cards had
not yet been printed. The former charges—all lower than the new
ones, of course—were simply crossed out and corrected.

The leading girls' boarding schools now average $2,500 for tuition,
room, and board, with many edging close to the $3,000 mark. This
is an increase of about $1,000 in the last two decades. The boys'
schools cost less, because of heavy endowments. The average is
$2,200. Tuition in the fashionable day schools starts at about $500
in kindergarten and rises to $1,100, mounting steadily grade by
grade. That is a nationwide average. In a city such as New York
charges run higher than that.

Saving up the price of tuition does not mean that a parent can
afford to send a child to private school.

As one mother explains it: "The tuition is only the beginning. You
might call it a jumping-off place."

Extras are anything but extra. In a girls' boarding school these
can amount to well over $1,000. The mother of a student at Con-
necticut's Ethel Walker informs me that the cost of tuition, room,
and board is $3,000, but charges of $400 for uniforms and $85.00
a month for upkeep of a horse bring the total up to more than
$4,000.

There are many other unexpected expenses. One father reports
bitterly that he was charged for his daughter's participation in a
fancy-dress ball. Then he had to pay for the costume. The cost of a
child's transportation to and from home can be a considerable factor
if the school is far away.

Assessments are by no means uncommon. At one of Boston's
private girls' schools a couple of years ago the board of directors
decided to start a retirement fund for the teachers. The plan was
worth while, everyone agreed. Teachers should get generous pen-
sions. The only catch was that the fund had to come out of the
parents' pockets. The board of directors decided how much each
family could contribute, and then called up and requested that
amount.

Private schools can do that sort of thing nowadays. They do not need to worry about losing students. Society's pet school, Foxcroft, in Virginia, turns away four out of every five applicants. Fashionable Madeira, just outside of Washington, D.C., is in a position to reject three out of four, and Massachusetts' Concord two out of three.

Nowadays many socialites—even some with *Social Register* listings—do not come from the old families. But they have usually gone to the right schools.

In the early years the school gives a child entree to the dancing classes and junior athletic clubs that are standard extracurricular activities for future members of society.

The headmistress of a top-ranking day school admitted to me that she is regularly asked for recommendations for boys and girls who have applied to the accepted dancing classes and clubs.

"I just won't do it," she stated flatly. "All I'll say is that the child in question is a student here."

In most cases I have found that this is quite enough. The names of these schools carry great weight. All invitations committees insist on the right kind of educational background. This means on the elementary and secondary-school level. Even debutante ball invitations go out before college.

Of course the individual contacts that are made are even more important in obtaining the desired invitations. In some schools almost all the students expect to be debutantes when they grow up. Their mothers have powerful friends on the invitations committees for the major balls—or serve with these groups themselves. The classmates of their daughters get preferential treatment in either case.

Foxcroft, Westover, and Ethel Walker produce bumper crops of debutantes. And certain of the day schools do not lag far behind. When looking over a recent list of debutantes presented at Los Angeles' select Las Madrinas Ball, I noted that out of twenty-nine girls eighteen were graduates of Marlborough, the local prestige day school.

Although boys do not share the debut problem, going to the approved private schools is just as important for them as for their sisters. Attendance per se at any of these can make a boy's social life. The boys at the leading boarding schools are often invited to "everything," and those at the private day schools do well, too. This frequently comes as a surprise, albeit a pleasant one, to parents who are not in the social swim.

"How do they get on all those lists?" one mother asked me curiously.

It happens in the most natural way. The world of junior society suffers from a manpower shortage. At most parties the correct ratio of boys to girls is three to one. And it is particularly difficult to achieve this proportion, because most young ladies want to go to parties and many young men do not.

The girls in this set not only want dates the way all teen-agers do, they simply must have them—if they are to go to the exclusive dances. It is customary for them to invite male escorts to the formal affairs. And so subdebutantes and their mothers are ever on the lookout for boys. They give parties, urging the boys they invite to bring classmates as extra men. Brother's friends in prep school are called on regularly. Mothers and aunts dragoon the sons of friends to fill additional gaps. If a boy slips just once and goes to a party to oblige Aunt Susan or Cousin Amanda, he is a marked man. The select private school set in any city is small, and names are passed from one mother to the next. In addition, these schools exchange invitations, on a class-wide basis, for social events. The attractive boys quickly get on the individual party lists.

The social secretaries, too, are always searching for escorts. They view the private schools as the best single source. And although these schools all maintain that they do not give out enrollment lists, yearbooks and a few good contacts make the refusals quite meaningless. The social secretaries do try to use some selectivity, but almost any boy who is known to a client or who attends a big party soon appears on the lists. And, as has been described in an earlier chapter, the filing cards kept by the social secretaries are consulted by hostesses.

But getting to parties is, of course, only one example of what the prep schools can do for their students. Attendance at the right secondary school helps a boy into a top-flight college and gets him into the right group there. A youngster in the inner circle or even outer circle of society is expected to become a student at an Ivy

League college. That is taken as a matter of course. To achieve status, a boy must make a club such as Porcellian at Harvard, Cottage at Princeton, or Fence at Yale.

Members of these clubs are accepted wherever they go. They are almost automatically desirable as guests at inner-circle homes. They are given preference at the social clubs, which are the nub of society in city after city. Even the alumni clubs of the Ivy League schools are not open to just any graduate. An applicant must be proposed, seconded, and passed by a vote. None of this is a problem to the man who belonged to the proper club in college. In addition, that club membership provides a boy with contacts who can help him in his later business career. Preparation for this kind of acceptance must be started down at readin', 'ritin', and 'rithmetic level.

Boarding schools are the real society schools, particularly for boys. Members of the inner circle in most cases use day schools for the elementary grades only. It is of incalculable benefit to a young man to attend a school such as St. Paul's or Phillips Exeter in New Hampshire; St. Mark's, Groton, Phillips Academy (Andover), the Hill, or Deerfield Academy in Massachusetts; Choate, Hotchkiss, or Kent in Connecticut; Lawrenceville in New Jersey; and for Catholics, Portsmouth Priory in Rhode Island.

For girls, the absolute top schools (in social terms) are also boarding schools. Foxcroft and Madeira in Virginia; Ethel Walker, Miss Porter's, and Westover in Connecticut; and St. Timothy's in Maryland are typical of those favored by Old Guard families.

But the reluctance of some parents to send girls away from home enhances the prestige of the day schools. A number of them are also as "right" as can be with the inner circle. These schools include New York's Brearley, Chapin, and Spence; Los Angeles' Marlborough; Boston's Brimmer and May, and Winsor; St. Louis' Mary Institute, and Dallas' Hockaday.

Newcomers find it very difficult to get a child into one of the socially approved schools, because there are so few of them.

This may sound odd when one considers that there are about 3,000 private schools in the United States today. But the fact is that barely 130 of them can pass society's rigid tests. (I have made up a directory of these schools. It can be found on page 265.) In some cities, even in some entire states, there are only one or two schools that teach the three r's to tomorrow's socialites. And most of them admit an incredibly small number of students. St. Timothy's takes only 120 girls, Miss Porter's, 220; Groton accepts a mere 200 boys; and St. Mark's, 205. As the members of the old families get preference at the high-ranking schools, there are only a few places left for all other applicants.

How do newcomers get in? In general, recommendations from friends (either social or business) count most heavily, directors of admissions agree. And it is best if they are from parent of a student or alumnus. The second choice is someone of recognized standing in the community.

I know one mother who started a system that has since been adopted by a number of her friends. When her daughter was still of tricycle age, she began to keep a card file on both day and boarding schools. On each card she put down all particulars, such as location and cost, and then the key facts—the names of people she knew who had some influence with the school. Whenever she met someone with such a connection, his name was added to the appropriate card. And so when application time rolled around, she was ready with the needed references.

Press agents and social secretaries can, and often do, help.

"We got the daughter of one of our clients—a family that was absolutely nowhere socially—into one of New York's top schools." A member of Count Lanfranco Rasponi's public-relations firm dropped this bit of news casually in the middle of a conversation.

The account executive was quite surprised when I singled out that statement. It was obviously standard operating procedure.

Most newcomers try to get an early start. The little socialite goes step by step from nursery school to a prestige day school until he reaches the boarding-school goal.

A newspaper society columnist confides that early in her career she laughed off a frantic letter from a subscriber asking for names of socially acceptable nursery schools. It was only later that she realized how pertinent the question really was. The day schools do take nursery years seriously. Directors of admission consult with the heads of the pre-schools. The child who has gone to an approved school often has the edge over the one who has spent her toddler-hood in the sandbox in the back yard.

In a fashionable suburb the small local nursery school is a virtual who's who of the area and is the right one to use. But today many communities have almost as many nursery schools as they have children. Perhaps the best rule of thumb for the newcomer in city, suburb, and small town alike is to consider the church nursery school. Any one connected with a prestige church is extremely desirable.

In general, the social acceptability of the nursery school follows that of the church. In most parts of the country that means the Episcopal Church, followed by the Presbyterian and Congregational. In New York City top nursery schools include those of the Brick Presbyterian Church, Church of the Heavenly Rest (Episcopal), Madison Avenue Presbyterian Church, Central Presbyterian Church, and Christ Church Methodist.

The classes are small. The Brick Church Nursery School takes only five boys and five girls for its three-year-old class. Children of church members are given preference, but others are admitted when there is room.

A few years ago there was talk that society's favorite Episcopal church, St. James, was considering starting a nursery school. Many would-be socialites were all agog about it—and rightly, too.

With or without nursery-school background, newcomers have the best chance of acceptance if they apply for the first grade offered by a given school—be it pre-kindergarten, kindergarten, first grade, or ninth.

Application blanks, by the way, can be obtained from any school simply by writing or telephoning the director of admissions. At this point no personal introduction or recommendation is needed. Most of these schools will also send catalogues and rate cards on request.

"Some schools are particularly hard for newcomers to crack," a leading social secretary told me. "In New York City, for example, Brearley, Chapin, and Spence take most of their students from Old Guard families. Of the boys' schools, I'd say Buckley, St. Bernard's, and Browning are the most formidable."

I find that teaching at the day schools tends to be conservative. From the very first grade on, the teachers are preparing the students for prep school. In some schools, first-graders who have trouble learning to read are coached. Progressive schools tend to attract fewer of society's offspring. There are, however, a few exceptions. In New York City the Dalton School is extremely progressive—and yet has fairly high social standing. A teacher commented to me that Dalton and Chapin have much the same clientele, even though their teaching methods are radically different.

Starting French in the first grade is an all-but-universal private-school touch. Even in kindergarten little ones play games in French and pipe up with *"Frère Jacques."* Other features of the curriculum are daily dancing and music.

Whenever I visit private day schools, I am struck anew by the fact that the physical plant and equipment are not so good as in many of the public schools. This frequently comes as a shock to the parent spending a large sum of money for his child's education. Science laboratories, for example, seem to belong to the era of the horse and buggy rather than the jet plane. A space map on the wall is often the only sign of the coming of the age of sputnik. The teachers, luckily, more than make up for the lacking equipment.

Good manners are stressed from the very start of schooling. Even six-year-olds are trained to stand up when a visitor enters a classroom, to step aside in the hall to let a grownup go first.

"Raise your hand and not your voice" is a watchword in almost every school.

Uniforms are worn in some but by no means all of the day schools. In New York, they are still required by Chapin and Brearley, not by Spence. But even when uniforms are worn, they are of surprisingly little help in sparing parents the expense of dressing a child—particularly a girl.

The lives led by most private school students demand a fairly extensive wardrobe. As a result, such shops as the Chapin-Brearley Exchange have sprung into being. The mother of a Brearley student has described to me the way these operate: A mother brings in an outgrown but still good-looking coat or dress. In the Exchange the women in charge decide that this outfit could be sold for $20.00.

And so the mother gets a credit of twenty points. She can use these to buy a coat or dress for her child. If the item she selects costs more than the points she has accumulated, she can pay the difference in dollars. Many dresses sold in the shop cost about twenty-five points or dollars, although there are a good number for less.

"The Exchange is used mostly for the little children," the woman added. "By the age of eleven most girls rebel against hand-me-downs, and so the parent must be prepared to pay for a lot of clothes—in quiet good taste, of course."

As the child grows older, most society parents prepare for the shift to boarding school. At New York's select Browning School, for example, enrollment in the lower grades totals 130 boys; in the higher, 35.

Attendance at a prestige day school helps an applicant into prep school. This is a source of worry to parents in areas without good elementary schools. Some of them, therefore, turn to the junior boarding schools, such as Eaglebrook or Bement in Massachusetts. These are best described as preparatory schools for prep school. All the ones I checked reported that every graduate was successful in achieving this goal. Most are for boys, but a number are coeducational.

The military academies are generally conceded to be slightly easier on applicants than are the big-name prep schools. They are also lower in cost. While not on a par with, say, St. Paul's or St. Mark's, they do have social acceptability, particularly in the South and Midwest. Graduates of the top military schools get into the Ivy League colleges. And in many communities Army and Navy personnel are accepted by the old families, who would not consider associating with any other outsiders. A boy who attends this type of school may not be planning to make the armed services his career, but the military aura can aid him socially during the years when he is making his first contacts.

Whatever the type of school chosen, admissions directors have individual preferences, which can be discovered by the observant parent. In some, the personal appearance of the child is apt to be the clincher. In others, sports ability is highly valued.

"We rode our daughter into Foxcroft," one parent admits cheerfully.

This fashionable boarding school is known from Cold Spring Harbor to Grosse Pointe for its exclusiveness. Riding is the key sport there. Many students come from the horsy sets of Long Island, Far Hills, New Jersey, and Lake Forest, Illinois. Half of the horses in the school's stables are owned by individual students. Parents of applicants often put a child on horseback at the age of three. By the time she is ready for Foxcroft, she is recognized at horse shows as an accomplished horsewoman.

Although principals like to say it is not so, an appearance of wealth is apt to prove helpful at the initial interview for almost any of society's schools. Many of them need money, even when they are not overt about asking for it. Despite sky-high tuition rates, it is difficult for private schools to make money today. This is particularly true of the girls' schools. Most of them have small endowments and alumnae who limit support to attendance at an occasional tea or theater party. General checks are not forthcoming. Alumnae get married—frequently to alumni of the boys' schools. A student of the double standard can make what he will of this, but the couple's support usually goes to the husband's school. In many cases contributions (or what is really the hope of future gifts) speak louder than old-line antecedents or high I.Q.

I know one couple who hired a Cadillac limousine to drive up to Miss Porter's for an interview.

"I didn't think we'd stand a chance in our own Plymouth," the wife commented afterward.

Another mother tells of an interview granted her at a leading day school. She had a recommendation from the parents of a student. "Within a few minutes the headmistress had told me how devoted she was to this couple. Why, their contribution to the last reconstruction fund drive of the school was $10,000," the mother reports. "She implied that the school likes to have parents who donate freely. She seemed to be curious about whether I would be able to follow the example of my friends."

The gifted child has an edge. A good number of the nation's leading private schools give intelligence tests to pint-size applicants for the first grade. Brearley, Buckley, and Browning in New York City are just three of the many schools that give I.Q. tests to applying four- and five-year-olds.

Brains alone are not enough even then. As every parent in these Freud-tossed days know, adjustment is essential literally from the cradle to the grave. A five-year-old who is not so good a glad-hander as a forty-five-year-old Elk is at a distinct disadvantage. At most of these schools the child spends a morning visiting the class he will enter the following year. This gives those in charge a chance to see how quickly the little one adjusts.

The mother of one applicant tells that her daughter did well in the intelligence tests but flunked the social session. She was too shy. The school suggested that the child be sent elsewhere for the first two years. By then she might be better able to adjust—and her I.Q. would not go down.

With each passing year the child's ability becomes more important to his social-academic future. The big-name boys' prep schools are particularly concerned about their academic standing and favor students who will be acceptable to the Ivy League colleges.

It is possible for the brilliant child to display his talents in a series of examinations. Many schools select applicants at least partly on the basis of their ratings on standard tests.

About 200 private schools use the Secondary School Admission Tests, usually known by their initials as the SSAT. These include some of the nation's top-ranking schools, such as Groton, St. Mark's, Choate, Lawrenceville, Andover, Exeter, St. Paul's, Anna Head, Kent, Lake Forest, St. Timothy's, Cranbrook, Asheville, and the Hill. Applicants can write to the Educational Testing Service, 20 Nassau Street, Princeton, New Jersey, to find out where to take these tests. The Service sends reports to any number of schools, adding an extra charge after the first six.

Some schools use the Educational Record Bureau Tests, and others favor the Secondary Education Board Tests in English, mathematics, French, and Latin.

Good test scores help but do not guarantee admission. Schools consider many other factors. Religion is one of the most important of these—and not only in its obvious sense of prejudice and quotas.

Many of the top-notch private schools have a religious affiliation and give preference to members of that faith. Some were actually started as church schools and have clergymen as headmasters. An Episcopal priest, the Reverend John O. Patterson, heads the famous Kent School, for example; the Reverend Matthew Madison Warren is rector of St. Paul's. Some other well-known Episcopal schools are the Bishop's School, Cate, Katharine Branson, and Marlborough in California; St. Timothy's in Maryland; Groton in Massachusetts; Cranbrook in Michigan; Chatham Hall, Stuart Hall, and Episcopal High School in Virginia. At Episcopal High, sons of clergymen get a 30 per cent discount. Proctor Academy in New Hampshire is Unitarian and allows ministers' sons $1,000 scholarships; Wayland Academy in Wisconsin is Baptist. Best-known Catholic schools are Portsmouth Priory, the Marymount schools, and the Convents of the Sacred Heart.

Attendance at the right school—with scholarship assistance—is perhaps the only way for newcomers without a great deal of money to break into the inner circle. But it is apt to be a hard way. It requires a truly mature child and parent to withstand the pressures of associating with people who think nothing of flying off to St. Moritz to ski at Christmas or who honestly believe that *"all* the kids go to Bermuda for the Easter holidays."

A number of schools operate on what is frequently called the "Kent plan." This is a students' work plan that originated at the Kent School, Connecticut. The students themselves do the cleaning, wait on table, wash dishes, and mow lawns. This reduces costs and makes it possible for tuition to be scaled to each family's means.

Scholarships are offered by virtually every one of the top-ranking schools. In practice, this is not quite so democratic as it sounds, particularly in the cases of the smaller, most exclusive schools. An alumnus of one such school tells me that he believes that most scholarships go to the sons of graduates whose financial position has slipped or to society's favorites: children of impoverished aristocrats. Nevertheless, many gifted boys from unknown families do attend big-name prep schools on scholarships. A number of these schools are so heavily endowed that they can afford to admit the poor and gifted, in addition to the rich and gifted. Exeter, for example, has an endowment of more than $22,000,000 and gives scholarships to more than 170 boys a year.

Andover also has a liberal scholarship program. This school sends a detailed four-page report to scholarship applicants. It makes the point that: "The procedure used in determining the size of the award ... resembles, for most cases, that used with Form 1040 in computing the Federal Income Tax."

The school has a table computing how much a family with a given income should be able to contribute to the child's schooling. A family with two children and a yearly income of $10,000 is expected to contribute about $1,370 a year. The school grants a scholarship large enough to make up the difference between what the family pays and the regular charge for tuition, room, and board. Scholarship boys must work about four hours a week in the office or dining hall, but at no time are they considered "second-class citizens."

I have it on good authority that about 20 per cent of the students in boarding schools get financial help. Even some day schools offer at least partial scholarships to about 15 per cent of their enrollment.

Students interested in obtaining a scholarship should write to the school in question (addresses are given in "A Directory of the Right Schools," starting on page 265), or consult the School Scholarship Service, 186 Centre Street, Milton, 86, Massachusetts.

The applicant and his parents cannot be inhibited. Glancing over typical application blanks, I note that questions are asked about the father's (and mother's) income, salary, inheritance, investments, bonuses, real-estate holdings, and automobiles. Parents are queried on the amount of mortgages outstanding on home or property and the number of payments due on the car. The student himself must be outstanding in his school work and character. His personality, and at some schools, his athletic ability, can be the deciding factors.

Once the student is accepted—with or without a scholarship—the school tends to put its stamp on him.

"I can always spot a prep-school graduate, sometimes even tell which school he attended," one society matron told me.

The speech, posture, dress, even the handwriting of alumni are of a kind. The schools are small and paternalistic, and supervise every aspect of a child's life very closely.

As many of the schools have a religious affiliation, chapel going is likely to be compulsory. At Catholic Portsmouth Priory, for example, attendance at both morning and evening prayers is required; even at nondenominational Choate there is daily chapel.

Most of the boys' schools have a work program for all the students. They clean their rooms, work on the grounds, wait on table. This rule is observed in the most exclusive schools, including St. Mark's, Choate, and Connecticut's Pomfret.

In some of the schools, such as St. Paul's, St. Mark's, and Groton, the younger boys sleep in cubicles in a dormitory; the older boys have their own rooms. In others, such as Middlesex in Massachusetts, all the students have individual rooms.

A classical education is still given by almost all of the society schools. The teaching method seems more like that generally associated with college than high school. Seminars and round-table discussions are used at Exeter, Lawrenceville, and many others. The ratio of teachers to students is high. At Andover, for example, there is one teacher to every nine boys.

Sports are emphasized at practically every one of these schools— an excellent preparation for the high society life that will be led by most of these boys. The campuses have every imaginable sports facility. Take Exeter: There is a swimming pool, artificial ice rink, twelve playing fields, and twenty-three tennis courts. At Middlesex boys not only engage in hockey, basketball, squash rackets, skiing, skating, and shooting (if parents permit), but they may also join the Yacht Club.

The girls' boarding schools are still battling the finishing-school label with more or less success.

Allegra Maynard, director of the Madeira School, insisted in an interview recently: "It is very much in the air here to work as hard as you can and to respect endeavor and achievement. It is fashionable to do well."

At Emma Willard in Troy, New York, Anne Wellington, the headmistress, proudly points out that every single graduate goes on to college.

At some of the other prestige boarding schools, though, there is still considerable stress on the "finishing" aspects of a nice young lady's education—with dancing, music, art, good manners, sewing, cooking, and home economics.

"I think it is possible for a girl to go through boarding school learning relatively little academically," the mother of three daughters comments sagely, "but all of these institutions now offer good courses for those youngsters who are interested in studying."

The girls lead a more cloistered life than is generally believed by those who imagine them on a continual wild subdebutante spree. Weekends off campus are strictly limited. St. Timothy's, for example, allows freshmen and sophomores two weekends a year away from school, juniors three, and seniors four. Garrison Forest School in Maryland permits only two a year, as does St. Mary's Hall in San Antonio.

Rules on allowing boys on campus vary considerably. Men are for the most part shooed off the Foxcroft grounds; at Concord they can visit on campus much of the time.

Even the amount of money the girls may spend is limited by many of the schools. Parents of students at Baldwin in Bryn Mawr, Pennsylvania, are advised to provide spending money of $6.00 a month for younger girls, $10.00 to $15.00 for older; at Chatham Hall, in Virginia, the allowance limit is set at $8.00 to $12.00 a month.

Uniforms have long been a distinguishing characteristic of many of these schools. They are worn at most of them—Westover, Garrison Forest, St. Timothy's, Baldwin, Agnes Irwin in Wynnewood, Pennsylvania, and Annie Wright Seminary in Tacoma, Washington—to pick just a few at random. But I find some indications that the uniform regulations are being relaxed. At Ethel Walker, where uniforms once meant everything from underwear out, the girls are now allowed to choose the color they wish to wear in the required short-sleeved V-neck dresses and tailored skirts. At Masters, in Dobbs Ferry, New York, blazers must be worn, but considerable variety is allowed. Those who work on the student newspaper wear Black Watch plaid blazers; those in the glee club, maroon. At Emma Willard uniforms are not required, but students must wear cotton shirtmakers in fall and spring, and a flannel skirt, a blouse, and a gray school jacket in winter.

A ban on make-up, except on weekends, is enforced almost everywhere.

"It's not hard to stick to this rule in boarding school," one teacher told me. "After all, we have boys on campus only on weekends."

It is quite a different story in the day schools. All of them have rules, but I find that these are obeyed only by those girls who are late to mature anyway. I know one school that insists that the students must wear flats, hats, and *no* make-up even when they are out of school. But I have never seen a teen-age girl who observed this regulation. Many schools are more lenient, allowing seniors to wear lipstick "with restraint" and high heels, letting the younger girls put on lipstick before leaving school, if their parents approve.

Sports are every bit as important to the girls as to the boys. Those schools in cold-weather country, such as Miss Hall's at Pittsfield, and Abbot Academy at Andover, Massachusetts, stress skiing and skating. Riding is, to be sure, the favored sport at almost all the girls' schools. It is a "necessary" extra charge practically everywhere. An annual horse show is held at Garrison Forest. Students who are really at home in the saddle are allowed to take part in the elite Green Spring Valley Hunt. The qualified riders at Oldfields in Glencoe, Maryland, may join the fashionable Elkridge-Harford Hunt Club.

The girls' boarding schools view it as their responsibility to prepare the students for their well-to-do futures. And so most of them try to inculcate a sense of community responsibility. Many of these youngsters will grow up to devote much of their adult lives to the socio-philanthropic functions of the rich.

Charity, therefore, begins at school level. Foxcroft girls work in a baby clinic; at Miss Porter's they help out in a home for crippled children; at Westover they sew and knit for the poor. Emma Willard students work with underprivileged children and raise funds for the needy, both in the United States and abroad. At Miss Hall's they work with the hospitals, the Coolidge Home for Crippled Children, and other local charities.

And then, of course, there is college. About 90 per cent of all private-school graduates now go on to higher education.

The schools naturally pride themselves on getting graduates into the ranking colleges, and the principals usually keep close tabs on which college each member of the senior class might be able to make. The youngsters are advised accordingly.

I know one student who was—contrary to all school claims—turned down at all three colleges to which she had applied. On the last day of school, she was sadly gathering her things together when the headmistress came by and asked her what she planned to do the following year.

"I don't know," she replied. "I couldn't get into college."

The principal immediately named a nearby top-ranking college.

The girl promptly applied and was admitted. Somehow the headmistress had made it her business to find out that this particular college had fewer talented applicants that year than usual. I have found that this kind of prescience is almost commonplace among the women running these schools.

The private-school student is prepared both for college and the kind of life he or she will live thereafter. The boys are expected to go on to high-level professional careers, the girls to debuts and marriages to men of substance.

The private-school set in many cities is self-contained. Its members are influential in top-level society life, and they favor one another: The "old school tie" concept is traditionally British—but it exists, in an invisible form, throughout the United States.

That is why social secretary Mrs. Tew told me: "Nowadays many girls who become debutantes do not come from the old families. A good school makes all the difference. The school wins social acceptance for its students."

CHAPTER VII

The Social Whirl Starts

"WHEN our little girl was ten, we decided we'd like her to make a debut," the mother of a recent debutante told me wearily. "But it was hard going for people without a high society background. If I knew then what I know now, we'd have started planning when she was five or six."

When I quoted this statement to a society matron with whom I was having lunch a day or two later she looked incredulous. "But that's ridiculous!" she exclaimed. "Why, my own Anne insisted that she wasn't going to make a debut until she was nearly seventeen. She was a real tomboy before that. When she changed her mind, I just phoned some of the women on the committee for the Grosvenor and told them about her. There wasn't any problem. It wouldn't have made any difference if I'd 'planned' for years, as your friend put it."

When I challenged the socialite to produce other such examples, she promptly came up with a Rockefeller connection who had come to New York from the West during her debut year. "She was accepted for absolutely everything, of course. She was even a member of the Assemblies."

Such a case is hardly typical. The brutal fact is that only the child whose mother was presented at the Junior or Philadelphia Assemblies or whose father is a Drexel, McCormick, or Rockefeller can skip up and down the road that leads to the debut at will.

For others, the ball invitation comes only after long and careful planning.

Sending a child to one of the recognized private schools is the first step. But what is done outside of school hours is almost as important. I have known a number of mothers who successfully used sports as the entering wedge into society for their children. Games can be played for society's sake as well as for the game's sake. A child simply cannot be too young to engage in sports. Members of the inner circle take these activities seriously. And so they introduce their youngsters to skating, riding, and tennis at an early age. Their children are to be found on the membership lists of the junior clubs maintained by many prestige athletic clubs.

Take the Skating Club of New York for an example. Its social position is such that membership is usually included in the newspaper wedding biography of a socialite.

Another indication of the caliber of the membership of the Junior Club can be gotten from a statement Mrs. Robert F. Luce, director, made to me recently: "At sixteen the members can advance to the Senior Club. But as most of them go away to boarding school, there is a gap."

They come back to join the Senior Club and keep on going until the infirmities of old age put an end to active sports. In the Skating Club some of society's oldest names join some of its newest names on the ice. And so membership has helped many social careers.

"The same can be said for many other sports," a club member commented privately. "But you have to have some athletic ability to be good at tennis or golf or hunting. *Anyone* can learn to skate."

The Junior Skating Club is hard to get into, but many newcomers have succeeded in doing so. All of them started their children as early as possible. That used to be at five, but the club has become so crowded that the age minimum was recently raised to six.

"A mother should put in her application when the child is four or five anyway," Mrs. Luce advised me. "To be considered, the youngster must be proposed and seconded by members. Even so, there is such a long waiting list that we can't accept everyone."

In many parts of the country newcomers make their way into society on horseback. Children are prepared for competition in the junior events at horse shows. Some little ones are placed in the saddle before they have attained a good seat on a tricycle.

Riding is used more successfully as a social lever in the suburbs and in smaller cities than it is in New York.

The real society way of doing it is to have one's own horse, and this is rather hard to manage in a crowded city. I remember that when I was a child only one of my friends had a horse of her own, quartered at a nearby stable. And she was in society already—or so she used to tell me—and her family felt it essential to have some member competing for the junior trophies at the horse shows.

One woman who has been working her way up the social ladder slowly but surely told me that she had seriously considered buying a horse for her daughter. But when she learned that it would cost her $80.00 a month to keep it, she changed her mind. She tried to talk her daughter into sharing a horse with a friend whose mother felt the same way, but both girls turned it down. She also admitted that she began to worry when she heard about a top-society family which had kept two horses in the city for their daughter and had to send the horses away when the girl began flirting with the stableboys.

"The best way to handle the horse problem is to keep the horses at your country home or farm," suggests a woman whose children are accomplished riders. "The youngsters get enough practice in the summer and on weekends to compete in the local horse shows. And many of these are extremely social. I have friends who have succeeded in working up to the Fairfield County, the Oxridge, and even the Meadow Brook Hunts."

I know of one high society family, split by divorce, in which the father insisted on keeping the horse. He felt that this would lead his former wife to encourage his daughter to visit him, instead of discouraging her. And he was quite right.

As society continues to be a man's world, parents of boys are understandably less tense about their children's futures than are parents of daughters. Boys who have not bothered with junior athletic clubs or dancing classes have, nonetheless, been swamped with subdebutante party invitations once they reached prep school.

Still the old-line families send their sons to the private military drill classes. And this remains the prestige thing to do.

The oldest and best-known of these classes is New York's Knickerbocker Greys, which has been attended by sons of New York's first families since 1881. Boys join at the age of eight and continue until they are sixteen. They drill every week from October to May under the direction of Colonel William H. Warwick (U.S.A. Retired) at the Seventh Regiment Armory.

The cost, as I have found true of most fashionable groups, is not exorbitant. The problem is to get in. Dues come to $60.00 a year, and uniforms add another $110; swords are rented for $5.00.

Admittance is based on letters of recommendation from parents of cadets and on a personal interview. But even a telephoned recommendation from the mother of a cadet will bring a handwritten note urging that the applicant be brought into the Armory to meet the board of directors.

Experience has shown that the private school attended by the youngster makes the difference. At some of the city's fashionable day schools (see my Directory on page 265) it seems that "all" the boys go. The directors—who are mothers of cadets themselves—are, therefore, likely to know the applicant or can find out about him easily.

The president of the Greys is Mrs. Andrew M. McBurney and the treasurer is Mrs. Albert C. Santy, whose name figures prominently on many top-bracket charity and dance committees, such as the Junior League Ball committee.

All such extracurricular activities are helpful, but the real battle of society is fought in the dancing classes.

"To become a debutante, a girl needs three things in her background," Marianne Strong, society press agent, declares firmly. "A, dancing school; b, the right school; c, money."

I cannot agree that dancing school deserves top billing, as the other two are really more important. But there is no question that future debutantes and their escorts are made on Friday afternoons at Miss Souther's, Barclay's or De Rham's.

"You usually find yourself going to the subdeb dances and then the debutante parties with the same group of girls you started out with in dancing class," a recent debutante pointed out.

And so in Philadelphia, for example, the goal of would-be social-ites is an invitation for their daughters to attend the Tuesday-afternoon dancing classes held at the Merion Cricket Club. Girls then advance to the Friday and Saturday dances. All of these are steps on the way to the Philadelphia Assembly.

Attendance at the classes where little Wanamakers, Astors, and Whitneys learn to waltz or rhumba is by invitation. The women or men who run the classes welcome almost any boy of reasonably good family, sisters and daughters of former students, and children from *Social Register* families. Newcomers can apply for admittance, and if the youngster is recommended by mothers of students, she may be accepted. Knowing parents put in their applications long before a daughter is old enough to attend. In some cases, this is early indeed. A number of the teachers believe that if a child can toddle she can fox-trot; others favor waiting until fourth grade.

One reason for the great prestige of the best-known dancing classes is that they change hands so seldom. Generations of socialites are trained by the same women. To be a teacher of a society dancing class is equivalent to drinking at the fountain of youth.

When I was a child attending Brooklyn's Berkeley Institute, the right dancing class for little girls and boys was run by Miss Elsie Hepburn. At the time, of course, I assumed that she had no first name. Dancing teachers are never referred to as anything but "Miss ———."

When I began to investigate current dancing classes for this book, I asked out of curiosity who had taken over Miss Hepburn's classes.

"Taken them over?" was the surprised response. "Why, she's still teaching."

In Boston Miss Marguerite Souther runs dancing classes for Boston socialites just as she did for their mothers twenty years ago. In Westchester Miss Covington held classes for fifty years from the early 1900's. Her classes have only lately been taken over by Mr. and Mrs. William Meeker.

Almost every city or suburb has one, or possibly two, dancing classes patronized by the children of local society. For the un-initiated, they are surprisingly difficult to find.

The wife of an executive who was transferred to New York from Dallas told me that she spent months trying to find the right dancing class for her children. "I started with the New York classified telephone directory. There are more than three pages of listings and advertisements for dancing instructors and schools. But I couldn't get the slightest idea from them as to which were the society dancing classes and which were strictly commercial."

I do not find that surprising, as not a single one of New York's ranking classes—in society terms—is listed there at all.

At that, the person from out of town is in a better position to find out the names of these classes than is a native. She at least has an excuse for asking, whereas anyone who has been brought up in the city is simply expected to *know*. This can pose quite a problem for people who decide that they want a society life for their children even if they never had it themselves.

Private-school principals are good sources of information, unless they disapprove of emphasis on social life—and many of them do. Classmates and their parents are the best ones to ask—if some likely excuse for not knowing can be found. Newcomers to those suburbs where even society children go to public school often find that someone in the office of a social or country club can supply the name. Many of the dancing classes are actually held in the clubs. The local Junior League or Service League can also furnish the information.

But old hands usually advise the newcomer to go slow in starting a child in dancing class. She must be certain which one is "right." Society's rules are very rigid when it comes to such essentials as dancing.

In New York City the two dancing classes with society's highest seal of approval are De Rham and Barclay.

"De Rham has the edge," a society matron states flatly.

She reports that the student body includes youthful Astors, Ban-crofts, Dukes, Goulds, Paines, Rockefellers, Roosevelts, and Whit-neys—not all at the same time, I must add.

These classes are now being run by Mrs. William de Rham, who took over in 1958 after the death of her husband. They are held in the fashionable Colony or River Clubs and in the Piping Rock Club in Locust Valley. Waiting lists are long and children's names are often sent in when their dancing is still confined to the playpen. This is not so much in advance as it sounds, because Mrs. de Rham starts classes at the three-year-old level.

Many parents have admitted that they find the De Rham classes conducted with an iron hand. Oddly enough, this seems only to enhance their prestige. Mothers and children share an anticipatory thrill of nervousness before class.

One afternoon last winter I was visiting a friend whose little girl in party dress and white gloves was being spruced up for dancing class.

"If they correct you about anything, just answer with 'yes' or 'no.' Don't try to explain," was the admonishment offered the little one.

But as "everyone" goes to these dancing classes, few parents even think that an unhappy child might better be removed.

One mother confessed that her son got so upset at one famous dancing class that he developed a facial tic, which he had for four months.

I question whether dancing class alone could be at the root of such extreme nervousness, but the mother believed that it was. Nonetheless, taking the boy out of class never entered her mind.

The only other dancing class that compares with De Rham in terms of prestige is run by John Barclay. He holds classes at the Colony Club and in the New Jersey suburbs as well. He, too, has a high society clientele—most of whom are completely devoted to him. I have yet to hear an unkind comment about Mr. Barclay.

The newest of the dancing classes is run by Mrs. Henry Duncan Wood, III, a dynamic woman who fills a real need. She is selective, but not so forbiddingly so as the others. As a result, a large group finds a happy haven with Mrs. Wood, who runs her classes in approved society style.

None of the prestige classes provide the Arthur Murray type of instruction designed to turn out juvenile mambo or cha-cha-cha experts. Dancing is almost secondary, particularly in the earliest

years. The aim is to teach the social manner that the "beat" generation has forgotten.

It seems to me that entering a dancing class is like stepping into
another era. All the teachers are firm in their insistence on polite-
ness and good manners. The little girls wear party dresses; the little
boys are in dark suits, with white shirts and ties. White gloves are
required of both. There is usually a ten-cent fine for forgetting
gloves. From the seventh grade on girls must wear stockings.

At a typical dancing class the children come in and sit down
quietly to wait until all the students have arrived. Then they rise
and go to a receiving line, made up of the teacher and one of the
mothers. Each boy takes a partner. The girl curtsies and the boy
bows. Then each says politely: "Good afternoon, Mrs. ————. My
name is ————."

The dancing then starts. In the younger groups the girls are
sometimes lined up opposite the boys and each dances with the
nearest one. In the older groups, the boy picks a partner. The
girls are given the sad facts of life right away—they cannot decline.
But partners are changed frequently. After each number the boy
takes the girl back to her chair, waits for her to be seated, and thanks
her for the dance. She thanks him, too. At the end of the class there
is a grand march. After that the children again go down the receiving
line to say good-by.

The cost of the dancing classes is by no means commensurate
with their social importance. In New York City $70.00 for a course
of fifteen lessons is typical. In some suburbs or smaller towns the
same amount of instruction costs $40.00; in others, $30.00.

The dancing classes change with the advancing years of their
students. From weekday afternoons boys and girls grow into the
Friday evening classes and then graduate to Saturdays. At this point
classes are more like parties than anything else.

"Saturday night at De Rham's is the Park Avenue version of
hanging out at the local store," one boy asserts. "Everybody you
know shows up there."

From dancing class girls and boys move on to subdebutante
parties. These are run in just about the same way in all cities and
suburbs that have a formal social life for this age group.

In a number of cities, subdebutante activities are not organized at all. This is the case in Richmond, for example, a call to Mrs. Allen C. Goolsby, society editor of the Richmond *News Leader,* revealed. She reported that subdebutantes may be invited to the debutante dances; there is nothing specifically planned for them.

But by far the majority of cities and suburbs do have a rigid subdebutante party setup. Each affair is a dress rehearsal for the main events of the debutante year.

In Boston the subdebutante dances are virtually continuations of Mrs. Souther's classes. She holds a series of afternoon parties called "Eliot Halls," the name of the place where they are held. Bostonian society matrons delighted in telling me that Mrs. Souther runs the parties with a no-nonsense approach.

"If a girl is a wallflower or does not seem to be pleasant and charming, Mrs. Souther may call a taxi and send the luckless subdeb home in the middle of the dance," they noted, clearly feeling that this is just the way it should be.

In Cleveland youngsters attend the National Recreation League parties. Feeling runs high about these, as girls who are admitted automatically go on to debuts at the Assembly. In Bloomfield Hills, a chic suburb of Detroit, the junior set goes to the Cotillion Club dances, directed by Florence Schoolfield Young.

New York's subdebutante life is one of the most actively organized in the country and is the best example of this period in the life of a socialite, junior grade.

The subdebutante parties are the first real hurdles for the would-be debutante and her parents. And hurdles is just what they are. If I were to select the social events that cause the most nervous strain, I would give that dubious distinction to the subdebutante dances.

A leading society public-relations man confirmed this for me: "I can make a girl into a debutante, but I would not even attempt to make her into a subdebutante."

The key social affairs for the youngest set are even harder to break into than are most debutante balls. They are almost completely controlled by society's Old Guard.

The most recent list of the committee for New York's Junior Assemblies is an inner circle Who's Who: Mrs. Lyman C. Bleecker, chairman; Mrs. Ethan Allen Hitchcock, Mrs. Alexander P. Morgan, Mrs. Rodman Montgomery, Mrs. S. Hazard Gillespie, Mrs. Andrew Y. Rogers, Mrs. Hoyt Ammidon, and Mrs. Robert Lee Patterson, Jr.

When I compared this list with the committees for the top sub-debutante affairs, I found an astonishing number of duplications. Take the Holiday Dance group, for instance. Mrs. Bleecker, Mrs. Hitchcock, Mrs. Gillespie, Mrs. Ammidon, and Mrs. Rogers are all on that influential committee.

And when I checked back over the subdebutante committee lists for the last few years, I found that many of these women had served on the same committees time after time.

"A woman is likely to stay on these committees until her youngest daughter has made her debut," reports a woman who is intimate with many of the committee members. "I'm not implying by this that these ladies serve in order to assure their children's acceptance. For this group that is a foregone conclusion. But they feel that during these years they know most of the subdebs and debutantes personally and are really qualified to select.

"Of course," she adds, "some women get to relish the position of power to such an extent that they just stay on indefinitely."

The problem of the applicant is increased by the fact that almost all the ranking subdebutante parties are controlled by a very small group. The same women serve on at least two committees the same season. In a single year, for example, Mrs. Robert Palmer, Mrs. Graham Mattison, and Mrs. Theodore B. Russell all served on both the Junior Bachelors and the Cosmopolitan Dance; Mrs. George A. Carden served on the Bachelors and the Get-togethers, and Mrs. Jose Ferrer (not the wife of the actor) on the Junior Dinner and the Junior Bachelors.

As all of these women are recognized in society, the girl who wins their approval as a subdebutante has gained social acceptance for years to come. And this approval is not easy to obtain. Mrs. Bleecker, for example, even overawes members of the Old Guard. She is the wife of a clergyman and lives in Cold Spring Harbor, an inner circle suburb. This influential matron follows in the footsteps of her mother, Mrs. Walter Phelps Bliss, who was a social arbiter of the old style.

Mrs. Bleecker and her fellow members of real society are in charge of activities for subdebutantes. Some of the teen-age groups are just like social clubs. Children become members and then attend parties, year after year, until they reach debutante age. Annual dues cover the cost of attending the dances. There are also individual dances, given each year for a carefully selected list of subdebutantes.

Invitations are handled in this way: The mother sends an application to the invitations committee of each group or dance she wishes her daughter to attend. But if it is to count for anything, the request must be accompanied by three letters of recommendation from personal friends of three different members of the committee. An interview with the committee is given only after the letters have been received.

"I hate to think of all the hours I spent on the telephone when my daughter was in her early teens," I was told by a mother who succeeded in launching her daughter despite a middle-class background. "I called anyone who might be willing to write a letter for her. Just as soon as I'd think I had one nailed down, she'd sail for Europe or go to the country for four months with the letter unwritten, and it would have to be done again!"

Friends met through school and dancing class, church, and charity work are the likeliest letter writers. And when these fail, business contacts are frequently tried—usually with at least limited success.

This happened in the case of one girl whose story is typical of new society. Her father headed an investment house, but he was not native-born, and the "foreign" label is disastrous in the inner circle (unless, of course, it means British). The wife of one of his employees was a key member of one of the subdebutante committees. With her patronage the girl was accepted to that group. But she did not get to any of the other subdebutante affairs. The committees are so interrelated that the inside story got around and did not help the youngster's chances.

Although she later made a debut at a fairly social ball, she is still viewed as a member of the international set rather than of real society.

The business push works better when the people involved are

not hampered by a foreign background. I was surprised to learn that a girl who got to "everything" last year comes from a family that has never been in society before. Here, too, her social career was advanced by an impoverished gentleman who worked for her father. But this employee had many high society contacts that he was prepared to use for his employer. In addition, he was very well liked. And then, the subdebutante's family was solidly American and, luckily, Episcopalian as well.

"Some of the committees view themselves as liberal," a society matron revealed. "I wrote a letter of recommendation for a Jewish boy and he was accepted for an exclusive dance. I know of a Chinese girl who got into the Holidays. And there is an understanding that some Catholics will be admitted to each subdeb group. A few Catholics usually serve on each committee."

But many applicants whose letters are good enough to produce a personal interview for them have an additional problem: their daughters. Some are not interested in a society future and refuse to cooperate. When they are dragged by their mothers to meet committee members, they make a poor impression. This can be intensified, in the case of those girls who flower late, by a poor complexion and puppy fat.

"Susan couldn't have been more awkward," wailed the mother of an ugly duckling. "I'm sure the committee thought we were lying when we said she went to Chapin and to Mr. Barclay's dancing classes."

Appearances count for so much, she went on, referring to the example of a woman whose daughter had been accepted, even though the family was brand new to society. But the girl was so pretty and poised that she charmed the whole committee.

"Well, I'll just have to try again, though it gets harder every year. And Susan keeps insisting that she doesn't want to get involved in what she calls 'that debutante ratrace.'

"It wouldn't be so bad if I could just take her refusal at face value," the woman continued bitterly, "but I've been around too long. I've seen so many girls who aren't interested at fourteen, fifteen, or sixteen. And then all of a sudden, at seventeen, they discover that all their friends at Chapin or Ethel Walker are coming out, and they are frantic. By that time it's almost impossible to arrange a big debut—unless you're solidly entrenched in society or can afford to hire a top-notch social secretary or press agent. For people like us the time to break in is during the subdebutante years."

In some cities there is only one subdebutante group; in New York there are many. But no list of them has ever been published. In addition, the committees shun publicity to such an extent that outsiders—and many would-be insiders—have only the vaguest idea of what these "clubs" are really like.

Not long ago I called on a member of the invitations committee of one of the subdebutante groups. While I was there, she got a telephone call from a girl who wanted to join.

"How old are you, dear?" she asked kindly.

Her jaw dropped at the answer. After she hung up, she told me that the "girl" was thirty-five. "I wonder if the word is getting around that we run a lonely-hearts' club," she remarked drily.

I think that the "girl's" ignorance is quite understandable. I have known mothers of subdebutantes who were not quite sure when to apply to what.

The first subdebutante year for girls is when they are in the ninth grade in school. Boys are considered as escorts in tenth grade.

The Holidays, which I have mentioned earlier, is everybody's favorite.

"I think it's the nicest of all the subdeb groups," declares a society matron. "The youngsters enjoy the parties. And there is simply no question as to its standing."

The Junior Holidays accepts 125 girls, thirteen and fourteen years old, and 275 boys a year older. This is one of the only subdebutante groups that requires applications from boys as well as girls. The same youngsters, with possibly a few additions, advance to the Middle Holidays at fifteen for girls, sixteen for boys. At sixteen and a half or seventeen the girls move on to the Senior Holidays, but by then they must invite their own escorts.

Two formal supper dances are given for each group every year. Both are held in the ballroom of the Hotel Plaza. They are kept very simple as far as decorations go. The first dance is held during the Christmas vacation and the second at Easter.

Mrs. Montgomery Willcox, a socialite herself, is the paid secretary of the Holidays and does much of the work of organization. She has been with the group for so long that she has considerable power herself in the selection of subdebutantes.

I was discussing the Holidays with a socialite whose daughter had just been invited, when her husband, a distinguished gentleman in his forties, came in.

"Why, I attended the Holidays when I was a boy," he broke into our conversation cheerfully.

"Who was running them then?" I asked.

"Oh, Mrs. Willcox, of course," he replied. "And she wasn't young then."

The Holidays date back more than sixty years, I later learned from Mrs. Willcox.

"Even at that time a number of society families were giving up their ballrooms, and they wanted to hold carefully supervised parties for their children," she explained. "And so they started a series of invitation dances to be held at the Rose Room of the Hotel Plaza."

In the beginning these parties were attended only by the children of the group of friends who had started them. But as time passed, the number grew until it became necessary to use the invitations committee system that has since become standard for subdebutante and debutante affairs.

Most of the groups have teas at which applicants meet the committee, but the Holiday teas are viewed as the classic of their type. They are held in March of the year preceding admittance.

"If you're in, you don't need to go," one old-line New Yorker states flatly. "As a matter of fact, it's *déclassé* to go. I think they only invite those girls whom they're planning to turn down."

I have found that this statement is quite untrue, but the belief is widespread and adds to the tension and anxiety of those being interviewed. Emotions run high. The headmistress of one of New York's top day schools has described the teas to me as "barbarous."

"I remember the Holiday tea as one of the most ghastly experiences of my life," another mother told me heatedly. "It was held at the home of an ancient lady on the committee. The invitation said to come between three and three ten. I heard afterward that the next mother-daughter combination was to come between three ten and three twenty. The questions they asked my daughter were trivial. They asked where we spent our summers, and did she like Europe? But actually it was clear that they were sizing us up. Were we overdressed or underdressed? Did we have too much or too little make-up on? After a few minutes they suggested that we have tea. But as we were also asked not to stand around, we didn't. I don't think anyone else did either.

"I know a couple of women who went to those teas and had nervous breakdowns later. I don't think the teas were the cause, but they certainly didn't help."

She was so vehement that I was sure that her child had been rejected. But it turned out that she had been accepted. Only the price in nervous strain had been too high.

"One reason that the Holiday group is so hard to get into is that we must give first preference to children—now it's grandchildren—of former members," Mrs. Willcox informed me. "That leaves very few openings to be divided among all the other applicants."

Invitations are issued only after a vote taken by secret ballot.

A similar type of club membership characterizes the Get-togethers, popularly known as the "Gets." This long-established group descends from the almost legendary Benjamin dancing classes of the 1890's.

"The Gets are not so hard to break into as the Holidays," social secretary Mrs. Tew points out.

The Junior Get-togethers are for girls fourteen and fifteen years old, and this group then advances to the Senior Get-togethers for another two years. Boys are invited by the girls, but must be approved by the committee. About 500 boys and girls attend both of the two formal supper dances held for each group annually at the Hotel Pierre. Mrs. M. W. Openhovski is the secretary who masterminds the whole thing.

The Gets' practice of having the girls invite the boys to the parties is followed by almost all the other subdebutante committees. It leads to untold anguish for everyone, except the juvenile Peggy Bancrofts.

"I've drafted the sons of my best friends so many times that I'm afraid to look them in the face," one mother sheepishly admits.

"But there are just so many parties that my daughter should go to."

I have been told the same anecdote several times—either in scorn or envy—about the mother of ten-year-old girl who had already made up a list of suitable future escorts for the child and was carefully cultivating them all. My first reaction naturally was that everyone was talking about the same woman, and that this was becoming one of those apocryphal anecdotes that society people love to repeat. But upon checking back I discovered that each socialite was talking about a different person. This leads me to wonder if such calculated preparation might not be standard operating procedure in some sets.

The problem is intensified by the fact that even a subdebutante is expected to attend an affair with at least two escorts.

The most exclusive party for fourteen- and fifteen-year-olds is the Junior Bachelors Dinner Dance, held each year during Christmas vacation. About 75 girls get the coveted invitations. Letters of recommendation are not required. The girl (or her mother) must be personal friends of the committeewomen. Most of those accepted have known at least two members for two years.

"I knew only one member, but she really went to bat for me!" the mother of a girl who was accepted exclaimed gratefully.

The subdebutantes provide their own escorts. The boys must be members. But the committee will consider for membership any young man suggested.

"Is it hard to get a boy in?" a woman asked innocently.

Her question was greeted with laughter.

Two other top-bracket subdebutante affairs for the youngest age group are the Junior Dinner and the Cosmopolitan Dances. The two committees work very closely, so that a girl is usually invited to one or the other—not to both. Each takes 75 girls. The Cosmopolitans have two dances a year, the Junior Dinner only one.

Just to keep everyone thoroughly confused, there is also a Junior New Yorker Dinner Dance group, run by Clementine Miller, a social secretary who specializes in handling dances. This is for fourteen- and fifteen-year-old girls. Those who start at fourteen continue for a second year. Boys can go for three years. The Junior New Yorkers take 125 girls, and maintain the minimum society ratio of two boys to every girl. Two dances are held each year at the Hotel Pierre.

"Girls can't apply to the Junior New Yorkers," emphasizes Miss Miller. "They have to be invited by the patronesses' committee."

Insiders murmur that this is not too hard to arrange.

Still another group, called the Merry-makers, is made up of girls who attend Brearley, Chapin, Lenox, Miss Hewitt's, Nightingale-Bamford, and Spence. Any girl attending one of those schools can join the Merry-makers in her first year of high school and can go year after year until she is of debutante age. Two formal dinner dances, one at Christmas and one at Easter, are held at the Hotel Pierre each year. Mrs. Openhovski of the Get-togethers also arranges these affairs.

Although not truly exclusive, except in the sense that those day schools are exclusive, the dances are attended by the girls who are doing the subdebutante circuit.

Catholic would-be debutantes are eligible for the Gothams, a group run in much the same way as the Holidays.

"Applications are usually sent in two years in advance," Mrs. William J. O'Shea, president, informed me. "We're hearing now from granddaughters of former members."

There are two groups of young Gothams, one for fourteen- and fifteen-year-olds, and the other for sixteen- and seventeen-year-olds. Usually the girls admitted at fourteen keep right on going. Sixty are accepted each year. They may invite boys, subject to committee approval. Membership dues, which run in the neighborhood of $50.00 a year, cover attendance at the two formal dances held annually for each group. These are benefits for the New York Foundling Home.

As Catholics can be accepted for all the other subdebutante parties, a number of socialites say frankly that they do not view the Gothams as a high-prestige group.

In addition to running dancing classes, Mrs. Wood holds her own subdebutante affairs, the Masquerade Dances, during Christmas vacation. Three dances are given, one for each age group, starting with eighth-graders. No letters of recommendation are required. Mrs. Wood makes up an invitations list, based largely on her dancing classes, and she looks kindly on applicants who attend any of the fashionable schools. The girls pay $30.00 for the dance; this price includes an escort.

At sixteen and seventeen girls become eligible for two of New York's most highly regarded subdebutante dances: the Metropolitan and the Colony. There is no general agreement as to which is more exclusive. Among a group of society women I questioned, the Metropolitan seemed to have the slight edge, but it was not conclusive.

"The Metropolitan Dance is smaller," said one.

"But Mrs. Earl, who is secretary-treasurer of the Junior Assemblies, handles the Colony," pointed out another.

Both of them are attended mostly by daughters of the Old Guard.

Members of the old-line families can pick and choose among all these subdebutante affairs. I asked a number of inner-circle society matrons which ones they favored. Without exception they selected the Holidays, the Junior Bachelors, and either the Junior Dinner or the Cosmopolitan for the fourteen- and fifteen-year-olds; for the following year they added the Colony and the Metropolitan. These are the six top-ranking subdebutante affairs in New York.

Some girls who get to comparatively few of the prestige parties are able to make up for that lack by their own efforts—and good looks.

"The prep-school dances can do wonders in launching a girl. And you don't need to pass muster with an invitations committee either," a recent debutante disclosed, with a gleam in her eye. "The most important is the Groton-St. Mark's dance, which is held in New York. If you're invited to enough of these dances, you'll get on the subdeb and debutante party lists."

It is customary for girls to give parties before or after the subdebutante dances. A number of mothers have used these parties to maneuver their daughters—and incidentally themselves—into the inner circle. One woman whose daughter had been accepted by the Get-togethers held parties regularly. Her guest list was limited to members of the Gets whose parents were high society. As she gave extremely lively parties, the youngsters were anxious to come. Only a few of the families balked. One Old Guard matron told me that she discovered on the day of the party that her daughter had accepted an invitation without her knowledge. She promptly phoned and canceled, with a transparent excuse. The girl just as promptly called back and said she was coming.

"I let her go," the socialite said later. "After all, the girl for whom the party was being given is attractive and harmless. But I had never realized the mother had actually gotten everyone to allow their children to visit her. I suppose that she'll be expecting us to give recommendations for the Junior Assemblies."

I learned later that the woman did make a try for the Assemblies. She did not succeed, but she did get her daughter presented at another quite highly regarded group ball.

The system works more easily when it is handled by somebody besides the mother. One family came to New York from the South. They knew only one solidly entrenched society couple. But as these people were prepared to help, that was enough. They arranged to get the fourteen-year-old daughter into one of the subdebutante groups. And *they* gave the pre-dance parties to introduce the girl to the children of their friends. Within a few years the newcomers were leading an old-line life.

Parties are held more often for a short-term gain—to provide a date for the dance. A mother can easily give a little party for the daughters of her friends, and can suggest that a brother or cousin be brought along as an extra man.

"Cocktail" parties are particularly popular. The first year or two the quotation marks are quite correct. Tomato juice, Seven-Up, Coca-Cola, and other soft drinks are served. But by the the time the youngsters reach the senior groups the boys expect hard liquor. They look down their noses at the sherry or dubonnet of an earlier era. It takes a firm parent to hold the line.

The cost of going the subdebutante rounds is not so great as outsiders believe it to be. Several socialites obligingly went over checkbook stubs for me, adding up what they had spent on dues and dance tickets. The total came to slightly under $100 a year.

As far as clothes go, the subdebutante needs at least two new evening gowns each season. During the first two years most mothers do their shopping at Miss Bergdorf's of Bergdorf Goodman or the Junior Departments of Bonwit Teller's and Saks Fifth Avenue. I would say that $65.00 is a pretty average price paid for a dress. The girls still want to look pretty much alike, and pastel pinks and blues predominate. Therefore, the sophisticated look is the thing, with strapless ball-gowns demanded. Shopping is done at the higher-priced departments at Bonwit's and Saks', at Henri Bendel, and at Bergdorf's. Some dresses may cost "as little as $100" (the quote comes from a socialite); others much more.

"But you can't calculate the cost in dollars and cents," the mother of a subdebutante lamented. "The real cost is in wear and tear on the nerves—and it goes on for so long!"

Nevertheless, most families are prepared to take it. They know that the child's debut and her whole social future hang in the balance. There is no substitute for long-range planning, at least for newcomers.

The right school, the dancing classes, the subdebutante affairs are prerequisite courses for debutantes. They must be passed before a girl can go on to the debut.

CHAPTER VIII

The Debut

"IT'S impossible to get any work done this week," a professor at Fairleigh Dickinson University complained to me one day last spring. "Everybody is worked up about the Fairleigh Dickinson Debutante Cotillion. Two of my students are debutantes and keep cutting classes to attend rehearsals. When I object, I am looked upon as a monster."

I discovered that any girl on campus can become a debutante, provided her grades are good enough. The student body of this New Jersey university is made up of children of families with moderate incomes. The existence of a debutante ball there is a clear indication of just how far the debut trend has gone.

Everybody wants to get into the debutante act. Even the American Institute of Architects has taken to sponsoring a ball, named, as might be expected, the Doric Debutante Cotillion. The oldest members of the Old Guard have capitulated, too. The august Society of Mayflower Descendants is no longer content to bring out its daughters privately or at the Junior Assemblies; it, too, presents the young ladies at its own annual dinner dance (though it insists that this is not a debutante ball).

Apparently there is no town too small to support such an activity nowadays. Even when given by a local country club with only a few hundred members, each cotillion is modeled after the fabulous balls of New York, Philadelphia, Charleston, and Baltimore.

To millions of Americans the debut stands as the ultimate in

social recognition. Today, presentation at one of the major debutante balls has come to be *the* criterion by which a girl becomes
known as a member of society. And this acceptance carries over
to her family as well.

The debut craze is of fairly recent vintage. It began after World
War II and gained momentum during the 1950's.

"Oh, ours is one of the old balls," a Rochester, New York, post-
debutante told me blithely.

But a quick survey reveals that the first Rochester Symphony
Ball for debutantes was given in 1952. The Denver Symphony Ball
was started in 1956, the Englewood, New Jersey, Cotillion in 1957
—and so it goes.

I made a spot check of major cities, towns, and suburbs throughout the United States to find out if any local debutante balls were
being held. In every single community I discovered at least one,
and sometimes two and three. (I have drawn up a list of cotillions
as a result of this study; it can be found on page 295.)

Contrary to popular opinion, though, the balls in themselves are
not debuts. A debut must be a private party. Parents of a girl
coming out at a mass ball usually give a small dinner party of their
own before the dance—and that counts technically as the debut.

The mass debutante balls fall into two categories. The first is made
up of balls given by the Old Guard for its members, and any girl
who attends is "in." The Philadelphia Assembly, the Junior Assemblies, and the Saint Cecilia Society Ball are the classic examples
for this category. The other type of mass ball, loosely called group
presentation, is a much more recent development. These affairs were
started to enable parents to avoid the fantastically high cost of
individual large debuts. Twenty, 50, or 100 girls come out at a
single party, and the parents share the expenses.

But nowadays status means more than economy. And a high-
society aura has a way of growing around the group presentation,
too.

"Of course I want a debut party of my own," a popular subdebutante said to me not long ago. "But I'll just die if I don't come
out at something big!"

Parents are less extravagant in their mode of expression, but many of them share this opinion. They know that they, too, gain in prestige by bringing out a daughter at a recognized debutante cotillion. And so they besiege the invitations committees of the mass balls. In fact, newcomers are prepared to contribute thousands of dollars to the charity being benefited by the ball in order to have their daughters presented "economically."

The group presentation balls gain social standing because members of high society—even rich ones—use them, too. The daughters of the inner-circle families, like most young girls, simply cannot get enough parties. They want to go to "everything." And their parents are quite willing to indulge them. Invitations committees welcome them with open arms, well aware of the advantage of having big names on the list.

A short time ago I read a newspaper biography of the daughter of an Old Guard family. The young woman was, of course, a member of the Junior Assemblies and was presented by her parents at Newport in one of the most lavish debut parties of the season. Nonetheless, she also came out at the Debutante Cotillion and Christmas Ball, the International Ball, and the Junior League Ball.

The country-club debutante cotillions for daughters of members are perhaps the only ones given for the sake of convenience and economy. And even at that, when the country club or suburb is exclusive, these have high standing and are attended by top-bracket local society.

All over the United States insiders and outsiders vie with one another to be accepted for presentation at the major balls.

"I'd hate to tell you what I did to get my daughter in," one newly-rich matron admitted to another, referring to one of the nation's most exclusive balls.

The other did not point out that she had already heard the story on the grapevine. Her friend had bought the girl's way in. She did not do this by slipping the members of the committee an unmarked envelope with huge bills inside. But her method was not much more subtle. A large sum of money was paid to the favorite philanthropy of a key member of the committee.

Sometimes the method used is a more obvious one. Social "middlemen" are approached by others of less impeccable social but

more impeccable financial standing. One man with connections on
the committee of an inner circle presentation ball was offered up to
$20,000 to get the daughter of a friend accepted. His version of this
incident, given to an intimate, is that he did get the girl in but
did not take the money.

In some communities only one ball is given, so all efforts are bent
on gaining acceptance to that one. In New York, Boston, Philadelphia, Los Angeles, and other big cities there are a number.
Newcomers try for the most important ones first. If they fail, they
just keep on moving down the list—from the Assembly or social-
club ball to the charity-sponsored benefits on down to the balls
given by individuals as business ventures. In some parts of the
country, particularly in the Midwest and Southwest, socialites also
must consider the civic festivals where the queen and her maids
have what would be debutante ranking elsewhere.

As society rules by conformity, I was not surprised to find the
same procedure governing ball invitations all over the country.
This is the way it works: The mother puts in an application several
years in advance. She also must get letters of recommendation.
These should come from friends of the committee members. If
mother and daughter are not known to the group, a personal interview is required.

Newcomers begin rounding up letters when the debut is still a
distant dream.

"Ask me when she's three (if you want me to recommend her for
the Assemblies)" is a pet society witticism. But it cannot be dis-
missed as a joke. Committee members can only be swayed by requests from really old friends.

New Yorkers think of the invitations committees as being made
up of dowagers. And this is true in such big cities as New York,
Boston, Philadelphia, San Francisco, Washington, and Chicago.
But particularly in the South, society is ruled by men. The St. Cecilia
Ball is managed by an all-male board; the New Orleans men's
krewes run the Mardi Gras balls; the Norfolk German Society
selects those who will come out in that city; and the Idlewild Club
presents Dallas' leading young women. But men are not more
lenient as far as debutantes are concerned. In Charleston, for

example, only daughters of members are considered for the St. Cecilia Ball. In Norfolk the men in the German Society believe they know personally anyone who might possibly expect to be presented. And so the system operates in just about the same way, whether men or women are in charge.

In New York there are a number of key balls. They run the gamut in terms of prestige. New York's debutante life serves as a model for such activities all over the country, so it will be considered in most detail. Regional differences are described in the chapters, "A Society Gazetteer."

At first glance it seems that it should be easy for a girl to be accepted for one of New York's many cotillions. But out of the city's teeming millions only about four hundred girls are presented at the major balls. Another four hundred come out at lesser affairs. The number of debutantes cannot be arrived at in IBM (International Business Machine) fashion by adding up the number of girls presented at each ball, because some debutantes come out at several. A girl can be presented at the Grosvenor, the Mistletoe, and be honored as a provisional member at the Junior League Ball in the same year. She can also attend the rest. I should say that about 150 of the season's debutantes go to almost all of the parties—a tribute to their tremendous stamina as well as their personal popularity.

The most sought-after and fought-over of the balls are the Junior Assemblies, started more than fifty years ago. Any girl who is asked to "become a member," as it is called, automatically enters the inner circle.

"If you want to know who really counts in New York society, watch for the list of the names of the families who give the dinner parties before the Assemblies," a knowing social secretary advises.

The Assemblies are not "coming-out" balls, its members proudly insist. Girls are simply invited to attend two big dances each year, one at Thanksgiving and the other at Christmas. They are not even required to wear the white gown that is the debutante uniform. But the Assemblies function as presentation balls nonetheless. A member of the Junior Assemblies is counted as a debutante, even if she does not make a private debut.

The cost of attending the Assemblies, by the way, is quite low, considering their importance. Only $135 covers attendance at both balls, which are held at New York's stately Hotel Plaza. And as these things go, they are modest and free of ceremony. At the first Assembly there is a receiving line, and the girls dance the first waltz with their fathers.

"We take one hundred girls each year, and most of them are known personally to the committee," Mrs. Lyman C. Bleecker, chairman of the invitations committee, told me. "Girls whose mothers or sisters are members obviously have a better chance. Applications are made only one year in advance, during the girl's last year in high school."

The Assemblies are almost barred to newcomers. But a few slim figures have slipped through that "almost" over the years, giving hope to others.

Assemblies members are horrified by the persistence of tales about outsiders gaining acceptance and do their best to avoid any new ones. A prominent woman on the committee privately tells that the niece of an Assemblies member was turned down when she arrived for the interview in a Rolls-Royce, wearing a mink stole, real pearls, and huge aquamarine rings.

"We were all offended," the committee member says. "After all, the Junior Assemblies have never been made by money."

As is true of most of the Old Guard society groups, it is hard to find a Jewish name among the Assemblies members.

Feeling about these balls runs unbelievably high—unbelievable to those who are not of the world of society. Every season I hear at least one anecdote about the matron who has made it her life's work to keep the daughter of a woman she disliked out of the Assemblies. Another perennial tale is about the newcomer who has spent years struggling to get her daughter accepted—and fails. She promptly insists that the girl (who luckily is always engaged) get married immediately. In this way she has a valid excuse for not appearing at the first Assembly the Friday before Thanksgiving.

Is all the fuss worth it?

"Somehow our members make every debutante list," Mrs. Bleecker commented to me in a matter-of-fact way.

That is only the beginning of what becoming a member of the

Assemblies does for a girl. It is a symbol for her and her family of complete acceptance by society. It will count in her favor in whatever she does socially in her lifetime, and it will outlive her. Children inherit the Assemblies' mark of approval.

The second-ranking debutante ball is the Grosvenor. I have always felt that its position is at least partly due to the small number of girls presented. Only ten, or possibly twelve, girls are accepted as Grosvenor debutantes by a committee headed in recent years by Mrs. Sigourney Romaine.

The small size of the group makes possible a preball dinner for all the debutantes, with twenty guests allowed each one. And this dinner counts as the real debut. Held the Saturday after Thanksgiving at the Hotel Plaza, the ball is run as a benefit for Grosvenor Neighborhood House. The committee tells me that the cost to the father of each debutante is $1,400, which includes the preball dinner. Guest tickets are an additional $25.00 apiece.

The Grosvenor is so highly regarded that just being invited to it as a guest means a good deal socially. About 150 debutantes are hand-picked by the committee to attend as guests. Nearly all of them are known personally to someone on the committee.

Inner-circle members engaging in a bit of top-level in-fighting value invitations to the Tuxedo Autumn Ball, held at the Tuxedo Club in Tuxedo Park.

One day I went to call on a society matron whom I knew to be rather stuffy. I was amazed to find her literally wild with excitement.

"My Evelyn has been invited to the Tuxedo Autumn Ball!" she practically shouted at me as I entered the house.

This ball has tremendous snob appeal among the knowing. It is the oldest of New York's mass debuts, and was started in 1886. Its prestige derives from the fact that Tuxedo Park was specifically built to provide homes for the Old Guard of the 1880's, and has always occupied a unique place as a high society suburb. The ball is attended almost exclusively by daughters of the original Tuxedo Park families and a very few of their friends. About fourteen girls come out in a typical year.

The weekend of the ball, house parties are held at nearly every home in the Park. Parents of debutantes give dinner parties before the dance as well.

The mother of a recent debutante has described to me the style of entertaining that is standard at these affairs: "Mine was a small party, held at the club for my daughter, five other girls and the essential minimum of twelve boys. The dinner itself—the food, that is—cost me $500. I also had to provide each guest with a drink book. Every time one of them ordered a drink, a ticket was torn out of his book and charged to my account. After the dinner the group went on to the ball. I naturally bought all seventeen guest tickets at $25.00 apiece."

These inner-circle balls are not for newcomers.

"But most of the other balls are possible," society press agent Marianne Strong reports.

One would never learn this from talking with members of the invitations committees for any of the big balls.

"Oh, I suppose someone new could break in. But I've never seen it done," the secretary of one of the largest cotillions said to me blandly.

With stoic self-control I did not tell her that I had made a careful check of the invitations list sent out by her very own committee, and it gave the lie to her words. A large number of the girls invited did not meet two thirds of the triple criterion she went on to mention of "birth, breeding, and good schools."

How did they get to the ball?

"Money and hard work," one woman admitted frankly. "A social secretary or press agent can help you—if you've really got an awful lot of money. But you can go it alone. I should know. I did it. You just have to know where you're going, and never lose sight of your goal. You must decide well in advance which ball you're going to aim at.

"That decision was really made for us," she continued. "When my daughter was fifteen, she was invited to attend the debut of an older friend from Brearley, who was being honored at one of the group presentations. This meant that we could be sure of at least one recommendation. So I concentrated on finding others who had contacts with that invitations committee. Then, as I knew the ball was a benefit, I worked for the charity involved."

It is often hard for the newcomer to society or the city to determine which ball might be suitable for her. The published material on these cotillions is a poor guide to their relative standing, and certainly gives no indication of the committee's attitude toward people without old-line connections. Speaking with socialites, ball chairmen, members of invitations committees, social secretaries, and press agents, I therefore made a point of investigating not only the prestige but also the invitations policy of each of New York's leading mass presentation parties.

The New York Junior League Ball has the highest ranking among the affairs that are not limited to daughters of the Old Guard. It was started in 1948, and is always held on the night before Thanksgiving at the Hotel Plaza. Members insist that this is not a debutante ball; it is simply a party for those forty-odd provisional members of the Junior League who happen to be eighteen years old. But when not on guard, even the most ardent League members do refer to this as their "debutante ball," and the girls are required to wear the white gown that is the symbol of the debutante.

In order to be honored at the ball, a girl must be accepted as a member of the Junior League. That means she must indicate an interest in community welfare. Volunteer work done after school or in the summer means a lot, a recent debutante has told me. A number of the girls work as helpers to nurses' aides or help at the Lighthouse and the Yorkville Youth Center.

"I don't want to imply that girls just do this so as to be presented at the ball," the Junior Leaguer said with a worried look. "But if you do happen to be interested in volunteer work, it counts an awful lot in your favor. And of all the girls I know, I can think of only two or three who were cold-blooded about it."

When New Yorkers talk about *"the* cotillion," chances are that what they have in mind is the Debutante Cotillion and Christmas Ball, given for the benefit of the New York Infirmary. Started in 1935, it has served as the prototype for dozens of balls throughout the country.

The charity connection is closer than at most other balls, as the

Infirmary itself runs the affair. Applications are sent in several years in advance. Each year 100 girls—occasionally it has gone up to 103— are accepted for presentation at the cotillion. An ushers committee of about 22 boys is formed. The ball committee chooses only the chairman. It is up to him to select all the other ushers. At the cotillion they help to introduce the debutantes. All five ballrooms of the Waldorf-Astoria are given over to the ball and four orchestras provide the music.

The cotillion's presentation ceremony is generally accepted as the classic example of how this is done: Each girl is gowned in white, without so much as a bow in another color. Long white gloves are required. The debutantes are announced, one at a time. Then each girl walks down four steps carpeted in red velvet and goes to sit in a small gold chair. Her escort, who is in full dress complete with white gloves, stands behind the chair. After all the girls have been presented, the dancing begins. A high point of the evening is reached when the debutantes perform the cotillion figures. They finish by forming a Christmas star on the dance floor and singing Christmas carols. Another tradition is the singing of the "Coming-Out Waltz," written by Virginia Scarlett, daughter of chairman Mrs. Eugene W. Ong.

> We're coming out tonight,
> We're having a fling!
> Debs dressed in yards of white,
> Waltzing we sing . . .

This fling costs each father $95.00, which includes a ticket for one escort. Of course no girl would dream of appearing with fewer than two or three. Guest tickets cost $25.00 apiece. In addition, parents of the debutantes take the boxes overlooking the ball-room, paying $275 for the first tier and $175 for the second. And pre-ball dinner parties are so standard that the Waldorf's large Sert Room is reserved for that purpose on the night of the cotillion.

Catholic debutantes have an extra ball of their own. They can make their bows to society at the Gotham Ball, held on Thanksgiving night at the Hotel Plaza. Many of the girls are former members of the subdebutante Gotham's social group. Nonetheless, I observe a scattering of comparatively new names on the list. Between thirty and thirty-five girls are presented each year to Francis Cardinal Spellman. His Eminence is chairman of the board of the New York Foundling Hospital, which receives the funds raised by the ball.

"His Eminence comes in with an honor guard at the beginning of the ball," Mrs. William J. O'Shea, ball chairman, says in describing the Cardinal's role. "The debutantes are presented to him. He stays a little while and then leaves before the dancing starts. In deference to his presence, modesty in dress is required. No strapless gowns are allowed."

One of the oldest of the group presentations is the Debutante Assembly and New Year's Ball which has been given annually since 1931 by Mrs. Thomas Webster Edgar.

A few months ago I ran into an old friend who had come out at that ball. With this book in mind I promptly asked her how she had gotten to be a debutante.

"I never went to the Holidays or the other big subdeb affairs; we didn't have the money for them," she confessed quite openly. "But as for my debut, Mother arranged that years in advance. I can't remember when I didn't know that I would come out at the Debutante Assembly and New Year's Ball."

"How did your mother arrange that?" I asked.

"Oh, she knew Mrs. Edgar through her church. They both belong to the Church of the Heavenly Rest," my friend said.

To be presented at this ball, she explained, a girl really should join the Assembly at the age of twelve. Each year she attends the teas given for her age group at the Junior League Clubhouse, the York Club, or in private homes. Sometimes picnics or wienie roasts are held. The mothers of the girls in the group (and some others, too, of course) apply for presentation at the ball. Thirty girls are accepted and notified in March of the year preceding the debut. There is no separate charge for the presentation. The yearly dues to the Assembly covers the cost.

"The ball is held at the Waldorf," my friend reported. "It starts with a reception at which the girls are presented by their mothers. I don't know of any other deb affair at which this is done. The fathers usually perform that role. After the presentation there's a dinner dance. Escorts must be approved by the committee."

Although this is one of the long-established balls, the committee is not so formidable as are those for, say, the Grosvenor or Junior League Balls.

A new cotillion obviously offers opportunities to rising socialites during the period while it is getting established. The newest of the mass coming-out parties is the Mistletoe Ball, given for the benefit of the Youth Consultation Service of the Episcopal Diocese of New York. It was first held in 1954, then discontinued for three years, and started again in 1958. About nineteen girls from New York City, Westchester, Long Island, Connecticut, and New Jersey are presented.

"The number of debutantes to be accepted each year has not yet been definitely set. The ball is still in the process of building," Mrs. Charles A. Dana, Jr., who has served as co-chairman of the ball, has informed me. "Our aim is to have each girl presented become an active member of the Youth Consultation Service."

At this time most of the eligible girls are suggested by members of the Service. The committee then writes to the mother, interviews both mother and daughter, and goes through the customary screening procedure. Despite the affiliation with the Episcopal Diocese, I learned that there is no religious qualification.

Prices, particularly for the newer balls, are likely to change at any time. For the first year or two, anyway, the family of a Mistletoe debutante made a donation of $500 to the agency. Tickets for the ball were bought for an additional $25.00 apiece.

The International Ball is another new group presentation. It differs from the others in being just what its name suggests—a cotillion for girls from the United States and abroad. The affair was the brainstorm of Beatrice Joyce, a former society press agent–social secretary.

"I started it because I got the idea that if girls of good families from all over the United States and from foreign countries as well could get together at a deb ball, it would contribute to better understanding between peoples," Miss Joyce gave me as her original reason for launching the affair. "These girls are going to be the mothers of men who will have great influence in the world of the future."

As foreign girls from noted families attend—the niece of West Germany's Chancellor Adenauer, the granddaughter of Archduke Franz Joseph, the daughter of the Infanta of Portugal, the children of ambassadors—the ball borrows their prestige and gets considerable publicity.

When it was started in 1954, the problem was that of getting enough debutantes, Miss Joyce admits. The first group was largely gathered through her personal contacts.

"But by now applicants are writing to me," she reports. "Some of my foreign debutantes write to recommend their friends and the American girls have suggestions, too."

The committee is still easier to approach than are those for the older balls.

More than fifty girls come out each year. The cost to each debutante is a $100 donation to the National Kidney Foundation, beneficiary of the ball, and a minimum of three tickets. These have been priced at $35.00, but Miss Joyce expects them to go higher in future years.

Mrs. Henry Duncan Wood, III, of the dancing classes and sub-debutante Masquerades, has recently inaugurated a debutante ball of her own. It is called the Greensleeves Ball, and the Old English ballad of that name is played as each debutante is announced. This affair is ostensibly for graduates of her classes, but other girls are presented, too.

The Greensleeves Ball gets considerable publicity, owing partly to Mrs. Wood's careful choosing of debutantes. Their photogenic and publicizable qualities are not overlooked. In 1958, for example, she brought out Natalie Trundy, one of the "glamour" debutantes of the year. Mrs. Wood invites those girls whom she would like to present. Others approach her, and agreement is eventually reached.

The cost of presentation is $600, which includes a champagne supper and a favor for each girl. Guest tickets are $15.00. A pre-ball dinner dance is also given for the debutantes at a cost of $20.00 apiece.

Although not strictly speaking a presentation ball, many debutantes of the season attend the Mayfair Assembly, a New Year's Eve subscription dance, run since 1941 by Clementine Miller. Girls do not apply for this one in the usual sense. The committee of patronesses simply invites one hundred girls to subscribe.

"Of course a woman can 'suggest' to a patroness that she would like her daughter to be considered," hinted a mother coyly.

Miss Miller selects a group to serve as the nucleus of the committee. These women ask their friends, usually choosing those with daughters, to join them. There are at least twenty-six patronesses. Most serve for four years, although I have known women with many daughters to remain longer than that.

"As it's New Year's Eve, each girl just brings her best beau, instead of the usual string of escorts," Miss Miller informed me. "After the dinner they wander. By that I mean that it's the custom for them to go to one another's houses."

No matter how many debutante balls exist, there always seems to be room for one more.

"Why shouldn't my little girl be a debutante?" is the view of many fathers who have risen from modest beginnings to tycoon rank.

As a result, there are more potential debutantes every season. All of them cannot possibly come out at the long-established balls— even if they could get by the eagle eyes of the committees. And so many women nowadays are starting cotillions of their own. Some of these are planned as a business venture; but just as many are intended as a solution to a pressing personal problem. Wherever there is a group of women with daughters, and without entree to the existing society balls in the region, sooner or later somebody begins to ask: "How do you start a debutante ball, anyway?"

As Mrs. Wood has recently organized a cotillion, I called on her in her pleasant apartment on East Seventy-seventh Street and asked how a ball can be started from scratch.

She shook back her bright blond hair and considered for a moment before answering. "The first thing you need to do is to form a committee. This is easier than it sounds. Every community has a group of mothers who would like to bring out their own daughters either that year or in the future. They are anxious to be connected with a debutante cotillion. Of course you will want to ask women who are fairly social. Members of a service league or of the Parent Teachers' Associations of the private or parochial schools are your best bets."

Each mother on the committee provides the names of suitable girls she knows. Contacts at any of the fashionable private schools can also suggest the names of students who might become debutantes. In order to give the ball a society aura, the lists of girls being presented at other cotillions in the area should also be considered. Many of these debutantes will attend a second, third, or even fourth ball.

"I always check over the invitations list of the Debutante Cotillion and Christmas Ball, the Junior League Ball, and Cholly Knickerbocker's debutante list," Mrs. Wood states.

The *Social Register* is another good source book for those looking for likely debutantes.

In suburbs and in smaller cities without *Social Register* editions or debutante lists the membership of social and country clubs can be consulted in the same way.

The person starting a new cotillion must send out a large number of invitations, as many of the girls approached will not accept.

"A good list of patronesses for the ball is needed to give it prestige," Mrs. Wood advises.

She finds hers among her own friends, the mothers of current, future, and—after the first ball—of past debutantes.

In a small town there is usually only one club or hotel suitable for the cotillion. But in a big city the place must be very carefully selected. Only a few hotels have high society reputations. In New York, these include the Pierre, Plaza, Sheraton-East, Waldorf-Astoria, St. Regis, Carlton House, and Astor. The ball must be held at a hotel of this caliber if it is to count at all. Society editors of newspapers are in the habit of reporting on social events held at the approved hotels. And then, of course, most of these have press agents or managers who promote the ball as a part of their job in publicizing the hotel.

Mrs. Wood holds the Greensleeves Ball at the Sheraton-East, one of society's favorites. Miss Joyce told me that after a year or two elsewhere, she moved the International Ball to the Hotel Astor, which was then being managed by Colonel Serge Obolensky. And he did wonders in building up the affair.

In most cases the hotel does its own catering, and in some, the florist, too, is prescribed. Where there is no restriction, any of the known caterers or florists can be used. In New York, Sherry's or Day-Dean's often handles the food and service, and such firms as Wadley & Smythe, Judith Garden, H. Carl Holpp, or Helen Cole provide flowers and decorations.

As for the dance band, it is a good idea to employ one of the few ranking society dance bands, such as New York's Meyer Davis, Lester Lanin, Emil Coleman, Ben Cutler, or Joe Carroll. This is one of the best ways of getting additional publicity, as most bands employ top-flight press agents.

"In a city like New York, the hotel, florist, and band have to be signed up a year in advance," Mrs. Wood counsels.

Although public-relations men for the hotel and band will help, they are really no substitute for a press agent of one's own. He can launch a debutante ball in much the same way that he can give social standing to an individual. A good press agent does not limit his work to the getting of publicity. He has solid contacts and can obtain a good date for the ball in one of the society hotels. Some can even help to round up patronesses and debutantes. Mrs. Wood uses the services of Emmett Davis, who also promotes the Junior League's Mardi Gras Ball.

The publicity buildup for the ball must be started well in advance. The Greensleeves Ball is held on December 30, and press reports begin to appear in the summer. Meetings of debutante committees are held, offering opportunities for newspaper photographs. And the individual debutantes are publicized as much as possible.

In communities where press agents are not used, the women running the ball usually get in touch with the society-page editors themselves. Most editors encourage local social activities and are quite ready to give newspaper space.

In a number of small towns and suburbs women starting a ball look for a charity tie-in. They interest a local hospital or philanthropic organization in having a cotillion held as a benefit. There are a number of advantages to doing this, a suburban friend explained to me. A benefit ball is more likely to attract socialites than just a ball. The inner circle supports local charities and looks kindly on fund-raising ventures. Members are usually willing to have daughters come out there (in addition to the Assemblies, of course). The presence of these girls in itself brings prestige to the new affair.

There is also the fact that tickets to a charity ball become tax deductible, an inducement to parents in the upper-income brackets.

"When a benefit is involved, it often becomes possible to run the party in a more lavish way," my friend added. "Florists, decorators, and dance bands are apt to charge less or even to donate their services.

"The charity itself is almost sure to have trained personnel who will take over some of the organization work. At the very least the organization can provide a good mailing list."

In most suburbs the prestige charity is the hospital. And I have observed that most of the newer and smaller benefit cotillions are given for local hospitals.

"The chairman of our ball committee called on the man who handles fund raising for the hospital," my informant told me. "It wasn't hard to get to see him. He realized that a benefit would be in his interest, too. He has to find ways to attract the support of wealthy and social people."

In connection with this I have seen the other side of the coin—the viewpoint of the potential beneficiary. In one small town I happened to meet the director of the local hospital. He was particularly concerned about the fact that somehow the hospital had no society support.

"What we need is a debutante ball," he told me. "I'm not just thinking of the money it would raise. I'm more interested in the prestige it would bring, which would be an aid in fund raising in the future. I've been suggesting a cotillion to several of the women in town, and sooner or later I'm sure that one of them will pick up the idea."

This is the era of the debutante cotillion. Women starting new ones have a better chance of success than ever before.

So many balls are springing up that it is not surprising that the whole idea seems funny to some. Yale, Harvard, and Princeton sophomores strike back at their debutante friends with the Guards Ball, which they attend as "dubutantes." The ball is run by a group of fifteen boys from each college, and is directed by Clementine Miller. The committee is selected by the boys who served the previous year. Members are chosen on the basis of family background and college standing.

"This doesn't mean academic standing!" a boy exclaimed, in fear that I might misunderstand. "It means that a man is popular on campus."

About five hundred debutantes from the New York area and the large eastern colleges are invited to the ball, which is a costume party. Eighty girls are specifically asked to be in the pageant, which is a high point of the evening. After a trumpet fanfare these young women are presented as debutantes. Then comes another fanfare, and out come the boy "dubutantes" for their presentation. They perform a military drill, for which they have been coached by Colonel William H. Warwick of the junior Knickerbocker Greys.

The satirical aspect extends to the refreshments. Chicken in the basket is served, along with beer poured into champagne glasses.

The Guards Ball is known to all the younger set as "a fun ball." They leave it refreshed to start out on another round of cotillions.

But though group presentation balls grow in number, they cannot do away with the private debut parties.

Many of the girls presented at the balls have debuts of their own, in addition to the small pre-ball dinners. Certain segments of the Old Guard view the private party as in better taste. And the girl who does not come out at a major dance can only become a debutante of the season if her parents bring her out.

With the aid of a good social secretary, even a newcomer can secure enough socially prominent guests to give her debut some standing. Each year there are a large number of debuts with guest lists of from five to seven hundred people and a price tag in five figures.

It has reached the point where even those who would like to be economical find it very hard to cut corners. Society's rule on how parties are to be given is rigid. If the home is not large enough to accommodate several hundred guests, the party must be held at one of the few acceptable debut hotels or such social clubs as New York's Colony, Cosmopolitan, or River. None of these is noted for Automat prices. The big-name florists and dance bands also are not for those on a strict budget.

"The only price variables are number of guests, decorations, and size of band," comments social secretary Katherine Palmer.

But even music must be performed in a way that makes it as high priced as possible.

"One band is expected to play continuously," Meyer Davis tells me. "There is no such thing as a band break. The theory behind this is that if the whole orchestra goes off, the party may break up. As all the men don't need to play all the music, they take turns going out for a rest. Sometimes a hostess suggests a half-hour intermission while supper is being served, but most want supper music.

"At a typical party the band is hired for a six-hour period, say from ten to four. But it is customary for the hostess to ask us to keep on playing until five. The cost of the music, of course, goes up with each additional hour."

The length of the party also adds to the price. If it goes on long enough, another meal—breakfast—must be served.

How much does the music cost? "It could be as little as $500 or as much as $15,000," states Mr. Davis. "At the average debutante party the band numbers between eight and fifteen men. For a twelve- to fifteen-piece band, the cost would be about $2,500. My organization has fifty bands—eighty in season—and the choice of the band leader affects the price considerably. If I go myself, or if one of my most popular conductors is requested, it obviously adds to the cost."

Not all the expense is for the party itself. Clothes may not make the debutante, but it is hard for a parent to put this idea across. To attend her own and other parties, a debutante feels that she needs a substantial wardrobe. I know of one girl who attended fourteen parties in her seventeen-day Christmas vacation, and some debutantes claim to have beaten that record.

"You don't need anywhere near the number of clothes people think you do," one recent debutante said to me earnestly. "I only got six new gowns my year. Of course I wore the same white coming-out dress at all three of the balls where I was presented. But everybody does that."

That practice does save money—when it works. I remember one mother who bought her daughter a $275 coming-out ball gown a season or two ago. The girl, who was to be presented at both the Grosvenor Ball and the Debutante Cotillion, wore it to the first and decided she did not like it. Her special escort had paid a great deal of attention to another debutante, and she blamed his indifference on her dress.

"I look fat in it," she maintained.

Faced with this abject misery, the mother did not have the heart to refuse to buy another gown. She made up some of the loss by giving the first one to a resale dress shop, which managed to dispose of it for $125.

It is quite the thing, by the way, for a debutante to wear her mother's "beat-up old ermine wrap."

The mother is usually the key figure in making debut arrangements, with fathers coming in to pay the bills. And the men often complain more about the waste than about the actual expenditures. One Manhattan father last year, who spent more than $10,000 for a debut, talked only of the $562 he was charged by the caterer for dinners intended for guests who did not show up. This is a major debut problem. Despite prep-school backgrounds, young socialites are given to accepting invitations and not bothering to attend or to notify the hosts that they will not.

Gate crashing is an unfortunate side effect of a big party, particularly one that has been widely publicized. Some teen-agers view breaking into a dance as a challenge to their ingenuity. There are many back entrances to hotel ballrooms through kitchens and pantries. Once discovered, the secret passes from friend to friend. Fathers with long memories inform their sons.

Miss Palmer tells me that she can often arrange with the police to have men stationed at the back doors of the big hotels. Pinkerton men are also placed at strategic spots. And she wanders around herself, eying the unfamiliar face suspiciously. Large parties in private homes in the suburbs are much harder to police. But the same effort is made.

In some parts of the country gate crashing is almost out of control. Last year it got so bad in Palm Springs, California, that the City Council was considering an ordinance making it a misdemeanor to attend a party uninvited.

Another problem for the host and hostess is what to do with out-of-town guests. There are usually many of these—family connections and boarding-school friends of the debutante. In the distant suburbs guests from the city need housing for the night, too. A certain number stay with the hosts, and friends usually take the overflow. In this set houses tend to be big enough to accommodate a goodly number.

When the guest list is too large to be handled in this simple manner, nearby hotels may be booked for the night. And I know of several occasions when parents have taken over the dormitories of boarding schools in the area. At one summer debut in Virginia not long ago girl guests spent the night in the Foxcroft dormitories, while the boys camped in temporary "barracks" set up on the fields.

Men are a hidden debut expense. Girls must invite the boys both to the mass debuts and the private parties. In addition, to have a successful party, a hostess must provide extra boys.

"I'm particularly careful to see to it that the out-of-town girls are taken care of. Otherwise, they can look pathetic and deaden the party," I was told by a mother in Buffalo who has brought out four daughters. "I invite a specific escort for each of them, putting his name on the girl's invitation."

For the balls, the girl's father usually buys the boys' tickets. And at the private parties the escorts are, of course, additional guests.

Surprisingly enough, top society encourages boys to be what another social group would describe as "free loaders."

"They're supposed to ask you for a date to pay back for a debut invitation," one debutante says meaningfully. "But the attractive ones get so spoiled that half of the time they don't bother."

"We have to pay our own traveling expenses to the out-of-town parties, and that adds up," one boy defends himself.

So do the girls. But, then, it is their golden year.

CHAPTER IX

Society's Big League

"WHY do I remain in the League? To help the daughters of my friends get in, of course."

Cynical, perhaps, but this private comment of a sustaining member of the Junior League underlines a basic fact about that prestige-laden organization. In today's social climate the League occupies a peculiar position. Its high standing makes it the natural prey of social climbers. And yet the Junior League has been able to use this seeming disadvantage to turn itself into one of the most worthwhile organizations of volunteers in the country today.

The League's standing has never been higher. I have actually seen a recent study by sociologist Myrna S. Minnis that reveals that the Junior League has the highest prestige of four hundred women's organizations in the United States and Canada. It is the center of society in many communities. Particularly in small towns and suburbs its members control top-level social life. League membership has become one of the few tangible signs of being accepted by society.

The truth of this appraisal struck me anew not long ago when I was talking with a woman who is generally conceded to be a major figure in society. With the promise of anonymity she confided in me that her background is anything but old line. Her father was an immigrant and owned a small store in Brooklyn. She started out in public school. As business improved, her father entered her in Packer Collegiate Institute, one of Brooklyn's more social private schools. It never occurred to her father that she might make a debut—nor did she do so. But after graduation many of her former classmates joined the Brooklyn Junior League, and on their recommendations she was accepted as a member. She became interested in a recreational program for children at Kings County Hospital and devoted a good deal of time to it.

When the League's annual ball for provisional members was given, she was asked to serve on the committee. Women who are active in the organization's projects are frequently given this opportunity. As a portion of the proceeds of the ball was to be contributed to her special interest, the Kings County Children's Program, she worked very hard. Her efforts were rewarded with a more important position on the committee the following year. In time she became chairman of the ball.

"I never really had the urge to break into society the way some people do," she insisted. "It somehow came my way. The girls I met at the League were members of the old families, and they invited me to their homes. They talked me into joining their pet charities, and I was eventually asked to serve on committees. My name began to appear regularly on the society pages.

"It still comes as a surprise to me that many people now view me as real society. And I know that it all stems from my position in the League."

Of course, it is undeniable that many people join the League in order to make the grade socially. Here, for instance, is the candid admission of one young mother I know:

"Let's face it. I really struggled to get into the League, so that I could be sure of bringing out my daughter at a cheap and easy debutante ball that wouldn't be viewed as second-rate."

As the daughter in question is only five years old, this confession may seem odd to those unfamiliar with the workings of society. But this soul-baring mother knows that launching a daughter successfully is a long-range program. And contacts made at the League can help a family through every step. League members can provide the needed recommendations for admission to private school, the top dancing classes, the junior athletic clubs. Among them are many who will in time become members of the invitations committees of the subdebutante affairs and the debutante balls. They will move into key roles with the leading charities and social clubs.

Even women who were not in the League themselves are likely to give preference to members. There is a feeling, shared by socialite and stenographer, that a Leaguer is in the inner circle. The main reason for this is that the League is one of the few society groups that everybody knows.

Although the Old Guard may not believe it, there are people today—even quite well-to-do and respectable people—who have never heard of the St. Cecilia Society or the Terpsichorean Club of Raleigh and who think that the Baltimore Cotillon is spelled with two "i's." But practically everyone has heard of the Junior League. For one thing, it is a nationwide group. For another, activities of the members bring them into contact with individuals on every economic level. And then there is something about the League that attracts publicity.

It has been fair game for cartoonists for years. "No, no, nurse, bring me the blue blood!" cries the doctor preparing to give a transfusion. "She's a Junior Leaguer."

And members' names appear in every section of the newspapers. Tarzan's latest mate is featured on the entertainment page—and it turns out that she is in the Junior League. Even the obituary of a notorious gangster plays up the fact that he was married to a former Leaguer.

"Everyone is interested in the League today. Why, when our Mardi Gras Ball was televised, hardly anyone in New York watched anything else," Mrs. Donald L. Wallace, chairman of the New York League's public-relations committee, informed me happily.

I am inclined to take statements by public-relations people with a grain of salt, so I called a contact at Columbia Broadcasting System to check. And sure enough, Arbitron (American Research Bureau) had given the League's showing a rating of 17.1, compared to 4.6 for normally top-ranking Jack Paar on another channel.

It is not surprising that membership in the organization has skyrocketed. From 1954 to 1960 membership rose from 63,000 women in 183 League chapters to 78,000 in 197. There are now 1,614 members in the New York League alone. The Boston League has 1,385 members and the San Francisco, 1,100.

Prestige and publicity are only a part of the story behind this growth in membership. The rise of the big corporation is another important factor. I was given this matter-of-fact explanation by the wife of one young executive:

"I had lots of friends in the League, but somehow I never joined it myself. I've lived in New York all my life, and I was perfectly able to get along without belonging to the League. But when Bob went to work for a big chemical company that has a policy of shifting its junior executives around, I changed my mind fast. I began to wonder how I'd get along in a strange city where I didn't know anybody. Since then, I've been hounding everyone I know in the League to recommend me for membership. Then, no matter where we'd go, I could transfer to the local chapter and get to know people of my type right away."

This view is confirmed by Mrs. Robert E. Dingman, who, as the professional finance consultant for the League, travels from one to the other: "Husbands of the girls often tell me that nothing was of more help to them in making a place in the community than their wives' membership in the League."

The same situation holds true in the suburbs. The growth of the suburbs has brought changes to the League. In some cities the membership has scattered to outlying districts to such an extent that units have been set up within the chapter. The Chicago League, for example, has fourteen units, the Los Angeles, eight.

Leaguers moving from city to suburb greet strangers who happen to be fellow members as if they were long-lost sisters. And the enthusiasm is usually returned and backed up with invitations to join local clubs, dancing classes, and charities. In a suburb where there is no Old Guard of long-established families, the League is the inner circle.

Members do not spend all their time solidifying their position in society. After all, the basic aim of the group is to help women to become constructive workers in their communities. Many of those in the organization are genuinely dedicated. Spokesmen for the League were eager to point out to me that 67,100 volunteer jobs are performed in a typical year, in cooperation with more than 14,000 community agencies.

"The leading debutantes often do not join the League; they are not willing to devote the time to it," an official stated flatly. "Why, a couple of years ago, when *Life* magazine ran an article on eleven young leaders of New York society, most of them were *not* members of the League."

But the debutante label has been pinned to the League since its beginnings in 1901. And despite all disclaimers, the organization perpetuates this reputation by its policy of reserving the right to choose who will be allowed to do good works. Exclusiveness is not a part of the spirit of true charity. But few League members see it that way. And those who are aware of the contradiction feel that the snob appeal does more good than harm by attracting people with money—social climbers though they may be—to participation in community service.

Even when the motives for joining the League are not of the purest, membership often produces surprisingly pure results. The national leadership is aware of the situation, and makes the most of it.

"Many girls do join the League to advance themselves socially," concedes a spokesman at national headquarters. "But then they find themselves interested in the work. And they are changed by this—for the better."

"The League has made it chic to do good," asserts another.

Whatever the motives, vast numbers of young women knock at League doors every day seeking admission.

Just how does a girl become a member? I went down to national headquarters in the Waldorf-Astoria Hotel in New York, and had the officials spell it out for me. This is what they say:

In the first place, the applicant must be young enough. The age limits are between eighteen and thirty-five, but it is best to be closer to eighteen. The League wants members to have many years of active work ahead of them. After thirty-five, women become sustaining members, paying dues, but doing no volunteer work. (I have noticed, however, that in suburban units or chapters the age level of new members tends to be higher than in the city. Many provisionals are well along into their twenties.)

The applicant must be proposed and seconded by women in the League. Really solid recommendations from members—preferably from those who are themselves well liked—count more heavily than anything else. I know several girls with no previous social background who became members of the League on the sponsorship of former classmates at Wellesley or of women in the same car pool in Montclair. The number of seconders required varies from one chapter to the next. In New York a girl must have a sponsor and letters from *five* members who are not relatives. A detailed application blank is filled out by the proposer and seconders. They comment on the girl's "compatibility, conduct, general standards, and interest."

In some Leagues provisional members can only be seconders for one friend. In a number of chapters each member in good standing can sponsor or write letters for five girls a year. Those unfamiliar with the League might expect a stampede to result. But that is not the case.

"As most members know the same people, it doesn't get out of hand," explains a spokesman for the New York League.

The next hurdle is the admissions tea. Each member of the admissions committee sits at a small table by herself. The applicant comes in with her sponsor and is introduced to the first Leaguer. From then on she is on her own. She goes from table to table, talking to each committee member in turn. Tea, cookies, and little sandwiches are served, but most girls are too nervous to eat. I was in the clubhouse one afternoon just before an admissions tea and noticed that only a dozen tiny sandwiches had been prepared for the entire group of applicants. If a girl does not make a good impression at the tea, she can be turned down. And this is not an idle threat. It has happened many times.

The final hurdle is a vote taken by secret ballot. An applicant must receive a "yes" vote from three quarters of the committee.

This sounds clear enough, but, as with all official explanations, it leaves out the intangibles. The fact is that there *is* a Junior League type. Even if she never made a debut, a girl should look, talk, and act like a debutante. A private-school background is absolutely essential. Most of the members come from families that have been in America for three, four, or more generations. If arrival on this continent is more recent than that, the heritage is far likelier to be British or French than Italian. And as in most such groups, Episcopalians, Presbyterians, and Congregationalists have the edge.

"The membership list of each chapter reflects the thinking of that community," League officials assured me, "and so some have more Jews and Catholics than do others."

But as I went through the lists of marriage and birth announcements sent by all the chapters to the League magazine, I could spot a mere sprinkling of Jewish names. And most of the ones I checked were either questionable (common Jewish names spelled in an unusual way) or were obviously mixed marriages. There was a similar shortage of Italian names.

The factors that make a girl the League type are all considered by the applications committee.

"After all," a committee member emphasized, "the League has always been intended to be a group of girls of like interests working together."

"Are you writing about similar organizations as well?" another committeewoman asked me in an aside.

"What organizations would you view as similar?" I probed.

"Oh, I don't know—the D.A.R., I guess," she replied.

Apparently the League type and the D.A.R. (Daughters of the American Revolution) type are sisters under the skin.

Once a girl is accepted, she becomes a provisional member and must pay annual dues ranging from $10.00 to $100. The highest figure is for the New York chapter. The nationwide average is $17.50.

What is it like to be a member? The first year is largely devoted to learning. A provisional training course is now required. Headquarters is taking no chance of having any current members echo Mrs. Franklin D. Roosevelt, who has been widely quoted on her Junior League experience: "At nineteen, untrained, I plunged into teaching calisthenics and dancing to little girls from the East Side. As I look back, the results were sometimes quite ludicrous."

Today a typical training program is made up of twelve sessions, given over a period of six to eight weeks. Some Leagues, though, give as few as six sessions or as many as sixty-six.

A League member from Chicago wrote to me to describe the course that she had just completed: "First the president of the chapter gave a report on League history, procedures, and activities. Then a lecturer came in from the Chicago Historical Society to brief us on our city's history. A number of civic officials discussed community problems with us. We covered such things as housing problems, the implications of the St. Lawrence Seaway, crime in Chicago—juvenile delinquency, criminal rehabilitation. Lectures were given on educational facilities, family-welfare agencies, Chicago's role in national politics and international relations. One of the most interesting sessions was a panel discussion on culture in Chicago. The chairman of the board of the Chicago Symphony Orchestra was in on that, and there were people from the opera and art institute as well. We took field trips to neighborhood centers, the Dunbar Vocational School and Cook City Hospital."

At the end of the training course an examination is given. Questions are carefully worked out. The League has not yet fully lived down the jokes resulting from a question that appeared some years ago: "What would you do if your maid suddenly told you that she was pregnant?" No knowledge of obstetrics is required today, but the test is not easy. Girls can flunk the exam, and I have known a few who have.

Those who pass begin a provisional year. Each young woman tries different types of activities—welfare, art, education—to find out which she likes best. At the end of the year she has a placement interview and requests a specific type of project. This procedure is repeated each successive year. College students sometimes postpone the start of volunteer work until graduation. This is permitted, but the girls are not counted as active members until they do begin.

"When you start doing volunteer work," a friend in the League discloses, "you discover a very strange fact: Lots of the people you help would not dream of accepting charity from anyone else. But they feel flattered by getting attention from debutantes."

"They have to go to the *Social Register* to find someone good enough to help me!" is the unspoken but prevalent view of many people aided.

"I teach a night course in English to foreigners," my friend reports. "But the course isn't designed for just any foreigners. It is planned for highly educated people. A lot of my students couldn't bring themselves to attend classes in the public schools, even though their lack of English keeps them in bottom jobs. But they can go to the Junior League, to 'their own kind.' "

These students include a Czech college professor who had been working as a dishwasher in the Automat, a Russian engineer who was doing manual labor, and a Polish surgeon.

The Leagues do a lot of work with the aged in the communities, forming Golden Age clubs, or indoor garden clubs. And many old people, although poor now, are also pleased at attention from well-born young ladies.

Snob appeal is one of the reasons for the success of the Leagues' most consistent big money maker, thrift shops. There are now ninety thrift shops in operation. Their net: more than half a million dollars a year. Most of these shops have two sections: the nearly-new department, made up of clothes in good condition discarded by Leaguers, and the thrift department, containing garments that have seen much wear.

In small towns the nearly-new departments attract much the same clientele as do the famous resale dress shops in New York City. In Tampa, for example, these clothes are kept in a "Florida Room," decorated with a potted palm—a far cry from the dingy room normally associated with charity shops. In an effort to remove all stigma of charity some of the thrift shops actually stock some novelty and gift items.

Other activities engaged in by League members cover every aspect of community life. A Leaguer in Des Moines writes that she is working with emotionally disturbed children at a day care center. One in Dallas reports that she is active in a project to recruit teachers for the public schools. A former classmate in Pelham finds jobs for teenagers as part of her work with the Youth Employment Service. The Los Angeles League does recordings for the blind. In New York a halfway house is maintained to help discharged patients from mental hospitals to readjust to the outside world. In Cincinnati Junior League members put on puppet shows in the public schools. The Atlanta and Mount Kisco Junior Leagues sponsor art exhibits for local artists. In Kingston the League keeps a loan closet to lend wheel chairs, hospital beds, or crutches. More than thirty chapters conduct homemaker services, sending a housekeeper to a family when the mother is ill.

The most unusual project I have heard of is one in which milk is collected from nursing mothers and made available for feeding premature babies. The Milk Bank results from the personal experience of an Evanston, Illinois, Leaguer. A few years ago this young woman gave birth to a premature baby. The infant's hold on life was very slight and the mother was told it might do better with breast milk. She located eight new mothers who were willing to give some of their milk to the frail infant. Every morning she toured the countryside, collecting the milk. Her round often covered thirty-five miles. When one mother weaned her offspring, she found another to serve as a replacement. By the time her own baby was pronounced healthy, she had used milk obtained from twenty-four mothers.

By then the story of her efforts to save her baby was all over town. Other mothers with premature infants began to turn to her for advice. And so she developed the idea of a Premature Babies' Milk Bank with volunteers making the collections. In time this activity was taken over by the League. In four years more than sixteen hundred quarts of milk were procured from nursing mothers.

Money to support these many varied projects is frequently obtained by means of benefit balls and performances of follies and cabarets. As these things go, fund raising is fairly easy.

"I always find tradespeople willing to put ads in the program as soon as they hear the words 'Junior League,'" reveals a member who lives in a Boston suburb. "These are the women they want as customers. They know the buying power of this group."

Even in blasé New York, where business concerns have become hardened to the onslaughts of socialites with that "charity" gleam in their eyes, twenty sponsors at $2,000 a head are rounded up each year in record time for the Mardi Gras Ball.

A woman who has worked on that ball offers these clues as to how it is done: "League members, as a rule, have good contacts. And they really get out there and plug. They see the ball as a golden opportunity to rise from the ranks and become prominent in the League. As is true of many women's organizations, there's a lot of in-fighting. Becoming a member is only the beginning of the struggle for prestige."

Positions on the key committees are eagerly sought. And the women anxious to advance themselves work hard—again proving the League's axiom that whatever the motive, membership produces good results.

I checked into how a woman gets to be named Queen of the Mardi Gras Ball, one of the most desired League honors. I learned that a recent Queen had served as chairman of the nominating committee, chairman of the administrative structure study committee, secretary and vice-chairman of the admissions committee and member of the Mardi Gras committee. She had also worked on the League's toy room, glee club, theater group, the *Observer* magazine, committee services, and committee members' workshop, and had served two terms on the Junior League board of managers. In addition, she worked with the Girls' Service League Committee, was engaged in fund raising for the Museum of Natural History, Seeing Eye, Multiple Sclerosis, Community Service Society, Chapin School, and Red Cross. Her three children occupied whatever time was left from charity and League projects. It seems almost too much for one woman to do. But that is what it takes to be Queen.

There is virtually no limit to the amount of volunteer work done by Junior League members. The social standing attached to membership is the sugar coating to the pill of hard work.

This prestige means so much that young women in communities that have no League chapters often band together to start a volunteer organization. They hope that in time this group will be accepted as a chapter by the Junior Leagues of America. In a typical year two such organizations make the grade and become a part of the nationwide League setup.

I was not far into the research on this book when I realized that members of community groups with such modest names as

"Junior Service League," "Service League," "Junior Welfare League," "Junior Aid," or "Junior Hospital League" all harbor the dream of one day changing the name to "Junior League."

I asked Mrs. Ann Knight Park, who heads the committee that passes on applying groups, just how that transformation is made.

"In the first place," she answered, "the group must be in a community large enough to offer opportunities for active volunteer work. This has been interpreted to mean a population of no less than 50,000. Then the organization itself must have at least 50 members, most of them well under thirty-five years of age. That is what it says in the rule book. In practice, however," she added, with a smile, "most groups accepted have about one hundred members."

A seven-year apprenticeship in community work must be served. It is only then that the president of the group can request an information questionnaire from Mrs. Park's committee at the Association of Junior Leagues of America, Inc., Waldorf-Astoria Hotel, New York 22, New York.

The questionnaire is filled out and returned. If it is approved, AJLA sends out a second more detailed form. After this comes back, the committee decides whether to send a representative to observe the applying group in action. Before this visit an initial fee of $400 is paid. A number of inspection tours are made before the committee calls for a vote. It takes between two and four years for an organization to pass all the membership requirements. During this period the applying group pays an additional $1,200 in three installments, plus $4.00 for each of its members in two installments.

What is the League committee looking for? A new chapter that is just like the old ones. And so any group seeking membership must carefully follow the existing model.

"The best way to do this is the obvious one," points out a member of a recently approved League. "Just follow the procedure set down in the *League Handbook of Information* to the last detail."

This handbook can be obtained from AJLA headquarters for $1.00 (price subject to change). It describes the administrative setup, membership requirements, financial policies, committees needed, procedures, and types of projects.

I checked over the League publications and selected the following as particularly helpful to groups now in the process of formation: *Basic Provisional Course Outline* tells how to organize the required training course; *Financial Finesse* is useful to treasurers; *Placement Pointers* gives advice on arranging volunteer work; *Piloting Projects* tells how to organize projects; *Catalog of Children's Theater Plays, Catalog of Puppet and Marionette Plays, Radio Script Catalog, Surveying the Arts, Shop Talk, Design for Education, Public Affairs*—these give specific project information. In addition, League headquarters will provide record forms to be used by the committee placing volunteers.

I also learned that many city, state, and national organizations are eager to be of help to volunteers trying to organize a program of community service. Information is available in such fields as mental health, cancer, heart disease, child welfare, hospitals, music, and art. Many organizations will furnish handbooks and other literature explaining how to set up child-guidance bureaus, mental-health clinics, or art councils.

Browsing through the open shelves of a public library leads one to any number of books telling how to put on puppet shows or children's theater productions—both favored League activities.

The type of projects engaged in and the group's standing in the community are carefully considered by the visiting League representatives. And then the whole is broken down into its component parts: the individual members are screened.

"We do guard the membership carefully," Mrs. Park confided. "The members must be similar in education, interests, and background to those in existing Leagues."

The community itself is then subjected to careful analysis. One note of warning: the admissions committee is likely to turn thumbs down on the company town where one big family controls the leading mill or other industry. The feeling is that too few women of League caliber live there.

"The church is really more suitable there as a base for charitable work than a League would be," a member of the committee contended.

Some highly industrialized communities are also not favored. In such towns, too, women with sufficient education to meet League standards and enough time to do volunteer work are marginal in number. The factory workers (or wives of factory workers) who make up the bulk of the population are not viewed as suitable League material. This leaves only the executive group, which is often too small for safety—in terms of League continuity.

The vitality of the community is yet another factor that is considered. Small towns are in a state of flux. And the admissions committee checks to see if the young people come back after college or move on to other communities.

As for the suburbs, they run up against the League policy that the applying group must be in an identifiable community. It must not be completely dependent upon the central city. Until recently this eliminated most suburbs. At best they had units of the city League. But suburban growth is causing a gradual change. Many communities have become independent of the nearby city. Industries have moved there, and social and business life are conducted locally. In addition, some commuter suburbs are so far out that women are quite unable to come into the city to do their volunteer work.

A member in Washington comments that the city clubhouse is no longer the focal point of League activities. "It is the area meetings in the suburbs that count."

The manager of a League thrift shop reports that she finally resorted to renting a room in a suburban shopping center where members could bring their discarded clothes. She found that they simply were not able to get into town regularly to go to the shop itself.

League headquarters is aware of this change, and suburban groups have a better chance than formerly.

Final acceptance depends upon a vote of the board of directors. The group can then change its name to "The Junior League." It is "in." From then on the new League pays the Association dues of $6.50 per member per year.

Those are the rules governing admission to the League. But I wondered if it happened that way in actual practice. A friend of mine is extremely active in a suburban service league that is now a "group in process"—awaiting approval by the Junior League. I was able to get from her a behind-the-scenes account of how it really works.

"The story of our League starts about eight years ago when a couple of members of the New York Junior League moved to this suburb. They bought homes on the block where I live, and that's how I got to know them. The League meant a lot to them and they kept on going into New York City to do their volunteer work."

It was not easy for them. The trip is long—it took me an hour and a half each way to visit my friend. And suburbanites are all struggling with the additional problem of insufficient household help and baby sitters.

"They kept on getting stuck," my friend recalled, adding dryly, "I know, because hardly a week passed without one or the other of them coming over to deposit her children with me for the day. The baby sitter just hadn't shown up. As I have four children of my own, there were days when having an additional three—or in the case of one of them, five—seemed a little too much.

"After a few months of this it dawned on both of them that it couldn't go on. They would have to let their League membership lapse. There were several other Leaguers in the community, all of whom were having the same trouble, and they used to get together and moan. And then one of them had the idea of forming a local service league, with the hope of someday turning it into a Junior League. Perhaps as a reward for my baby-sitting activities, I was invited to get in on the ground floor."

The original group consisted of fifteen women. They conducted a personal survey of the need and opportunities for volunteer work. They visited the local council of social agencies, the nearby hospitals, the home for the blind. They consulted doctors, ministers, teachers, school principals, and social workers. At the end of four months of this kind of research they concluded that there was a real place in their community for a league.

"The problem at that time was that there were so few of us that no amount of dues could possibly cover the cost of organizing and setting up a number of projects," my suburban friend told me. "And so we decided that we needed a money-making scheme. The girls who had been in the Junior League claimed that a thrift shop was sure fire. There wasn't one in town. And we certainly had plenty of old clothes."

They rented a small vacant store, dividing up the cost of the first month's rent between them. And they found that the League's experience worked for them, too. Sales from the very beginning were big enough to cover expenses. And in a short time the shop began to show a profit and provide some working capital.

"The thrift shop gave us something besides money that we needed badly—a back room to use as a meeting place," she added. "Until then we had been meeting in one another's homes, trying to ignore small children, dogs, delivery boys, and phone calls from Mother."

The original members began to enlarge the group by inviting their personal friends to join. New members, of course, mean only one thing to a would-be League—the setting up of a provisional training course. A six-week course was developed, based on those described in the *AJLA Handbook*. A nearby college made room available. Local lecturers were found, and field trips to hospitals and police courts arranged.

A number of volunteer projects were started. The first ideas were simple ones, as the new organization began feeling its way.

"We bought thirty reproductions of paintings from an art museum," she remembered, "and rotated them among the nine public schools in the vicinity to foster appreciation of art. A golden-age club was formed for the old people in the community. We took turns picking up the members in our own station wagons and taking them to the community center for an afternoon of bridge, arts and crafts, or just plain talk. Sometimes we chartered a bus and took the old people sight-seeing. We set up a toyshop project to make or obtain donations of toys to be sent to hospitals."

By this time applications began to pour in. Women living in luxury homes and in small development houses were as one in their desire to become League members. The group soon had to follow the standard policy of setting up an admissions committee. They ruled that each applicant must be proposed by one member, seconded by two others, and passed by the committee.

Within a surprisingly short period of time the Service League became not only the focal point for volunteer work, but for social life as well. Townspeople viewed members as belonging to the inner circle. Country clubs in the vicinity began to consider applicants who were Leaguers more favorably.

"Most of the women in the group had young children and were worried about the lack of a suitable dancing class," my friend reported. "And so it seemed only natural for the Service League to organize a class of the type we had known in the city. We didn't mean to limit it to children of members, but somehow it worked out that way. We began to talk about setting up subdebutante parties and perhaps in time even a debutante cotillion."

As the membership grew, the organization was able to branch out into more ambitious activities. The group arranged for children's concerts to be given by a symphony orchestra in a nearby city. A League newspaper was started. Classes in Braille were established, and some members began to type textbooks in Braille for blind and partly blind children. Books were collected, and members manned a library cart to go through hospital wards.

Expanded activities required more funds, so benefit fashion shows and follies were put on. The services of Jerome H. Cargill, who produces follies for many Leagues, were called upon.

As the group approached its seven-year landmark, it began to think seriously of ways to improve its chances of acceptance by the Junior League.

"We knew that the League sends observers to check on a service league's position in the community, so we felt we should do something big," my friend explained. "We needed to find something that would involve the whole town. The best idea to come up was a jazz festival, which everyone could attend and enjoy. A festival would give our community the kind of publicity that civic groups would appreciate. In addition, it could be a tremendous fund raiser for Service League projects."

Members made lists of musicians playing in nearby cities. They then set themselves the thoroughly pleasant task of going in to late night jazz spots to see the performers in person and to ask them to participate.

"We were surprised at how many of them agreed right away, even though we couldn't pay them very much."

All contacts were used—and service-league members (like Junior League members) tend to have good contacts. Husbands working in television, on newspapers, and in publicity and advertising were able to arrange for the appearance of many big names in jazz. Some musicians lived in the neighborhood. One bass fiddler was brought in by his baby sitter, the daughter of a member. A junior committee was formed to interest school children in the activity. They helped to sell tickets and put up posters.

Long before the festival took place everyone in the community was aware of it. In addition, major publicity breaks in the New York City newspapers proved surprisingly easy to get. I remember having seen some of these stories myself. The presence of celebrities at a charity affair in itself produces newspaper coverage. And many of the jazz musicians had press agents who were ready to lend a hand. As the Junior League headquarters is in New York, such publicity is extremely valuable to a group.

Last year the Service League passed the seven-year hurdle, and put in an application to AJLA. Since that time, the two detailed questionnaires have been filled out and approved. Representatives of the League have visited the community and observed the group in operation. So far the applying organization has passed each membership test. But more lie ahead before the group can join the 197 Junior Leagues now in existence.

"My husband sometimes laughs at me," my friend admitted. " 'What's in a name?' he keeps saying. 'You'll still be doing the same things with the same people.' He's right, of course—but still ...Don't ask me why it means so much to me—to all of us—but it does."

Note: I have made up a complete list of the Junior Leagues. It can be found on page 300 of the Directory.

CHAPTER X

A Society Gazetteer: Part One

ONE day last fall I went to Times Square and stopped at the newsstand that stocks newspapers from all over the country. I staggered off loaded down with armfuls of *Heralds, Records,* and *News.*

As I went through the society news later, I had the feeling that none of these papers took me very far away from home. There was Cholly Knickerbocker in San Francisco and Charles Ventura in Philadelphia. Dorothy Kilgallen and Walter Winchell, who include society news in their columns, were regulars in Chicago and Dallas just as in New York. The doings of New York socialites were reported from the Atlantic to the Pacific, down to who attended which party with whom, wearing what.

I also observed that those sections devoted to local social activities were remarkably similar. It all backed up my conviction that the pattern of high society life is basically the same all around the country.

And yet my own travels and conversations with men and women from many different cities show that there are some regional differences. At the very least each city has its own social functions and clubs. These come to the mind of the socialite whenever that city is mentioned. And so I feel that some attention must be given to these specific activities. The well-informed member of society in Kansas City, Cleveland, or Amarillo must be able to identify such social landmarks at the St. Cecilia Society, the *Green Book,* the Baltimore Cotillon, the Mystick Krewe of Comus, and Caldwell & Company.

I shall therefore take a literary swing around the country, hitting a few of the society high spots in each city. This chapter and the next will serve as a guidebook—the exigencies of space make it a brief one—to social life in twenty-two major cities. I shall start close to home with Philadelphia, Wilmington, and Boston. Then I shall gradually work my way south to Baltimore, Washington, Richmond, and Norfolk. Getting into the heart of the South, I shall stop at Raleigh, Charleston, New Orleans, and Atlanta. After this I shall head west to Cleveland, Detroit, Chicago, St. Louis, and Omaha, swing into Texas for San Antonio, Houston, Dallas, and Amarillo and wind up my society safari in California with Los Angeles and San Francisco.

In some cases I shall limit myself to a brief analysis of the social or civic-social event that is known at least by name to socialites all over the country. In others I shall give a thumbnail sketch of the high society life and the personnel of the inner circle. And I shall indicate the degree of opportunity open to men and women who do not have old-line antecedents.

When I talk with socialites from cities other than New York I often find myself mentally paraphrasing the old Gilbert and Sullivan song: "A newcomer's lot is not a happy one."

After talking with people from all over the country, I have come to the conclusion that of the major cities in the United States (in terms of an organized society life), Charleston, Philadelphia, and New Orleans have put up the most impregnable walls around their inner circles. Then come Boston and San Francisco. New York ranks next. It is slightly easier in Atlanta and Houston. Newcomers have a little more of a chance of breaking into society in Dallas and Los Angeles. Chicago offers many opportunities for outsiders, and Washington, D.C., is, as these things go, wide open. That does not mean it is easy. Breaking into society is at best difficult, and, at worst, almost impossible.

"I should not like to be a newcomer to Philadelphia," a member of one of that city's best-known families told me confidentially. "Some of my cousins aren't even aware of people who are not related to the Biddle-Drexel-Cadwalader type of family."

Her words were backed up by an expatriate from Rittenhouse

Square whom I met a few days later: "Philadelphians pride themselves on their exclusiveness. They like to think that they outdo Bostonians."

There is certainly no question about the fact that Philadelphia society vigorously resists the inroads of the newcomer. It is, after all, the city where an art show can be completely given over to portraits of ancestors of members of the National Society of Colonial Dames of America. It is one of the few remaining places where one can attend dinner parties and find the ladies retiring after the meal to leave the men to their brandy and cigars.

Inner-circle society is characterized by the subscription dances. Most who attend have inherited their memberships from grandparents or great-grandparents.

The top-ranking men's club is the Philadelphia Club, which is one of the most exclusive in the country. The Rittenhouse Club is second. For women, membership in the Acorn Club is a sign of prestige. The Merion Cricket Club in Haverford is the leading suburban club. The dancing class for society's children is held there. As Philadelphia socialites like to ride to the hounds, the Radnor Hunt Club also has an elite membership list.

Those belonging to the Old Guard are active in charities. And the Main Liners, the really well-established families, devote much of their time to the cultural fields of music and the arts.

It is, perhaps, because of the city's excessive gentility that society there breaks its bonds periodically. Philadelphia is the scene of some of the most lavish parties in the country. The staid old Bellevue-Stratford's ballroom is transformed into anything from a tropical forest to the Jockey Club at Hialeah. The price for this redecoration can be as much as $50,000. And that is only one half the total cost of the ball. Guest lists at private parties have been known to go as high as 2,500.

Some of the fabled balls described repeatedly by social historians took place in Philadelphia. It was there in 1906, at Mary Astor Paul's debut, that ten thousand exotic butterflies were brought from Brazil and stored in a cylinder suspended from the ceiling to be released at the high point of the ball. Unfortunately, the butterflies died and their release brought chaos instead of joy. This tale has such appeal that it will never die. Fifty-four years later I find it cropping up as a current anecdote in socialite conversation and in articles about debuts.

Philadelphia's debutante system works somewhat differently from New York's in that it is more carefully organized. There is an official debutante list, published every year by J. E. Caldwell & Company, a jewelry and stationery store. Mothers register their daughters with George W. Rehfuss, head of Caldwell's stationery department, when the girls are twelve or thirteen years old. Ostensibly this is so that he can keep the party dates from conflicting. But it also makes him a debutante screener. There are usually between 110 and 130 debutantes a year.

"Private debut dances are favored—and a good thing, too—as the big debutante balls are almost exclusively Old Guard," a woman new to the city commented in relief.

The private parties are not for the economy minded.

"Even a modest debut is likely to cost between $10,000 and $15,000," the newcomer added.

Many of these are handled by crack social secretaries, Mrs. Edward J. MacMullan and Mrs. Wirt L. Thompson. Meyer Davis is the favored bandleader. Decorations for most are handled by Liddon Pennock, a florist-decorator, described to me as "fairly young, tall, slender, and handsome" by a recent debutante.

In addition to the private parties, girls dream of coming out at one of Philadelphia's mass balls.

The Philadelphia Assembly is the oldest ball in the United States, and presentation there carries tremendous social prestige. It is not only that the Assembly has top ranking in Philadelphia, but also that Philadelphia society itself is highly regarded by inner-circle groups all over the country.

The "Dancing Assemblies," as they were first called, were started in 1748 by fifty-nine colonial families, who belonged to the elite of that period. And the debutantes today are supposed to be descendants of those families. Although that claim may be a slight exaggeration, the Assembly is virtually closed to newcomers. A recent debutante, for example, was the ninth generation of her father's family and the tenth of her mother's to be presented at the ball.

But there are reports about newcomers who have broken in. I met a former Philadelphian who pooh-poohed the fabled exclusiveness of the Assembly and told me he knew two sisters who were presented, although not one of their forebears had preceded them. These girls had spent their summers at a resort attended by a large number of ladies who were graduates of the Assembly. The sisters so charmed the older set that these ladies got them invitations when the time came. I repeated this story to another Philadelphian, who, it seems, also knew the sisters. This man added the salient fact that these "newcomers" were from a *Social Register* family. That in itself is a commentary on the character of Philadelphia society.

The June Ball is another of Philadelphia's top-ranking affairs and is a benefit for the Emergency Aid of Pennsylvania. This, too, is virtually closed to newcomers, partly because it is so small. About sixteen girls are presented each year.

The old families still have tremendous influence on Philadelphia society. These include the Biddles, who have been identified with the city since 1737, the Drexels, the Chews, Morrises, Cadwaladers, and Rushes. A statistically minded reporter who took the trouble to count names in the Philadelphia *Social Register* came up with the interesting nugget of information that sixty Morrises, descendants of a signer of the Declaration of Independence, are listed.

But even in Philadelphia there are chinks in the wall around the inner circle.

"If a newcomer is to advance socially, there is really only one way to do it in Philadelphia," confides a native. "It is through business success. Top executives can work their way into society. If a man is important enough, he can even wangle an invitation for his daughter to the Assembly."

Philadelphia and Wilmington society are closely related. Even the same edition of the *Social Register* serves both cities. The Du Ponts account for forty-six of the Wilmington listings in that volume. Wags frequently call that city "Du Pontland" for reasons too obvious to mention.

The debutantes in the two cities go to one another's coming-out parties. And it is hard to see who is getting the better of the deal, as Wilmington is the scene of some of America's most lavish private debut balls.

"They don't stint on anything," Meyer Davis told me happily. "At Newport I am usually asked to supply a band of between eighteen and twenty-five men. In Wilmington, it's thirty to thirty-five. In the 1930's and 1940's the parties were even more lavish than they are now. In those days a Du Pont ball could easily cost $100,000. I remember one ball in which the ballroom of the Du Pont Hotel was made into a facsimile of the family's winter home in Boca Grande, Florida. The decorations alone must have cost more than $35,000."

But even in these austere times, frugality is hardly the keynote at Wilmington debut parties. At one recent dance for a mere six hundred guests, movies were taken during the evening. Long before "Good-night, Ladies" was sounded the pictures were developed and were shown on one huge wall of the ballroom.

The lives of Boston's debutantes are stationer-regulated much in the same way as in Philadelphia. The stationer involved there is M. T. Bird & Company. This firm, too, publishes an annual list of debutantes. Mothers register daughters several years in advance. Many of the girls are graduates of Miss Marguerite Souther's dancing classes and are attending the subdebutante Eliot Halls.

They go on to one of the two major balls: the Debutante Assembly, held at the Statler Hotel on the night before Thanksgiving, and the Debutante Cotillion, held at the Sheraton-Plaza Hotel in June. The Cotillion is comparatively new, dating back to the mid-1940's. Fewer than one hundred girls are invited by a committee whose membership is kept more or less secret.

Private debuts at home are popular, but are modest compared to Philadelphia-Wilmington-New York standards.

"I spent $3,000 on my daughter's debut!" a father in the fashionable suburb of Dedham exclaimed in horror.

When one realizes that any New York social secretary would throw up her hands in despair if given a budget of less than $5,000, one can get an idea of how sincerely Bostonians dislike ostentation.

Although Boston society is conservative and slow to change, I observe with interest that there are quite a number of new names on the debutante list.

If Boston lived up to its reputation, the life of the newcomer would be simply impossible. Not only in America, but even in Europe, the city's name is synonymous with exclusiveness.

"Boston is still exclusive. But it's not the way it used to be," a society matron complains. "In my mother's day, it took generations for a family to be accepted. But now! Why, I understand that some of the debutantes at the Cotillion come from families no one ever heard of before."

These families must have worked very hard to achieve this end. The father had to be an extremely successful business executive, the mother active in charities, and the children students at the right schools. A son at Harvard is a distinct asset, as Boston debutantes look for male escorts every bit as avidly as do their more flamboyant sisters in other cities. In order to advance to the inner circle, the boy really should make Porcellian at Harvard. And this is quite possible nowadays, an old member lamented to me. In the golden days— twenty or so years ago—only sons and relatives of members were taken into the club. But boys with no family connections can make it now—provided they have good contacts, the right school background, charm, good looks, luck, etc.

Participation in the cultural life of the city brings social dividends. Boston society admires intellectuals. The women attend the Friday-afternoon concerts of the Boston Symphony, sitting in the same seats their grandmothers once used. Membership on the board of trustees of the Boston Athenaeum, a library, is highly regarded.

In another vein, it certainly helps if a family is expert at riding and hunting. Boston, strange as it seems, is often mentioned to me as one city where girls can ride their way into society. Many socialites belong to the Dedham County and Polo Club or the Millwood Hunt.

But breaking in is harder than it sounds, because the influence of the old-line families is still strong. A count of a recent *Social Register* produced forty-four Cabots, nine Lowells, and many representatives of the Saltonstall, Frothingham, Forbes, Adams, and Gardner families.

The key philanthropies, such as Massachusetts General Hospital and Vincent Memorial Hospital, are in the hands of the Old Guard.

"Newcomers trying the charity route must have the patience to work up slowly through the lesser philanthropies," advises a knowing but new member of society.

The top social club for men is the Somerset, and the leading women's club is the Chilton. But old-timers say ruefully that some newcomers are admitted to membership nowadays.

In Baltimore the inner circle prides itself on having one of the oldest and greatest debutante balls in the country: the Bachelors Cotillon. It is the only cotillion, by the way, to use the French spelling.

This ball is antedated only by the Philadelphia Assembly and the St. Cecilia Ball. The Cotillon was started in 1797 by a group of bachelor officers and gentlemen. They formed a club to give parties, so as to be able to return invitations. The first dances were held in the Indian Queen Hotel. The Bachelors moved twice during the next hundred years, first to the Assembly Hall and then to the Lehman. In the early years of the twentieth century the group moved once more to the Lyric Theatre on Mount Royal Place, and has stayed there ever since. The orchestra seats are replaced by a ballroom floor. Each debutante has one of the boxes and it is completely blanketed with flowers.

There were originally five balls, called germans, a year. And the german held on the first Monday in December was the one to which the season's top debutantes were invited. The second german was also for debutantes, but was somewhat less desirable.

"You're supposed to call the Cotillon the 'Bachelors German,'" a debutante told me severely.

The secretary of the ball is virtually a social arbiter for Baltimore's debutantes. Every girl who is presented comes escorted by four or more—it can be as many as ten—men, all of whom are members of the Cotillon. And it is customary for each of them to send her flowers to fill her box.

Pre-ball parties are customarily held at the Mount Vernon Club, the Elkridge Club, L'Hirondelle, or the Sheraton-Belvedere Hotel.

In nearby Washington, D.C., society breaks out of the standard mold in which it is confined in most of the rest of the country. The reason for this is politics—the be all and end all of life there.

"If you want to make your way into Washington society, the fastest and easiest way to do so is to get elected or appointed to some office," a Washington correspondent points out.

There is, of course, an old-established Washington society. Members are generally known as the "cave dwellers." They traditionally live in Georgetown. This set includes such families as the Mackalls, Greens, Devereux, Dulaneys, Dorseys, and Beales. These people do lead the life typical of old-line society elsewhere, but they have little influence on the social life of the city as a whole. Members entertain one another quietly. Their activities tend to be overshadowed by the doings of the politicians.

A political appointee, even in a relatively minor position, is in the best spot to rise socially. Cabinet officers are at the top of the hierarchy and are invited everywhere. Lower officials have to work for social recognition, but they have the opportunity if they are willing to use it.

Senators and representatives can also make their way. When a man is elected to Congress, he is automatically invited to the congressional party given each year by the Women's National Press Club. From then on, he will get invitations to as many affairs as he could possibly attend.

High-ranking Army, Navy, and Air Force personnel do well, too. And though diplomats must tread carefully, they are desirable as guests wherever they wish to go.

Members of the press, radio, and television are in a better social position than elsewhere, because most politicians are extremely eager to get much and good publicity.

Almost anyone in any of these groups can have his daughter presented at a debutante ball if he tries. The Debutante Cotillion and Thanksgiving Ball, started by social secretary Mary-Stuart Montague Price, is the most highly publicized of these. And I note the names of daughters of political figures on the list every year.

A newcomer can also become active in the many charities and benefits which are a standard feature of Washington social life. It has frequently been noted that the city's leading philanthropies are supported by leading politicians and diplomats, rather than by the old-line families. This is a unique situation. And it is a clear indication of the fact that no stigma is attached to brief residence in the city.

Although Washington does have an edition of the *Social Register,* one hears much more about the Social List, known as the *Green Book.* The reason for this, I firmly believe, is that everyone is in the *Green Book.* The front section lists all Washington officials. Those who know are well aware that such automatic listing is meaningless in terms of social standing, but it does make it possible for any politician to claim with accuracy that he is in the *Green Book.* What counts is getting listed in the Social List that appears in the back.

The *Green Book* was started in 1930 by Helen Ray Hagner, and her daughter Carolyn Hagner (Callie) Shaw runs it today. About four hundred people apply every year, but fewer than one hundred are accepted. There is supposed to be a five-member board to pass on applicants, but most Washingtonians maintain that the "board is just Callie."

She has considerable power in Washington, somewhat augmented by her eager acceptance of the role of social arbiter and adviser. Her services are offered without charge to subscribers of the *Green Book.* As she puts it: "Assistance in the seating of small luncheons and dinners in accordance with 'who outranks whom' will also be given."

This is particularly important in a city where parties have become a way of life. It is essential for politicians and diplomats to meet people, so they attend one affair after the other—often going to several cocktail parties on the same day. It is not correct for a man to admit that he enjoys partying. Not at all. He goes to exchange ideas with important people. Many inveterate martini drinkers carefully point out, before reaching for another, that the idea of the International Geophysical Year was developed at a party in suburban Bethesda.

In Washington it takes thirty-five society reporters to cover the doings of those who give and those who attend social affairs. I was shown an estimate made by a Washington caterer revealing that in a typical December, 300 cocktail parties and buffet suppers are given, 120 official or diplomatic dinners, 62 diplomatic receptions, and 150 teas, dinners, and debutante dances. Hostesses must carefully check the "Red Book" in the Women's Department of the Washington *Evening Star* before scheduling parties.

The highly publicized Battle of the Hostesses is no joke. In no other city is a woman better able to break into society by giving good parties than in Washington. In addition to charm, it takes a sizable income and/or expense account—$100,000 a year, according to the generally accepted estimate.

In view of the interest in the Washington hostesses, I have compiled a Who's Who of the current leaders:

I must start, of course, with Perle Mesta, who is by way of being a legend in her own time. After all, she provided the inspiration for the musical comedy, *Call Me Madam*. Mrs. Mesta is originally from the Middle West and has served as United States minister to Luxembourg. A widow, she lives with her sister, Mrs. George Tyson, in a house called Les Ormes, furnished with the results of ten years of collecting.

The one criticism I hear about her parties is that they are too big: "Anyone can come."

The most discussed hostess of today is Gwen Cafritz, wife of realtor Morris Cafritz. She likes to throw huge and elaborate parties, attended by as many high government officials and diplomats as possible. They are encouraged to make little speeches after dinner. Mrs. Cafritz gives a regular Easter Sunday party. All her doings get tremendous press coverage. Mrs. Cafritz has joined Perle Mesta in the back section of the *Green Book*.

Quieter parties, featuring chamber music or art lectures, are given by Mrs. Mildred Barnes Bliss. She is the wife of a former ambassador to Argentina. Her dinners are small and intimate. Invitations are delivered by hand. Similar parties are given by Mrs. Virginia Bacon. Unlike Mrs. Mesta or Mrs. Cafritz, Mrs. Bacon is a Republican, widow of a Long Island representative.

Another noted hostess is Mrs. Marjorie Merriweather Post Close Hutton Davies May, heiress to the Post cereal fortune. Mrs. May gives huge and lavish affairs. She has been known to hire the National Symphony for her parties.

Credit for the longest reign as a hostess belongs to Mrs. Alice Roosevelt Longworth, known as "Princess Alice." She is the daughter of Theodore Roosevelt and widow of Speaker of the House Nicholas Longworth. Well along in her seventies, she is still a leading social light.

Mrs. Ruth Buchanan, heiress to the Dow Chemical fortune and wife of the State Department's chief of protocol, is one of the newest additions to the hostess ranks. So is beautiful Mrs. Nicole Alphand, wife of the French ambassador.

In Washington there is no reason for newcomers to despair. After all, there is always somebody else who is newer. The changes brought about by every election make Washington society a somewhat temporary thing.

It is very different in nearby Richmond. Society is somewhat less organized than in a number of other cities. But being the South, it is quite exclusive, nonetheless.

Asking natives what are the criteria for belonging to society produces only a blank stare. "People just *know* who is in" is the answer I usually get.

Members of society are, of course, to be found in the hunt clubs. They also belong to a number of key dance groups. The youngest men, both bachelors and married, belong to the Richmond Cotillion; the next age group moves on to the Richmond Assembly, which is for married men up to about the age of forty-five. The middle-aged belong to the Richmond Hundred, and the group ranging in age from forty-five to about sixty are members of the Society of Virginia Creepers.

In Virginia most debutantes now set their sights on the bigger balls held in Washington, Baltimore, and New York, but some still come out at the local affairs.

In Richmond there are between twenty-five and thirty debutantes each year. The ranking presentation ball is the Christmas German of the Richmond German Society. This debutante affair dates back to the late nineteenth century. It is held at the Commonwealth Club on the Monday before Christmas, unless that Monday is Christmas

Eve. The second major affair is the newer June "Bal du Bois" Debutante Ball, sponsored by the Junior Board of the Sheltering Arms Hospital. The dance is held at the Country Club of Virginia.

In Norfolk the German Society, a men's club, selects the girls who will be presented. This is an old group, and its members feel that they know everyone who counts. Girls do not put in applications. Members claim that they "remember" when a local girl is approaching debutante age. There are many occasions, though, when their memory may need to be jogged by anxious mothers. Between seventeen and thirty girls are presented at the first of the Society's four yearly balls. It is held in November at the Hotel Monticello.

"The year I came out five of the debs were in some way related to me," says a recent debutante. "But there were two newcomers— girls from the service families stationed in Norfolk."

Such girls got in by having a friend intercede for them with a member of the Society.

In North Carolina the Terpsichorean Club Debutante Ball is quite different from the quiet germans held in most of the South. It is unlike any other ball in the country, for that matter. Although held in Raleigh, it is not limited to local debutantes. It is a state-wide ball.

Offhand it would seem that the committee would be quite unable to discover eligible girls. But in practice it works out quite simply.

As one southerner explained it to me: "There are just a few big cities in North Carolina. The state is mostly made up of small towns, each dominated by one family and one industry. That is usually either textile, tobacco, or furniture. And everyone in the state knows the family in control. The daughters are quite naturally invited to the Terps. The girls may also go to nearby deb balls in Charlotte, Greensboro, or Winston-Salem, but no one wants to miss the Terps Ball. It's a fun ball!"

The Terpsichorean Club of Raleigh, which gives the ball, is naturally most influential in Raleigh proper. Selection of debutantes is made by a secret committee of club members. Invitations go out late, only a few weeks before the ball. This contrasts with the New York practice of selecting debutantes months in advance.

It is much harder for young ladies to become debutantes in Charleston.

"My sister has lived in Charleston for fifteen years," a New York society matron told me, "but she's going to bring her daughters up to New York for their debuts. She still has good contacts with the invitations committees here. And she'll never be able to get the girls into anything that counts down there."

Charleston is the classic example of a city with a truly exclusive society. The South always has been, and still is, traditionally unwilling to accept newcomers.

"But no other city carries this attitude to the same lengths," my socialite friend insisted.

Her view is backed by the oft-repeated statement that visitors to the city had better enter the famous and beautiful old homes during March and April when they are opened to the public for the benefit of the Society for the Preservation of Old Dwellings. It is hard to get into them in any other way, in view of Charleston society's attitude toward outsiders.

Until a very few years ago the St. Cecilia Society rule over Charleston society was absolute. If a father or brother was not a member of St. Cecilia, the family was not viewed as top drawer. This left out in the cold many old, well-established families who would have been inner circle anywhere else. For newcomers, it was hopeless.

As for the St. Cecilia Society debutante ball, it is certainly the most exclusive ball in the South—some say in the entire country. For many years it was the only ball at which a Charleston girl could properly make her debut.

The society traces its history back to an amateur music group started in 1737, but it did not become a formal society until 1762. This makes it second in age only to the Philadelphia Assembly as the sponsor of society balls. In the early years, though, the main event of the St. Cecilia was a concert. It was not until 1819, when President James Monroe visited Charleston, that it was decided to have a ball follow the concert. This innovation quickly showed that music lovers do not stand a chance against party-goers. Two years later the concert was dropped altogether.

The ball has always been run by a male board and attended by the women in the families of members. This made it exclusive enough for any place but Charleston. A few years ago membership requirements were tightened. Membership could be passed only from father to son, with no exceptions. This had the side effect of substantially reducing the number of girls eligible to come out at the ball.

The outcry was such that in the late 1950's there was at long last a revolt. Old Guard families who were not quite Old Guard enough to make the St. Cecilia challenged the society's stranglehold on social life. The rebellion was successful, to a certain extent anyway.

A non-St. Cecilia debutante committee was set up, composed of a group of mothers and a paid secretary. It determines the number of debutantes who may come out in a given season, on what appears to be a purely arbitrary basis. On checking, I learned that twenty girls passed muster in a recent year. This committee also arranges party dates a year or two in advance.

And so today a group of girls can go the whole debutante whirl, except for St. Cecilia.

But many members of Charleston's inner circle still maintain: "If a girl doesn't come out at the St. Cecilia, she's not a debutante at all."

This is a diehard view. The new liberalism is gradually being felt throughout Charleston. But it is the most exclusive form of liberalism ever devised. It has not reached newcomers yet. A few of the older families are breaking into society, despite the lack of a St. Cecilia father. Others can hope for the future. Whenever the base is broadened, opportunities begin to appear.

In New Orleans the native view of newcomers is similarly uncompromising.

"New Orleans is almost impossible to crack," reports a friend from Pittsburgh who has spent ten years in the Louisiana city. "People with money may succeed in getting their children accepted, but they can seldom do it themselves."

Society is controlled by a number of men's social clubs unlike any others in the United States. They are called "krewes" and observe a rule of strict secrecy. Those who belong are not even supposed to reveal membership to their wives. Not being married to a krewe member, I cannot vouch for the practical aspect of this.

Oddly enough, the flamboyant, highly publicized Mardi Gras

tightens the hold the krewes have on social life. This frequently comes as a surprise to people from other sections of the country who feel that the Mardi Gras is designed for tourists and has no society connotations at all. The fact is that only a part of the Mardi Gras is for out-of-towners. New Orleans society is centered around the exclusive balls given at that time by the top-ranking krewes. The queens and their maids are the city's leading debutantes.

As I find that people from cities other than New Orleans have only the haziest idea of these influential groups, I have made up a directory of the most important ones:

The oldest and most exclusive is the Mistick Krewe of Comus, started in 1857. The captain of this krewe is one of the most powerful men in New Orleans society although his identity is a jealously guarded secret.

The other top-ranking krewes were started in the 1870's. They are the Knights of Momus, the Twelfth Night Revelers, Proteus, Oberon, and Atlanteans. The membership is so select that even *sons* of members have not always been able to get in.

In the early 1900's men excluded from the older krewes formed several of their own. By now, as might be expected, these have become pretty exclusive themselves. This group includes the Mystic, Mystery, Mithras, Nereus, and Olympians. A number of krewes have been organized even more recently. Notable among them is the Krewe of Apollo, started in 1929 for men under twenty-one years of age.

All of these clubs are strictly male. In the last few years, however, the women have formed krewes of their own. One of the best known is the Krewe of Adonis, started in 1948.

Returning to the men, I must name the Krewe of Rex, which is extremely influential, but occupies a somewhat different position from the others. Rex is to a certain extent a civic enterprise designed for tourists. It was started in 1872, the story goes, to receive the Grand Duke Alexis of Russia, who had followed a popular singer, Lydia Thompson, to New Orleans. Her best-known song was "If Ever I Cease to Love," and this is still Rex's official theme and is played repeatedly during the Mardi Gras. The king of Rex is king of the whole carnival.

There is also another newer tourist-inspired carnival demonstration, known as Hermes.

Many of New Orleans' leading citizens belong to two or more krewes. Out of a city population of 621,000, about 25,000 belong to the male krewes. At least that is the best guess I could get. No one knows for sure. Membership in each of the major krewes is estimated at between 300 and 400 men. Dues are extremely heavy. They must cover the cost of both the Mardi Gras ball and the spectacular parade given by many of these clubs. Some krewes employ designers the year around to prepare the lavish floats, beautiful costumes, and settings for the elaborate tableaux that precede the dancing at the balls.

About sixty balls are given during the six-week Mardi Gras season —all of them in the Municipal Auditorium. To make it possible for two balls to be given at a time, the auditorium is divided by a sound-proof partition. On the last night of the Mardi Gras Comus and Rex hold their balls. At midnight the partition is knocked down and the two kings and queens meet in the climax to the Mardi Gras.

Invitations to the balls are highly prized. As an example of this, I was told about a man who lost his invitation to the Comus Ball and offered a $1,000 reward to the finder. Not all bids are so valuable. There are two types: The first is an invitation to *watch* the dancing; the second specifically asks the guests to dance at the ball. Those who receive these are known as "call-outs." They belong to New Orleans top society. At the ball, floor committeemen summon the call-outs to the dance floor. The Rex Ball is the only one where this system is not used. Anyone may dance.

Rex does not follow krewe protocol in other ways, too. The king is the only man who is not masked. All others can be expelled or fined if they take off their heavy wax masks in public. I asked how they drink, and was told that they do so in a separate private room off the dance floor.

Lady call-outs at the balls are given favors. Each krewe member carries a sack with the gifts inside tied to his wrist. In theory, the woman does not know who is giving her a favor, but as I have heard romantic tales about girls who received engagement rings on this occasion, that seems somewhat unlikely. There are also innumerable anecdotes told every Mardi Gras about the wife who got the gift intended for the mistress and vice versa.

The queen and maids for each ball are selected from girls whose fathers are active in the sponsoring krewe. Outsiders obviously have no chance at all. If a man belongs to several krewes, he can get his daughter made queen or at least maid at more than one ball. The captain of a krewe has tremendous power in the selection of the queen. The choice is made in complete secrecy.

A debutante's rating depends directly upon the importance of the ball she attends. The queen of Comus is, therefore, the city's leading debutante. She even outranks the queen of Rex, who is queen of the entire carnival.

The queens of Comus and Rex are notified months in advance, as gowns are designed and made for them. And the debutantes must practice sitting and walking in these creations because the heavy mantle tends to pull them backward. A steel harness is usually worn under the dress to help support the weight. But though the queen and her family knows, the girl's name is kept secret (theoretically). It is traditional for the queen to give a supper after the ball. And the invitations go out far in advance, with R.S.V.P. to a post-office box.

The Twelfth Night Revelers started the custom of having queens. They give the first ball of the Mardi Gras. This krewe maintains the fiction that the queen and her maids are chosen "by chance." The girl who finds a gold bean in her piece of cake is queen; those who find silver beans are maids. But as the fathers are informed in advance, this is rather a put-up lottery. The queen of Momus, on the other hand, is only informed at the last minute. The reason behind this, I was told, is that a member of the krewe once refused to let his daughter accept her crown because he could not afford to give the traditional queen's supper. If a man does not know his daughter's rank ahead of time, he cannot be expected to have a lavish party. The junior-age Apollo krewe selects a queen and maids from among the city's subdebutantes. The Mystic krewe chooses a married woman. The female krewes pick kings instead of queens.

The supper parties that follow the balls usually last until morning. Then the debutantes and those of their elders who are still on their feet go down to the French market to drink coffee and eat crullers at the Café du Monde and the Morning Call, both famous coffee houses.

The inner circle's emphasis on the Mardi Gras is very hard on the city's 10,000 Jews. They are excluded from carnival functions on the pretext that Mardi Gras is a Christian religious ceremony in which they have no part. Although technically true, the carnival aspects of the Mardi Gras are social rather than religious. The situation is so awkward that many prominent Jews actually leave New Orleans during the carnival season, when society's krewes take over.

In addition to membership in the krewes, the older families belong to the Boston Club, which jealously guards its membership. Started in 1841 with 400 members, the club has expanded over the century to only 525. It takes an applicant seven years from the time of nomination to be elected, no matter how good his contacts are.

The older fortunes in New Orleans were earned in sugar, cotton, and cypress wood. Now it is oil. In connection with this, I was amused to learn what happened to the family of a Mardi Gras queen of a few years ago. The original fortune was based on cypress wood. After several generations of vigorous exploitation, the last of the cypress trees was cut down. Shortly thereafter oil was struck on the same property.

As far as oil goes, though, it usually is not a case of "them as has gits." Newcomers "git" it, too. The old-line families do not quite approve, but they are fighting a losing battle. I understand that more than two thirds of the shareholders in a new club being built across Lake Pontchartrain are members of the oil industry. The oil influence is so strong that many Texans are involved in New Orleans society. Fully half of the members of the Petroleum Club of New Orleans are Texans.

Although the idea of money is anathema in most of the South, Atlanta has grown so rapidly over the last few years that society there is not quite so formal as in many other southern cities.

"Society is made up of clubs," explains a native, "but there are so many of them that almost everyone can find one. Social standing is based on which club you belong to."

The top men's club is the Piedmont Driving Club, started in 1887. This club gives dances every Saturday night, and presents the city's ranking debutantes at its Halloween Ball. The membership is restricted to 800, which is barely a fraction of the number of men who want to get in. By now membership is inherited for the most part.

In 1955 a group of the younger men got discouraged waiting for members to die and let them into the Piedmont Club. So they formed one of their own, the Cherokee Town and Country Club. They started out with 900 members, each of whom gladly paid an initiation fee of $600. Within four years the fee was raised to $840 without discouraging anyone. By the end of its first year this club had a waiting list, too. Now I understand that Cherokee is viewed as the ranking social club for the younger set in Atlanta, Piedmont for the older.

Although the most influential, these are not the oldest of Atlanta's clubs. The Capital City Club and the Nine O'Clocks antedate them. The latter is a bachelor's club with no fixed headquarters. Its Thanksgiving and New Year's balls are top-drawer affairs.

The Presbyterians, Episcopalians, and Catholics find it easiest to gain club membership, despite the fact (or, perhaps, because of it) that Baptists and Methodists are much more numerous in the city. The Jews, of whom there are more than 11,000, have their own clubs.

Opera Week in the spring is usually the high point of Atlanta's social season. The opera is brought in by the Atlanta Music Festival Association. A leading light in this group is C. Howard Candler, son of the founder of Coca-Cola. And natives tell me that no account of Atlanta is complete without a mention of Coca-Cola and the Candlers. Since 1886 the soft-drink firm has been an integral part of the city's business life; the family, of its society life.

CHAPTER XI

A Society Gazetteer: Part Two

"WHY is it that everybody talks about society in New York or Philadelphia or Boston or San Francisco? Studies of society always leave us out. Do they think that all we do is farm?" a Clevelander asked me indignantly.

I assured her that I would not overlook her native city, where an exclusive inner-circle group does exist. The lives of the younger high society set in Cleveland are ruled by the National Recreation League. Parents are eligible for the League when their oldest child is twelve or thirteen. They must be proposed, seconded, and passed by a super-secret committee.

It is extremely difficult for newcomers to break in. I personally know of only one who succeeded—though, of course, there must be others. In that particular case the father had an extremely important newspaper job, and the family's acceptance was based on that.

Background is the key to acceptance by the League. Most members are Episcopalian or Presbyterian. A debutante friend told me that there were four or five Catholics in her group and no Jews.

Both girls and boys are taken into the League. The sexes are about evenly divided, although a few extra boys are admitted. After two years additional youngsters may be accepted, as some of the original members drop out.

There are three divisions, each made up of children in two school classes, starting with eighth and ninth graders. A dinner dance is given at Christmas for each age group. A committee of girls works out the seating arrangement. The system is that the boy placed on the girl's right at dinner is her escort. The first dance is with him. The subdebutantes are in this way freed of the necessity of finding escorts. By the time the youngsters are halfway through high school, the dating system takes over anyway.

Parents pay dues as long as the child is eligible for League parties.

The year after the senior year in high school the party is the Assembly Ball and is the recognized debut. This means that League members automatically become Assembly debutantes.

Boys are invited to the Assembly, too. The girls are technically called "hostesses," not debutantes, and the boys are known as "hosts." Only the girls, however, are on the receiving line. In a typical year there are thirty-six girls and forty-five boys. Post-debutantes can keep going to the ball without paying for their tickets until they get married.

Expenses for the Assembly are divided among the parents of the "hosts" and "hostesses." The League's president is always co-chairman of the ball.

"They soft-pedal the idea of debutantes in Cleveland," says a young woman who came out recently. "They don't even use the word very much. A few years ago a big magazine planned to run a group of photographs of leading debutantes from major cities and its editors contacted the Recreation League. The members were simply horrified and no Cleveland girl's picture ever did appear. Most of the girls I knew had private cocktail parties. Only two had big balls of the type they have in Chicago."

Most members of Cleveland's inner circle have moved to the suburbs from the Bratenahl section on the lake front, although there are still some big estates there. Many society people belong to the men's social Union and Tavern clubs or the women's Intown Club in the city. In the suburbs they join the Kirtland, Chagrin Valley Hunt, Shaker Heights, Pepper Pike Golf, Oakwood, and Westwood Country clubs. Members of Oakwood are required to make annual contributions to charity.

The suburbs are centers of Detroit's society life. Grosse Pointe, Grosse Ile, and Bloomfield Hills rank among the richest and most

fashionable communities in the country. Fabulous estates line Grosse
Pointe's Lake Shore Drive on the banks of Lake St. Clair.

Most of the debuts in the Detroit area are private—and lavish.
A friend in Grosse Pointe estimates that there are sixteen local
debutantes in a typical season.

But high society is new rather than Old Guard.

"How can it fail to be?" a rising socialite pointed out in a matter-
of-fact way. "After all, a man's position in Detroit society is a direct
reflection of his position in the automobile industry. It can be helped
along by support of the arts and charity, but somewhere in the background there's a car."

Chicago socialites view Chicago society in much the same way
that Texans view Texas: It is the center of the country, that is all.
To hear them tell it, Chicago society is older than Philadelphia's,
more exclusive than Charleston's, more glamorous than New
York's. No socialites anywhere can compare with Mrs. Chauncey
McCormick or Mrs. Howard Linn (the former Lucy McCormick
Blair). No social affair anywhere is as exclusive as the Casino's
December Ball.

They are so convincing that a women's mass-circulation magazine,
in a recent study of society, accepted as gospel a Chicago social
secretary's statement that a wealthy family who had been in Chicago
for two generations simply could not make their daughter a leading
debutante because they had "put down no roots."

The fact is that no one's roots go down very far. Chicago society
only dates back to the second half of the nineteenth century—
completely *nouveau* in Philadelphia, Boston, Charleston, or New
York terms.

A former reporter for the Chicago *Daily News* told me flatly:
"Chicago society is a haven for newcomers."

The inner circle is best reached by an approach via charity. Hard
work on committees of the leading philanthropies, such as the Passavant or St. Luke's hospitals, is absolutely essential.

Those who are "in" society belong to the Casino, a city social club.
This is for couples and is not to be confused with the men's social
club, the Chicago Club, which is also top drawer. Membership in
the Casino is limited to 400 and is highly prized.

Chicagoans like to tell a possibly apocryphal anecdote about the man who offered to have the Chicago Art Institute air-conditioned if he were accepted as a member of the Casino. This did him no good, they assert righteously.

And yet, I note that Athlyn Deshais Faulkner, famed society editor of the *Daily News,* has reported several times that all ambitious newcomers hope to make the Casino's December Ball, and that some of them succeed.

Although a few outsiders do make it, the December Ball remains one of the most exclusive affairs in the country. Invitations go out to 450 chosen by a secret committee.

"Getting an invitation means much more than breaking into the *Social Register,*" a member of the inner circle commented. "There are more than 3,000 people in Chicago's *Register.* Only the top 450 of them are invited to the December Ball."

Another top social group is the Bachelors and Benedicts, limited to men under forty-five years of age. Its Thanksgiving Ball is a highlight of the season. Invitations are hard to come by. Yet I hear a persistent rumor that it is getting easier to become a member.

Shoreacres and Onwentsia are country clubs with heavy Old Guard membership lists. The Racquet Club is also very fashionable. The Saddle and Cycle Club near the Edgewater Beach Hotel is a hangout for lively socialites.

The hunt is the thing for a large segment of Chicago's inner circle. Most of the big names in society's younger set (younger to society would be middle-aged in lower economic levels) are at home in the saddle. A number of them spend a part of the year in Virginia's famous fox-hunting country.

As far as the real younger set goes, its sights are set on the Passavant Debutante Cotillion and Christmas Ball, sponsored by the Women's Board of the Passavant Hospital. Only thirty girls are accepted as debutantes. Mothers send in applications when their daughters are fourteen or fifteen years old. Cost to the father is $500, which does not include tickets for the family, escorts, or guests.

Emotions run high over the Passavant Cotillion. An expatriate from Chicago told me about the time a major newspaper decided to publish the list of Passavant debutantes *before* the committee made its public announcement. The girls had already been notified, so it was just a matter of calling all the likely debutantes and finding out which ones had the coveted invitations. The newspaper published an accurate list—with one exception. The Passavant committee called to say that it had never even heard of one of the young women named. It turned out that this girl's mother had got wind of the newspaper list and had managed to convince a reporter that her daughter was to be presented. She thought in this way to force an invitation out of the committee. Members did not yield to her pressure.

But Chicago recognizes many girls as debutantes who do not bow at the Passavant. One friend estimates for me that out of eighty debutantes one season, only thirty-five were from the old families.

Private debut parties are numerous and lavish. A supper dance in Chicago can easily cost between $20,000 and $30,000. Every year I hear of at least one family who imported a big band from the East for about $7,000, spent another $7,000 on liquor, $3,000 on food, and $2,700 for the marquee. Decorations add any figure the family cares to spend.

When it comes to private debut balls, it is hard to find any that outdo those given in St. Louis.

"They are absolutely tops in terms of lavishness," I have been told by John Jackson, publisher of the *Debutante Register,* an annual listing of the nation's debutantes.

For one party, to give an example, the host's entire thirty-four-room house was redecorated. Four orchestras were brought in to provide the music. Guests amused themselves by having a snowball fight with plastic snowballs. Beer—of course it is beer in St. Louis—gushed from dispensers whenever a guest placed a glass under the spigot. (A photo-electric cell was the secret.) Forty-five waiters and bartenders served roast pig, turkey, champagne, and the like.

The biggest event for debutantes is the famed Veiled Prophet Ball. The queen of the ball is the number-one debutante in the city, and the four leading debutantes are her special maids of honor. About fifty other girls are attendants. They are presented to the Veiled Prophet of Khorasson, who crowns the queen. Her reign lasts a year, and she is not supposed to get married or even announce her engagement during this time. Only one impatient girl ever broke that standing rule.

Both the queen and the prophet are chosen by a secret committee of St. Louis businessmen. And so it is not surprising that socialites at times accuse them of commercialism.

One debutante of a few seasons back told me heatedly: "I was supposed to be queen, but the girl chosen had more money, so I only got to be a maid."

That may, of course, be simply sour grapes, but this sort of accusation is common in civic events which develop society overtones over the years.

The ball was the inspiration of a man named Alonzo Slaybach, who in 1878 thought that St. Louis should borrow some of New Orleans' Mardi Gras spirit to enliven the Agricultural and Mechanical Exposition. A group of enterprising businessmen fell in with his plan. The theme they evolved is that each year a mystic veiled prophet should rise from the bottom of the Mississippi, visit St. Louis, crown a queen of love and beauty, and then return to his cave. The true identity of the prophet should never be revealed.

The ball is held in the huge Kiel Auditorium, which can accommodate ten thousand spectators. The night after the affair there is a huge parade. The queen rides on a float, together with her four special maids of honor.

Omaha's Ak-Sar-Ben coronation is another of the big civic celebrations, which has become a major social event. As those whose minds have been trained by advertising have already guessed, ak-sar-ben is simply "nebraska" spelled backward. And it is the name of the civic organization devoted to public service that puts on the ball.

Each year the daughter of a socially prominent family is chosen as queen, and a leading citizen is made king. The identities of both are supposed to be kept secret until the actual coronation night.

Moving on to Texas, I find it a state where initiative is admired, and the moneyed newcomer can make his way. Whatever difficulties exist result from the efforts of Texans to lose the reputation of being "crude" socially. As one might expect, society is just perverse enough to rank oil money below money earned in other ways. But as time passes even the Old Guard is breaking down under the onslaught of millions of dollars. The problem is that of saving face. The claim is made repeatedly that the late Hugh Roy Cullen did not gain acceptance in Houston society because of his $1,000,000-a-week income from oil. Not at all. It was because of his many philanthropies. The fact that one was completely dependent upon the other is simply overlooked.

All parts of Texas are not alike.

"You can't lump us together with Dallas or Houston," insists a resident of San Antonio.

Society in San Antonio is older. Some families can trace their lineage to the Canary Islanders who got land grants from the King of Spain in 1730. The next major wave of immigration was that of the Germans in the mid-nineteenth century. Big names in San Antonio are Clegg, Groos, Kampmann, and Tobin.

I asked about the clubs in San Antonio, which have the reputation of being extremely exclusive. The German Club selects the city's debutantes. Then there is the Argyle Club, the Order of the Alamo, and the San Antonio Country Club. Texans maintain that money will not buy into the Country Club. The Order of the Alamo gives the highly social Battle of the Flowers.

This begins with the traditional March of Silence to the Alamo where the names of the dead heroes are called. And wreaths are put down in their honor. The queen of the festival is the daughter of one of the city's most prominent families. Her garden party held on the lawn of the San Antonio Garden Club is a major event for local socialites. Former queens attend a Battle of Flowers luncheon.

This festival is the top-society affair, although much more is heard about the big Fiesta of San Jacinto, which is commercially sponsored.

San Antonio's inner circle struggles manfully against the inroads of newcomers with fortunes made in oil. The Old Guard refers to itself as the "400" and describes others as the "398-ers." Only the military can break into San Antonio society easily. The ranking officers of the many posts around the city are welcomed.

There is also a large Mexican-American group. The San Antonio Sociedad Patronata (Society of Patrons) actually forbids the use of English at its meetings.

Both Houston and Dallas have an Old Guard of families who were wealthy before the flood of oil poured over Texas. Timber and cattle are the basis of most of these fortunes. Next in the social scale come the so-called "old oil" families, who made money in oil before 1930. And last come the "new oil" people.

"Even in the 1940's I used to feel that anyone who invited the oil people to a party was *nouveau*," an old-line Houston socialite told me. "But by now I've had some of them to my home myself."

Houston is a mixture of the old and the new. Business success is the likeliest way to gain social acceptance. Top executives are taken in everywhere, except—in the inner circle, which remains as hard to crack as any. Although efforts made in 1950 to start a Houston edition of the *Social Register* fell through for lack of support, there is a *Social Directory* with about two thousand names listed. Well-known Houston families include the Abercrombies, Blaffers, Cullens, Hobbys, Mastersons, and Saffords.

Ima Hogg is always mentioned when Houston society is discussed. One reason for this is obvious: her name. It is stoutly maintained that she was not called "Ima" as a cruel joke, but because it was the name of the heroine of her father's favorite romantic poem, "The Fate of Marvin." Miss Hogg is noted for her patronage of the arts. She has been a moving spirit behind the Houston Symphony Orchestra, and has donated her art collection to the Houston Museum.

When it comes to debutantes, socialites insist that Houston is going counter to the national trend. They claim that the number of girls being presented declines every year.

"At one time there were fifty debs in a season," a society matron said to me. "Now there are only about a dozen."

Social arbiter for Houston debutantes is the Allegro Club. This club was started thirty years ago as the "Twenty Dollar Club." And that was the amount of the dues. Inflation, however, made that name embarrassing. By now the dues are $72.00. The ranking debutantes of the season are selected by a secret committee.

In addition to holding a presentation ball, the Allegro Club helps to keep Houston social life running smoothly. A committee has the date book, and socialites register their parties a year in advance.

Some of Houston's other clubs are extremely exclusive. The Eagle

Lake Club is one of that small group of men's social clubs in the United States in which membership must be inherited. This is also true of the Bayou and Rod and Gun clubs. They are small, with only about two hundred members.

The country clubs are cold to outsiders, too.

"You can't buy your way into the Houston Country Club," declares a member firmly.

The club is limited to eight hundred members and there is a waiting list of two hundred, all of whom have passed the requirements.

Newer money heads for the River Oaks Country Club, where the initiation fee is $10,000 and memberships have been sold for as much as $17,000.

Although Dallas is one of the country's cultural centers and is the home of the socially elite Idlewild Club, people are apt to associate that city with money. After all, the spectacular Cipango Club is located there. This club's demand on members is simple, direct, and unashamed: Membership is restricted to men and women with annual incomes of at least $100,000.

"For a person in less than the $100,000 bracket, the club has little to offer," insists director Eddie Zimmerman.

Anyone worrying about the state of the economy can take heart upon learning that Cipango's membership numbers one thousand.

Less flamboyant social clubs include the Terpsichorean for bachelors, the Slipper Club for women, the Trippers Club, and the Dallas Dinner Dance Club. The Tuesday Club also has social prestige. Women meet each week to play cards.

The leading debutantes of the season are presented each year at the ball given by the Idlewild Club. This is a men's social group, organized in 1884. At that first ball only five girls came out. Even today the Idlewild remains so exclusive that only eight or ten girls are presented a year.

The other ranking cotillion is the Terpsichorean Ball at which ten debutantes make their bows.

The lives of Dallas debutantes are regulated by Party Service, which is made up of society people. This group maintains lists of eligible debutantes and men, arranges dates for debut parties, and handles invitations. A friend in Dallas claims that it even assigns escorts.

Like everything else in Texas, society functions on a big scale. Balls and private parties are lavish. Most of the important ones in Dallas, Fort Worth, and Houston are designed by Joe Lambert. And he is a man who thinks big.

A few years ago a client got the yen to throw a Christmas party on the Fourth of July. On the Glorious Fourth seventeen truckloads of artificial snow rolled up to the door and started to unload.

And then I keep hearing of "simple" barbecues at which fifty steaks are cooked in fireplaces with grills on three levels, making it possible for them to be made either rare, medium, or well done at the same time.

Money talks in Amarillo in the Texas Panhandle. Huge oil and cattle fortunes are to be found there. The city is bigger than most easterners realize and has a club setup. But an Old Guard has not formed yet. Society is still at the stage of taking in anyone wealthy.

In Los Angeles money counts, too. But there is still a mighty struggle between new money and old. The real Old Guard is made up of those who trace their ancestry to the families who got land grants from the Spanish in the 1700's. But descendants of the early American pioneers of the Westward Ho movement are counted as Old Guard today, too. Then come those who made their money before the turn of the century. The well-established families include the Bannings, Chandlers, Dockweilers, Duques, Hancocks, Mudds, O'Melvenys, Otises, Pages, and Rowans.

And as old-line Texans fight a losing battle against oil, so does Los Angeles' inner circle wage a valiant struggle against the encroachments of the movie colony.

"If movie people attend, it is not a top-society function. That's all there is to it," a member of one of the old families said to me firmly.

But the society editors contend that they see movie personalities at a number of the most exclusive affairs. Some eyebrows were raised, but a well-known producer did succeed in having his daughter presented at the exclusive Las Madrinas debutante ball.

It is hard to keep the movie colony out, the columnists insist, as they have the money to become key figures in leading charities and civic drives.

When confronted with such reports, most socialites simply shake their heads. They point out that society editors cannot be impartial. Movie people do make the best copy.

The social clubs work hard to maintain their exclusiveness. Las Damas Pan Americanas is made up of descendants of the first Spanish families in California. It sponsors a most exclusive debutante ball. The Bachelors and its sister group, the Spinsters, are top drawer in Los Angeles as in many other cities.

The Bachelors was started in 1905, and its annual costume ball is still one of the highlights of the social season. Members of the Spinsters claim that the Los Angeles group is the oldest of its kind in the country. It was organized in 1926. Membership, of course, ends with marriage, leaving a steady stream of openings in the club.

"There were thirty-one new members the year I joined," one of these youthful old maids told me. "Eleven of them came from Pasadena."

The Assembly, which began in 1925, holds its membership to under one hundred women. The annual Assembly Ball is Los Angeles top society ball (except for some of the big charity benefits).

Some of the groups are charity-oriented. Tops among these is Las Madrinas, the godmothers, founded in 1930 by sixty prominent society matrons. The organization selects the city's ranking debutantes for presentation at the annual ball. This is held as a benefit for the Children's Hospital. About thirty girls get the longed-for invitations.

Women socialites in Los Angeles belong to a number of leagues, in addition to the Junior League. All of these combine social standing with social work. The Assistance League, started in 1918 by Mrs. Hancock Banning, has a number of auxiliary organizations, all manned by members of society.

The National Charity League is similar to the Junior League. Its annual Coronet Debutante Ball presents girls who work for the League. A minimum of fifty hours of social work is a requirement.

The Juniors of the Social Service Auxiliary have an annual Candlelight Ball, generally considered an upper-bracket affair. The League for Crippled Children gives a Crystal Cotillion every year to help the Orthopedic Hospital. This ball was originally called the Jack O'Lantern Ball and has been held regularly since 1940.

The Junior Flower Guild runs a heavily publicized headdress ball. The ladies who attend may appear in their latest Balenciagas or Mainbochers; all that they costume is their heads. Some of the more adventurous wear small-scale gardens in tribute to the Flower Guild.

Jewish socialites may bring out their daughters at the Cameo Ball, given by the Cheerful Helpers for Handicapped Children.

Many of the suburbs—and California is really all suburbs—have debutante groups of their own. At Pasadena, which is often described as Los Angeles' most fashionable suburb, the exclusive Valley Hunt Club gives the prestige debutante ball. It is restricted to daughters of members.

Although Los Angeles society resists money made in movies, business success is decidedly helpful in gaining acceptance. Not only industrialists but also doctors and lawyers have considerable social standing.

To the north is San Francisco, which likes to be called the "Boston of the West Coast." And it is every bit as hard on newcomers. As outsiders have seldom been prepared for this, it comes as more of a shock. The West Coast is traditionally the land of opportunities, so people expect to make their way there easily.

"You're thinking of Los Angeles. They don't even have a *Social Register* there" is apt to be the snide comment of San Franciscans.

Actually, the fact that California's history is a short one is the reason for the surprise. It is unusual for families to feel as old as all that so quickly. Compared to the first families of Virginia, Boston, or Philadelphia, all San Franciscans are newcomers. The well-known names of Crocker, Hopkins, Stanford, and Huntington date back to the gold rush of 1849. Some of the other prominent families in San Francisco today are the Laphams, who made their money in shipping, Spreckels in sugar, Hellman in banking, Folger in coffee, De Young in publishing (San Francisco *Chronicle*), and Blyth, Sutro, and Monteagle in finance.

The clubs have considerable influence. The Pacific Union Club, which occupies a red-stone building on top of Nob Hill, is one of the most exclusive men's clubs in the country. Another is the Bohemian Club, which belies its name. Young single men belong to the Bachelors and postdebutantes to the Spinsters. Similar groups are to be found in many cities from Baltimore to Louisville to Raleigh, but their influence in few places is as strong as it is in San Francisco. The Junior League occupies an important place in the city's social life. Socialites also belong to Marin's Lagunitas Club and the Burlingame Country Club.

There are many philanthropies and benefit balls, but the charity road to social success is a rocky one. Just joining an organization and working hard can be a dead end—in society terms only, of course.

"You simply must have the sponsorship of at least one member of an old family to advance to a key spot on a committee," a woman new to San Francisco told me.

But she added that this sponsorship is possible to get. She reports that about one third of the names on the committees and boards of some of the leading charities and benefits are those of newcomers.

The opening night of the opera is one of the high points of the social season, and the performance is usually preceded and followed by big parties. Society women feel they must put in an appearance at the Monday fashion-show luncheon held in the Mural Room of the St. Francis Hotel. This has been going on for a generation, and by now is so desirable that women make reservations months in advance. Getting a good table is viewed as an indication of social prestige.

The Debutante Cotillion, held at the Sheraton Palace Hotel, is the ball for San Francisco's top debutantes. Only twenty girls are presented. The dance is run by a committee of ten, most of whom are members of the old families.

In 1958 a separate ball was started for East Bay debutantes. Called the Winter Ball, it is held at the Claremont Hotel in Berkeley, and benefits the Children's Hospital of the East Bay. Twenty-six girls were presented the first year.

It is hard for newcomers to win invitations to any of San Francisco's major debutante balls, but private debut parties are popular and are extremely lavish. Many men spend between $25,000 and $50,000 to bring out a daughter in style.

It was in San Francisco, by the way, in the St. Francis Hotel, that I overheard a striking comment that seems to sum up much of what I have observed. A couple dressed in formal clothes was heading for the ballroom where an exclusive charity ball was being held.

The woman turned to her husband and said cheerfully: "It's just as I told you back in Des Moines. If you spend enough money, you can make it anywhere."

CHAPTER XII

A Fresh Start in the Suburbs

"I'M tired of being a nobody in the city," said a young mother, slamming down the lid of her last suitcase. "In the suburbs I'll be able to break into society."

This view may be a trifle optimistic, but the woman is not just indulging in idle dreams. There is much to be said for her reasoning. The base of society is broader in the suburbs than in the city. Family background is less important. Studies reveal that 12,000,000 people have moved outside of city limits in the last decade. And in a single year recently, 33,100,000 people changed houses. Who were their great-grandparents? When did the family arrive in America? Who can possibly tell?

Income stretches further—in society terms. A family can keep up with the suburban Astors on a bank account that would not make possible even outer-circle life in the city. People are not automatically rejected because of an income based on salary, rather than capital, because of a single part-time maid instead of a retinue of servants.

The president of a suburban service league (almost equivalent in prestige to the Junior League) confides that many members live in "development" homes. A father in a fashionable suburb spent $300 to have his daughter presented at the local cotillion and an additional $100 for the private debut party at home.

Many Americans who would not stand a chance of getting into the Union or Cosmopolitan clubs can slip into the inner circles in Darien, Manhasset, or White Plains.

"Would it be hard for a newcomer to break into the top social group here?" I asked a friend in a New Jersey suburb.

"I think it would be hellishly tough," replied the woman, her mouth tightening with the memory of her own struggles.

Just then two of her neighbors came over. And she caught herself short. "Why, nobody has any trouble breaking in," she hurriedly amended her statement.

Although an established member of the community, she was afraid to be heard giving the real lowdown on social life. The myth that the suburb is a wide-open friendly town with arms outstretched in welcome must be maintained at all cost.

The sad fact is that suburban dwellers do not like newcomers—even though in terms of years most of them are pretty new themselves. Nearly every person who moves to a suburb would like to be the last one to get there. The doors should slam shut behind him.

But they do not shut. The population keeps on growing. Each wave of invaders brings a large number of people eager to become part of an organized society setup—at the top level, of course. Many of them were not of the inner circle in the city. They did not even hope for such status there. But in the suburbs they believe they can achieve their goal.

Entry into suburban society *is* possible, but it certainly is not easy. The sheer weight of numbers of applicants prevents that. The small-town aspect of suburbia lends a terrible intensity to the struggle, driving many to tranquilizers or mental collapse.

"We moved to the suburbs to get out of New York's mad society whirl," says a new Westchester resident. "I wanted my daughter to get into dancing class, the subdeb dances, and the debutante ball without the wear and tear of trying to crack De Rham, the Holidays, and the Debutante Cotillion and Christmas Ball.

"My friends out here kept telling me that it was so easy. They said that any nice girl whose parents were reasonably well off would have no trouble at all. I'd like to make them eat their words. Though, come to think of it, two of the women have practically done that already. They've both had nervous breakdowns as a result of their efforts to get into the social swim."

One of these suburbanites broke down at a time when she had

succeeded in being accepted at the best local country club, was active in the charity favored by socialites, had placed her daughters in a good private school, and had managed to get the older one invited to the first of the subdebutante dances.

After six months in the sanitarium she was pronounced cured and returned home. Everything went well for three more years. Then she threw herself into the attempt to have her daughter presented at the cotillion. The strain involved again proved too much for her. She had to return to the sanitarium once more.

If this story is a sad one, it is particularly so, because it is not unique. Many fall by the mental wayside. However, it is encouraging to observe that such lapses do not affect the social rise in the least. Mental illness is perfectly acceptable, if the patient retires to a fashionable private institution or goes to the right psychiatrist. People come back to join the fray again, as if they had never been away.

The strain of living without acceptance in the suburbs is much more trying than in the city. The urban family can enjoy a full social life during the years of struggle for recognition by the upper crust. It is possible to have friends on many levels who are unaware of the striving.

"The growth of the suburbs is directly reflected in the increasing number of debutante cotillions," I was told by Mr. Jackson of the *Debutante Register*. "Many girls who are suburban debutantes would never be presented if they lived in the city. It's not just that it's easier for families to manage. It's that in a city, not so many people know if a girl comes out. But in a suburb of 4,000 families everybody knows."

In the wealthy suburbs *all* social life is dominated by the small set that is "in." As a rule, being "in" means being a member of the best country club.

"We bought a beautiful home just outside Detroit," says a former city dweller. "As we had friends who were members of the club there, we were not too concerned about getting in. But once we had moved, we found that the club had a long waiting list and our friends were not influential enough to get us taken in ahead of other eligible people. At first I wasn't too upset. But I soon discovered that all activities were planned around the club. We could only go there as guests, and people won't invite you year in and year out. It was even harder on the children. They were left out of so many things—like the dancing classes and the teenage parties."

As the suburb is prejudiced against newcomers, little effort is made to help out people like these. No matter how nice they are as individuals, the original inhabitants of old-line suburbs such as Grosse Pointe, Bala-Cynwyd, or Pasadena, are not glad to see them. They firmly believe that a suburb should remain just the way it was when first settled.

Many privately agree with the outspoken words of the chairman of the Planning and Zoning Commission of Greenwich, Connecticut: "Intruders from any direction must be held at bay."

The country-club set likes to tell of the suburb that actually cheapened its school program to discourage newcomers. So that the people living there would not be inconvenienced by poor schools, an active birth-control campaign was waged.

A builder in Rye, New York, sued the officials of the Westchester Country Club for having encouraged the sons of members—who like all sons need little encouragement at best—to "harass and annoy" him by "having smoke bombs, burned paper, and kerosene bombs" laid at his front door, in order to discourage him from putting up a housing development.

Zoning regulations and building requirements are the legal method of exclusion. In a New Jersey community the local administration owns one third of the land within its jurisdiction and sells only a dozen lots a year to buyers of its own choosing. A minimum lot size of five acres is common in many suburbs, as is a ruling requiring each house to be different in design from five of its neighbors.

It therefore is not easy for people to make a fresh start in a fashionable suburb. Discrimination against newcomers cuts across all lines of race or religion. Even white Protestants face difficulties in achieving status when they move to a suburb where they are unknown.

"It is true that some communities are very hard to break into," Madeleine Torrens, a leading social secretary in the New Jersey suburbs, said to me, "But after all no one forces you to move to one of them. You can't blame the people there if you are left out."

That view is the classic one held by the older suburban families. There are communities outside of Boston where the original settlers are so afraid of mingling with the newer groups that philanthropic organizations send socialites to call on them for fund drives, instead of using those volunteers who raise money from the newcomers.

"It is easiest to break into a suburb where there are a lot of people who work for your company," advises Miss Torrens. "Colleagues help each other out. Standard Oil Company personnel tend to settle in Plainfield and Union, New Jersey. They get one another into the Plainfield Country Club, which is a setting for many debut parties."

Most rising socialites, I find, do not feel that they have unlimited choice as to suburb. As I pointed out in an earlier chapter only a few communities are considered acceptable. A family's whole social future can depend on where it moves. Each person is immediately placed socially by the name of his suburb.

Winnetka, Dedham, Chestnut Hill, Bloomfield Hills, Chevy Chase, Oyster Bay—is there anyone who does not know what they stand for? And in just the same way, is there anyone who does not know what Rego Park or Levittown, Long Island, means in terms of its inhabitants? Why, the Levittown homeowners not long ago petitioned the post office to allow them to use a "Wantagh" mailing address.

The relative inconvenience of a suburb is also a definite clue to its standing—or lack of it. Americans take it as a matter of course that the most inconvenient one is the highest in the social scale—a view that would no doubt stun visitors from Mars. Some New York City executives, for example, consider Philadelphia a suburb—commuting daily. The definite implication is that anything nearer is not fit to live in. A simple rule of thumb is that men in prestige positions live farthest from the city where they work. Salesmen, white-collar and blue-collar workers cling more closely to the metropolitan area borders.

I have analyzed the society setup in a great many fashionable suburbs and have found strong similarities among all of them. But there are some variations. These depend upon the type of suburb involved. Considered in society terms, there are four major categories: the private-club suburb, the older suburb originally settled by members of the inner circle, the well-established commuter suburb, and the new low-to-moderate-income suburb.

At the top of the hierarchy is the private-club suburb, such as New York's Tuxedo Park, Cleveland's Waite Hill, and Los Angeles' Rolling Hills. These communities were originally developed by a group of families who were friends, and outsiders are still unwelcome.

At Rolling Hills, for example, a *Newsweek* reporter who got a peek discovered that uniformed guards stand at the gates and no one is admitted without an appointment. The only other significant fact that has dribbled out of Rolling Hills is that 80 per cent of the families own horses.

"About two dozen families bought property in Waite Hill between 1925 and 1930," one of the few residents of that village told me. "In the years since then the number of inhabitants has just about doubled. But there are no newcomers. The new families are made up of children of the founders and a very few of their friends."

The community has its own administration headed by a mayor, and a police force. Zoning laws are strictly enforced. Everyone who lives at Waite Hill belongs to the Kirkland Country Club, which is one of the prestige country clubs in the Cleveland area.

Tuxedo Park was started as an exclusive club in 1885. The guiding hand was that of Pierre Lorillard 5th, who bought 600,000 acres of property around Tuxedo and had it improved and fenced in. A club made up of leading New York families was formed, and only members could buy homes at the Park. The Tuxedo Park Association still handles all community problems, such as police, sewage disposal, water, and lights.

Social life in such suburbs is inner circle with a vengeance. As Tuxedo Park residents are members of the old-line New York families, they also participate in the city's top social affairs. Daughters come out at the local Tuxedo Autumn Ball and at New York's highest ranking balls as well. Waite Hill debutantes are welcomed at Cleveland's Assembly.

But such suburbs are really remnants of a bygone era. Tuxedo

Park residents admit sadly that their day of glory is over. Many of the families are moving back to the city.

"The last time I was there," a New York socialite comments, "it seemed to me that everyone was poorer. Why, there were actually families living in what used to be the gardener's cottage. They said they couldn't afford the upkeep on the big house."

Even so, just living in those suburbs guarantees status.

Almost as high in prestige are the old suburbs where the members of the inner circle have their homes. I place such communities in my second category. Detroit's Grosse Pointe, Boston's Brookline, Chicago's Lake Forest and Winnetka and Long Island's Cold Spring Harbor and Oyster Bay are typical. Most of the old families who live in these moved from the city well before the mass exurban migration, in order to find space for their estates. Nearby, and technically a part of the same suburbs, are sections settled more recently by people attracted to the society aura of the original settlers.

The next suburban category is made up of the commuter suburbs, which began their growth before World War II and completed it to a large extent in the late 1940's. They are dominated by a high-income executive group. Most of these people were not able to break into the inner-circle clubs and functions in the big city. But they were close enough to those who did to be aware of traditional society and to wish to be a part of it. And so when they moved to the suburbs, they promptly set up an organized society life.

The last group in the hierarchy is composed of the new, low-to-middle-income communities. The traditional forms of society have not seeped into these.

It would be well worth our while to take a close look at the second and third suburban categories. The private-club community is a survival of another era; the inhabitant of the low-income suburb is unable to afford the high society life (as soon as he can, he moves away). But in the other two there is a well-established social life.

In order to explain the social structure in a vivid, concrete way, I have decided to use specific suburbs as examples. I have, therefore, selected a group of Long Island's North Shore suburbs—including Locust Valley, Syosset, Glen Cove, and Oyster Bay—as most typical of the areas where big name society families have estates. The Connecticut suburbs—including Darien, New Canaan, and Stamford—are my choice as most representative of the fashionable commuter suburbs. The pattern of life described can be applied equally well to communities outside of San Francisco, Chicago, and Boston.

The estates of Old Guard socialites dominate the North Shore of Long Island, often described as the "Gold Coast." They are bounded on all sides by the homes of newcomers. The established families lead an inner-circle social life that is as hard for outsiders to crack as it is in the city.

One woman, who can afford to laugh about it now, admits in confidence that for several years after she moved to such a community not even the grocer was happy about waiting on her. This ostracism lasted until she became friendly with a local socialite, who was a fellow member of a P.T.A. committee. From then on her purchases of asparagus and strawberries were welcomed, while other newcomers were ignored.

Breaking into society is attempted in much the same way as in the city. Membership in the right church is particularly helpful. Top socialites in Locust Valley, Oyster Bay, and Glen Cove attend St. John's of Lattingtown, the Episcopal church. This has an active women's auxiliary.

"The Catholic church is not social out here," a Locust Valley resident comments.

Charity as a means both of doing good and making good contacts is tried by many. But as the suburban socialite's heart is apt to belong to an urban charity, that is not so easy. Members of the inner circle divide their time between suburban and city society. They are in a position to do this, being equally welcome in either place.

"My husband and I go into New York regularly to attend private dances or charity balls," a Syosset society woman told me. "Our friends have big apartments or town houses and usually put us up for the night. I often drive up just for the day myself, too. I like to skate at the New York Skating Club, join my friends for lunch at the Colony Club, and attend committee meetings of my charities. My neighbors in Syosset are active in city groups raising funds to fight cancer, heart disease, multiple sclerosis, alcoholism, and mental illness. Many of us support the Philharmonic Orchestra and the Opera. Even though we go into the city a lot, we also devote time to the local hospitals and family-welfare services."

The local charity affairs offer opportunities for volunteer work. A young woman in Locust Valley told me that she made friends with members of the elite by working on the annual Boys' Club Ball. This affair is held at one of the huge estates, such as the home of the Sherman Pratts or Mrs. Henry P. Davidson, but it is completely run by volunteers.

"About sixty men and women are involved," my informant reported. "Volunteers arrange for the marquee, decorate the place, plan the music, get the flowers, order the food and liquor. The same two people head the committee for two years running."

Sports are apt to be even likelier sources of good contacts than charity. The inner circle's enthusiasm for athletics comes into full flower in these older suburbs. Many socialites moved out of the city simply to guarantee themselves enough space to engage in these activities. There is a big horsy set riding to the hounds in the suburbs of Boston, Philadelphia, Washington, Chicago, and New York.

Children and adults have countless opportunities to display their accomplishments in horse shows. Long Island society attends the Piping Rock Horse Show held at the Piping Rock Club. It also goes to Huntington to the Thomas School of Horsemanship Junior Olympics, and the Rice Farms annual spring horse show. In case anyone should doubt the degree of local interest, the 1959 entry list at Rice Farms totaled 900 horses.

Such horse shows are to be found in any suburb dominated by the old-line families. In Wayne, outside of Chicago, the Dunham Woods Riding Club horse show has been a major social event since the early 1930's.

It is easier for children than for adults to gain social acceptance as a result of good horsemanship. Many of these shows are limited to men and women who have good family background in addition to athletic prowess. One wealthy horseman who was not allowed to take part in a famous horse show retaliated by establishing his own in a nearby community. The competition was followed by a ball—a standard practice. As the horsy set cannot resist horse shows, in the course of a few years this one became extremely social, too. In the beginning anyone could get a ticket to the ball. But by now it is by invitation only. And there is some talk of turning the affair into a debutante cotillion.

Although tennis is a sport for every man nowadays, the suburban tennis clubs retain their old exclusiveness. A Long Island resident maintains that court tennis is very popular there among the inner-inners.

Almost all the leading country clubs have excellent golf courses. Tournaments with calcutta pools are the thing. A calcutta means that golf teams are auctioned to the highest bidders at a pre-tournament dinner. The pool goes to the "owner" of the winning team. A member of the Jupiter Island Club on Hobe Sound told me that the calcutta pool there often totals more than $26,000.

Another popular practice is the holding of amateur-professional golf tournaments for local hospitals. A rising socialite comments that she plays every year in the competition held at the Piping Rock Club as a benefit for the Community Hospital of Glen Cove.

"Sixty teams enter, made up of one professional, one lady—that's me—and two men amateurs," she reports. "Each amateur pays $100 as his entry fee, and that is the contribution to charity."

Sailing is one of society's favorite sports, and yacht clubs are to be found in the suburbs of every city near water, such as Cleveland, Detroit, San Francisco, and Los Angeles. On Long Island the elite sailors moor their boats at the Manhasset Bay Yacht Club, the Cold Spring Harbor Yacht Club, and the Seawanhaka Corinthian Yacht Club.

"The dues are not expensive," one sailing enthusiast informs me. "They're only about $60.00 a year. The expense is the boat. In our set most of us belong to the 'frostbite' group and sail in the winter, too."

Several socialites I know in that area have given yacht club membership to their grown children as a gift. That is a very "in" thing to do.

Ice skating is popular in suburbs, whether near water or not. The Beaver Dam Winter Sports Club in Locust Valley has an artificial rink on the side of a natural one, so that nature's whims need not

affect club members. The Huntington Country Club has a separate
Winter Club on the grounds with an artificial outdoor rink. Memberships of the two clubs are separate.

"About 80 per cent of the women here belong to garden clubs,"
says a Syosset society matron. "We spend a lot of time gardening
and making flower arrangements. The flower shows are very important to us. And, of course, everyone hopes to have her house chosen
for a benefit home and gardens tour."

Country-club membership is essential, though in itself it does not
bring complete acceptance in those suburbs where background is the
prime consideration. The top families are in as a matter of course,
even though they do not view country clubs as comparable to their
city social clubs.

"I don't really use Piping Rock or the Creek Club much," a
Locust Valley socialite who belongs to both remarks coolly. "But
I usually do have dinner at one or the other on Thursday nights.
That's the traditional cook's night out, and people have gotten into
the habit of dining out on those nights. So you get to see your friends
at the clubs."

Although the Old Guard is casual, newcomers feel very strongly.
They know that being left out is a black mark against them.

"The membership list at Piping Rock is almost always closed,"
a woman who has just moved to Long Island told me with a worried look.

Admission is only one step along the path toward social acceptance. Turning a daughter into a debutante is much more important.
(Club membership is, to be sure, a help in achieving this goal.)

The whole pattern of dancing class to subdebutante parties to
debutante cotillion is followed, just as in the city. Many of the
dancing classes are actually imported. On the North Shore of Long
Island, for example, New York's Mrs. de Rham teaches at the
Piping Rock Club. Brooklyn's Miss Hepburn is to be found in
Garden City, New York's Mrs. Wood in Manhasset and Huntington, Long Island, and Rumson, New Jersey.

Is it easier to get into the prestige dancing classes in the suburbs?

"Not at all," says a resident of Locust Valley. "It's not so bad
if you have sons. All the teachers want boys. But for girls it's very

hard. You have to enter the child when she's in kindergarten. After the fourth grade, it's almost impossible. And when we moved here, my oldest daughter was already in the sixth grade. I called Mrs. de Rham and talked to her and she had a suggestion. If I could find a new boy student to balance the class, she would take my daughter."

The next hurdle, of course, is getting the child onto the subdebutante party circuit. The old-line society families bring their daughters to the city to attend the Holidays, Junior Dances, Colony and Metropolitan. But they also go to the Long Island Junior Assemblies.

"These are for girls and boys from all over Long Island, New York, and Connecticut," Mrs. Dewitt Bleecker, who runs the affairs, told me. "Most are from Long Island, naturally. The children are divided into groups, according to age. They start at fourteen. Three dances a year are given for each group."

A young matron in Locust Valley points out that girls have to subscribe to all three, while boys can sign up for one at a time. The cost is $10.00 a dance.

Youngsters in the dancing classes are likely to get invitations. At the very least, their mothers get some guidance.

"Mrs. de Rham told me about the Long Island parties," says a newcomer to Locust Valley. "She suggested that I call Mrs. Bleecker and tell her about my children."

In this type of suburb the "right" debut is either the private party or the debutante ball in the nearby city. Daughters of the top families are invited to New York's Junior Assemblies, Chicago's Passavant Cotillion, Philadelphia's Assembly, or Boston's Debutante Assembly. In addition, they come out at lavish debut parties on the grounds of their estates.

During Long Island's Little Season, which in a typical year lasts from June 13 through June 24, several debut dinners and dances are held every single night at private homes or country clubs. Some are handled by local social secretaries. But most are run by New York's Chapin and Palmer, Tappin and Tew, and Burden Littell.

Some of the newer residents in this category of suburb do, after years of effort, succeed in gaining acceptance by the inner circle.

But a much larger number do not. And so they set up a separate society that resembles the real thing as closely as possible. At its highest level this newer society is intertwined with that of the Old Guard. But it has an elite of its own, made up, naturally enough, of the older (in terms of residence) and wealthier of the newcomers.

It is in these suburbs that I have seen the traditional society setup started from scratch by the enterprising newcomers. Sometimes a group of mothers, allied only by identical interests, sets up dancing classes, subdebutante parties, and cotillions. More often members of a service league or country club are the moving spirits. The club, by the way, is not always the prestige club of the area. (Most suburbanites belong to some sort of country club, even if they are unable to get into the Piping Rock of the community.)

The first step is usually the formation of dancing classes. These are badly needed by those whose children are not accepted into the society class in the area. Invitations are sent first to friends or to the membership of the group involved. As word gets around, other women in the community apply for their youngsters, too. It frequently happens that the classes grow in size to the point where children of newer newcomers are rejected. In addition, children of Old Guard families who are unhappy in the society class switch over, bringing the prestige of their names. Many of these new classes gradually achieve high social standing.

"Our dancing class is run exactly like De Rham," a young mother on Long Island reports. "As a matter of fact, we were able to get one of the recognized teachers to hold additional classes for us. And I know some people in another suburb who simply hired an impoverished society lady who knew the dancing-class ropes."

Dancing classes lead inevitably to subdebutante dances. One of my friends on Long Island's North Shore was active in launching a series of parties, and so I was able to get from her an authentic account of how it was done.

She explained that in her community the North Shore Junior Service League, started in the early 1950's, is the nucleus of new society. Members of the group decided to start a rural version of the Holidays or Get-togethers. A dance committee of a dozen women was formed.

"We started out by sending invitations to children of members," she reported. "To our surprise, we were soon flooded by requests from women who didn't belong to the League. Apparently our children had talked about the dances in school and at the country clubs. So we realized that an invitations policy had to be formulated. We decided that a woman who was not in the League would have to get three letters of recommendation from members."

Two groups of subdebutantes were formed. Fifth-graders and sixth-graders were put in one; seventh-grade and eighth-grade girls and ninth-grade boys in another. Each group attends two parties a year.

"We decided to hold them at the Nassau Country Club in Glen Cove," my friend continued, "and for reasons of economy and convenience we give parties for both age groups on the same night. The younger group has the room from seven to eight thirty; then the older one takes over from nine to ten thirty."

The arrangements are kept as simple as possible. Refreshments are limited to cookies and punch. As Ben Ludlow, the band leader, lives in the neighborhood, it was natural to ask him to provide the music. The fall party is a square dance and he sends a caller. Mr. and Mrs. J. Thompson of Barclay's dancing classes are brought in to run the affairs. Cost of attending the two parties is $15.00 and children must subscribe to both in the fall.

"But as you might know, boys often call at the last minute and say they want to come," my informant added sadly. "I should say 'no.' But then you can never have enough boys at a dance."

There is talk now of starting a supper party for the older subdebutantes.

"In another year or two, some of the girls in the group will be of debutante age," my friend stated. "Then we will hold a cotillion."

That has been done in many of the communities I have studied. The founding of these cotillions is a part of the do-it-yourself society of the suburbs. Sometimes a single enterprising mother starts the ball herself, using the method described earlier. But most often the country club serves as the base of operations. And certainly a country-club group presentation is the easiest to arrange. As the club itself is geared to giving parties and catering them, most of these problems are taken out of the parents' hands.

Anyone who belongs to a club can suggest a debutante ball. The total membership does not even need to be very large. Five girls can come out at a time, or ten, or twenty.

"Having a small membership can be a problem, if the people involved are not very rich," I was told by a member of a club which gave its first cotillion two years ago. "That is true in our case. Last year there were only six girls of debutante age. The party was lovely, but it was awfully costly for the parents, who had to divide up the expenses. So this year we decided to include people in the community who do not belong to the club but who are friends of members."

This is how most of the great balls were started. At the country-club level one can see society in the making.

And as for costs, a spot check of a number of these smaller country clubs shows that a charge of $75.00 to the father of the debutante is average.

Moving on to the next category of suburb, typified by the Connecticut communities, I have discovered that society is surprisingly rigid. These areas were first settled in the 1920's and 1930's. A second stream of migrants moved out in the late 1940's. Since then immigration has been held down to a trickle by rigid zoning laws. The pattern of social life was established during the years when the suburb was growing. The debutante balls were set up at that time. Casual in the beginning, they gradually became exclusive.

The development of the Westchester Cotillion is a typical case history. In the 1930's a group of suburbanites in Connecticut allied themselves with a similar set in Westchester and organized a local mass debut ball for their daughters.

"We just started it for our friends," Mrs. Winfred B. Holton, one of the founders, said to me wistfully. "But in time we were just besieged by people moving into all these communities. So we had to set up an invitations committee and ask for three letters of recommendation. Even at that, the ball got so big that the Connecticut groups split off and formed cotillions of their own."

All of that was done some years ago. By now Mrs. Holton is able to say with considerable justification: "The debutante list for the New York suburbs is the Westchester Cotillion list."

Society in these areas has become inner circle in technique, despite its recent birth.

I choose to call these the "nervous-breakdown" suburbs. The people who move to them are unaware of the rigidity of the social life. They are deluded by the fact that the other residents are mere $40,000-a-year executives, just the way they are. They would expect to have trouble breaking into the communities where the old-line families have estates. But they are quite unaware of what they will find in the commuter suburb. In terms of ultimate success, their chances of making their way into the inner circle are much better than in the other category. But as they are unprepared for the difficulties they will face, the psychological cost is much greater.

In many of these suburbs the country club occupies nearly the same position in ruling social life as the St. Cecilia Society does in Charleston or the Piedmont Driving Club in Atlanta. Although country-club membership is not inherited, some clubs are so exclusive that it might as well be.

I know a couple who were recently admitted to a country club in an upper-bracket Connecticut suburb. Here are the requirements they had to meet: They needed to have a proposer, two seconders, and *ten* letters from members. In addition, the husband was asked to meet all the members of the men's committee and his wife all members of the women's committee. At any point along the way they could have been blackballed. That happens to many applicants. They, incidentally, had to be able to pay up the $1,500 initiation fee and $500 dues without straining the budget.

"The committee seems to have a sixth sense about people. It knows in advance who will spend a lot of money in entertaining and playing golf," says a club member. "The club doesn't want anyone who will just come in for an occasional meal."

Wee Burn in Darien, the New Canaan Country Club, and others of that type have no trouble finding members no matter what demands are made on applicants.

The newcomer in the community must become acquainted with

people in the inner circle before he can even be considered for membership. How is it done?

The church—Episcopal, Presbyterian, or Congregational, naturally —is just as influential as in all other types of suburbs, or cities, too, for that matter.

In Darien members of the older families belong to St. Luke's Episcopal Church, the Noroton Presbyterian Church, and the First Congregational Church. Newcomers flock to the church auxiliaries.

"The minister helped me a lot in ways I would never have expected," one woman told me. "He actually advised me about such things as dancing classes for my daughters."

"If somebody new were to ask me how to break into society here," an established resident states, "I'd advise her to become active in the Community Association. We take local problems very seriously."

This advice has the advantage of being very easy to follow. Anyone who lives in the area can join the Community Association. Dues are only about $10.00 a year. And there are more committees than there are volunteers to staff them.

"Everyone wants to take part in the activities, but no one wants to organize them," one newcomer discovered. "I'm on half-a-dozen committees—and I could be on more if I had the strength."

"What are the committees for?" I asked.

The woman ticked off the following activities: thrift shop, dental clinic, well-child clinic, hospital volunteer program, sixty-plus club, book club, garden club, writers' workshop, lecture program, choral group, and arts and crafts classes.

"And of course you'll meet the older residents working on zoning and community planning."

In one town a matron reports that keeping the local social date book is a community association project.

"I tried to get that job for years," she said. "If you're holding the date book, everyone in town has to call you. I thought I didn't stand a chance. But the woman who had it finally got sick of the work and was willing to turn it over to me."

In addition to the association there are always a large number of civic, service, political, and educational organizations that need and welcome volunteers. These include such groups as the Family

Counseling Service, Catholic Charities, Children's Services, American Red Cross, League of Women Voters, and Citizens for Good Education.

Some communities have women's clubs which may—or may not —have high social ranking.

"I found the alumnae association of my college particularly helpful," one new resident reveals. "Somehow the school spirit lives on. I was welcomed by girls I hadn't even known before, and they helped me to meet people in town."

Being a parent makes the newcomer's life much easier—and most suburbanites do have children. The reason I mention parenthood in this context is that the common meeting place between inner circle and newcomer is school. And it can be public school.

No social stigma is attached to public school I have been told by many socialites in both Connecticut and New Jersey. I was shown a recent study which revealed that only 4 per cent of elementary school children in Darien were attending private school, 7.8 per cent of junior high-school students and 19.6 per cent of senior.

Nonetheless, many parents maintain that it helps to send a child to private school. A youngster from a family new to the community can otherwise be overlooked.

"The committees for the subdeb parties look over the private school enrollments," says a new resident of Greenwich. "I know that because I have two daughters—one at private, one at public school. Only the one at private school was invited to the junior dance."

Some mothers have found that the presence in public school of the children of the older residents creates a whole set of problems. Youngsters whose families belong to the good clubs and who attend the dancing classes and subdebutante parties tend to form a clique, excluding all others. And so parents often do switch sons and daughters to private school.

In Connecticut the favored schools include the Low-Heywood School and the King School in Stamford, and the New Canaan Country Day School and St. Luke's School for Boys in New Canaan. In New Jersey the comparable schools are the Kimberley School in Montclair, the Kent Place School in Summit, and Newark Academy in Newark.

It is through the parents of school friends that newcomers can learn the particulars of local social life.

"When I first moved to the suburbs," one mother remembers, "I didn't know anybody. I was sure that there must be some dancing class that was favored by the better families. As I was too shy to question strangers, I asked the real-estate agent who sold us the house. He suggested the commercial dance studio! It took me years to find out where people *really* were going."

Getting a child into the favored dancing class literally provides her with debut insurance.

In Darien the top dancing classes are conducted by Mrs. Ashleigh Halliwell, a lady who is as aged and ageless as most of the others of her breed. Unlike many teachers who start pupils as soon as they put away their Teddy bears, Miss Halliwell takes children from the fifth through the seventh grades in school only. The course costs $40.00. To be admitted, an applicant must present two letters from parents of students in the classes. These are handed in a year in advance. Mother and child also have to go before a committee. First preference is given to children of former students and to younger brothers and sisters of those in the classes. Length of residence in the community is also considered. The waiting list is long.

"But newcomers with contacts do sometimes jump over others on the list," one Darien resident admits. "And aggressive mothers have been known to work miracles."

Those who are not accepted at Miss Halliwell's have a harder time advancing socially—but they can do it. In the suburbs there is always room for hope. Even in communities such as Darien, where the society structure is well established, new dancing classes, clubs, and parties appear from time to time and compete with the existing ones.

I observed the effect of the rise of such a dancing class in the Connecticut suburbs. A few years ago a teacher named Phil Jones began to give lessons in the public junior high schools, charging each student fifty cents. He also conducted courses in his own studio at a cost of $20.00 for anyone who cared to attend. Those who had been refused by Miss Halliwell naturally turned to Mr. Jones. That was only the start. An excellent teacher, he began to attract many children who wished to learn to dance. Most youngsters, after all, are not much interested in learning good manners and making suitable social contacts.

A number of his students were members of the older families and would have had no difficulty in getting into Miss Halliwell's.

Before the rise of Mr. Jones, the subdebutante party lists were virtually repeats of Miss Halliwell's enrollment. But after a few years it became apparent that some of Mr. Jones's students could not be overlooked either. The net result has been a loosening of the bonds holding the social structure together. Failure to get into Miss Halliwell's is no longer sure social death the way it used to be. Invitations committees must consider a much larger group of applicants.

I do not mean to imply that it is easy to get a child on the subdebutante party round. Most of the affairs were started long ago and have become exclusive.

"We began the subdeb dances out here," one of the older residents recalls, "because we felt that children should have big formal parties. And yet we did not want them to get into the rat race of New York's social life."

That was years ago. By now the Connecticut party setup has turned into that same old rat race. And this holds true for communities all over the country.

In these suburbs the earlier a child can slip onto the subdebutante whirl, the better. Once on the party list, a youngster is likely to get to everything. One reason for this is that every invitations committee favors the girls and boys who attended other local dances.

The first big party for teenagers in the Connecticut suburbs, for example, is the Cinderella Ball. The following year the Starlight Ball is the event for tenth-graders. Then comes the Mistletoe Ball for eleventh- and twelfth-grade students.

"In general," a committee member told me, "those children who attended the Cinderella go on to the Starlight and the Mistletoe. As a matter of fact, the same committee runs the last two."

Darien admits boys and girls from New Canaan and Stamford to its parties, and those communities return the compliment. Darien children are invited to such affairs as the Stamford Junior Cotillion and the New Canaan Snow and Silver Moon Balls. They also go to the Westport County Assemblies and Red and White Ball. Invitations are sent out by a Darien committee of the New Canaan, Stamford, or Westport balls.

"I was on the Darien committee for the Silver Moon Ball last year," one matron informed me.

Upon checking my notes, I was hardly surprised to observe that she had also served on the Starlight Ball committee that same season.

How does a child get that valuable first Cinderella Ball invitation? Her mother cannot put in an application; she has to be invited by the committee. This is made up of four women from each of the participating towns: Darien, New Canaan, and Stamford. Three hundred and fifty children attend. Both boys and girls are invited, as they are theoretically too young to date.

"The committee first considers the list of children who attended Miss Halliwell's classes. Since the dancing-class upheaval, that list is not quite so comprehensive as it was formerly," my friend on the committee told me. "So we also go over the public and private school enrollments, checking them to see 'who knows whom.'"

Children away at boarding school can be forgotten, unless a mother guards against this by "reminding" a member. Mothers in doubt of invitations usually do make a practice of asking a friend to phone someone on the committee to "chat."

The Cinderella is a dinner dance. It is held at the Wee Burn Club, and costs $7.50 per ticket.

Those who missed the Cinderella may yet make the Starlight Ball, though it is much harder. This happens most often to youngsters whose parents have been admitted to the Wee Burn Club in the interim. The dance is given under the auspices of this club.

"Being the child of a member helps, though we don't give preference," said a woman on the committee, using the double talk at which socialites excel. When pressed, she added that every Wee Burn member's child automatically gets on the invitation list.

Both the Starlight and the Mistletoe Balls cost $5.50 per couple, $4.00 for a stag. The Westport balls, I hear, run a bit higher—about $10.00 a couple. The girls, by the way, are expected to provide their own escorts and pay for their tickets. Stags are invited by the committee.

At the end of the subdebutante road lies the debut. Practically every one of the well-established commuter suburbs has its own ball. The goal of mothers in the Connecticut suburbs studied is the Darien-New Canaan Autumn Cotillion.

The committee for this is made up of two groups, one from Darien and one from New Canaan. Each can invite a maximum of 21 girls.

"Length of residence in the community is the main criterion," says a committee member firmly.

As might be expected, girls who attended the Starlight and Mistletoe balls have the best chance, as those lists are carefully studied. But girls who have missed out on those occasionally do break in.

"You can have a friend call a committee member and ask that your child's name be considered," one woman on the committee advises. "Somehow it's not the thing to call yourself."

Invitations go out in the March preceding the ball. But in January the chosen parents are asked if they would accept if invited. This allows time to find substitutes for those who view debuts with a jaundiced eye. It is also easier on the nerves.

"When my daughter came out," says the mother of a post-debutante, "invitations were sent to all those considered eligible, and the first twenty-one to accept were in. I remember running to my mailbox at delivery time day after day, holding a pen in my hand, so as to be able to accept without a moment's loss of time."

The cotillion is run as a benefit for St. Joseph's, Stamford, and Norwalk hospitals. This is a benefit to parents of debutantes as well. Cost of presentation is $300, and $160 of that is tax deductible.

"The ten days before the debut are ten days of sheer hell," the mother of a recent debutante confesses wearily. "Every deb has to give some sort of party, so that there isn't a moment's respite."

Parties range from formal dances to breakfasts, beach parties, and cookouts. Some years studied informality is the rage, and everyone attends all daytime affairs in Bermuda shorts.

Despite all the difficulties, the suburbs still offer the best opportunity to those who wish to lead the society life without benefit of old-line background. Many rising socialites (like most other Americans) move to the suburbs for "the sake of the children." But a father in this group does not limit his dreams to the universal Tom Sawyer image of carefree boys and girls swinging their books on a strap as they walk down the country road to school. In his mind he cherishes the picture of his pony-tailed daughter all grown up, in a white gown, dancing the first cotillion waltz with him.

CHAPTER **XIII**

The International Set and Café Society

ASK the man in the street to name members of high society. Chances are that he will come right back with the names of those prominent in the international set and café society. To the unsophisticated that is what society is.

The reason is not hard to understand. These are the people whose names appear regularly in society columns all over the country.

The columnists are not altogether happy about this state of affairs. There is nothing they would rather do than write about old-line society exclusively. Unfortunately, the inner circle does not do enough that is news producing. Members entertain at home, and sometimes even divorce in secret. And so the columnists have been forced to turn to the more flamboyant doings of the international set and café society.

Although the two groups overlap to a certain extent, they are not on a par in terms of prestige. The international set ranks much higher.

Its highly publicized parties, sun-drenched resorting, and lavish expenditure of money are so ostentatious as to appear low class. But the set does include so many bona-fide socialites that it cannot be written off as *nouveau riche* and nothing more. Many heirs to great fortunes do not need to earn a living and can spend their lives in seeking pleasure. They lend the influence of their great names to this group and so attract some hard-working self-made men and women and a number of celebrities.

Who is in the international set? I find it dominated by the figures of the Duke and Duchess of Windsor, Colonel Serge Obolensky, Princess Grace of Monaco, Elsa Maxwell, and the Greek shipowners, Aristotle Onassis, Basil Goulandris, and Stavros Niarchos. Royalty, even minor royalty, is in no danger of being dethroned. There is also a mixture of old and new society, including Margaret (Peggy) Bancroft, the Winston Guests, the Henry Ford II's, the William Paleys, the Henry Luces, Mrs. George F. Baker, the Cornelius V. Whitneys, the Herbert Scheftels, John Mortimer Schiff, and Angier Biddle Duke.

This group is relatively easy to break into. Socialites are welcomed with open arms. Others only need to have money—lots and lots of it. One magazine recently estimated an annual income of at least $100,000 after taxes as the bare minimum. To many in this set that would be living in a very sparse way indeed.

Lady Norah Docker, for example, shows up on the Riviera in a gold Daimler upholstered in leopard skin. I have never been on Mr. Onassis' fabled yacht, the *Christina,* but those who have report that an El Greco hangs in the master bedroom. There are eight guestrooms, each with its own marble bathroom with gold fittings. A mosaic dance floor can be lowered to become a swimming pool. Then there is the White Russian who recently built a villa on the Riviera and felt that the floors simply had to be of pure white marble. His bill for the villa? Estimates hover near the $500,000 mark.

At the Corviglia Ski Club at St. Moritz, the crowd that gathers on the terrace after lunch still likes to remember the exploit of a young heir to a mining and oil fortune. He won a $1,000 bet at a party by climbing up and down a pyramid made of six tables and a chair without spilling a drop from the brimming champagne glass he held in one hand.

The international set meets at resorts on a rigid time schedule. In winter it alternates between St. Moritz and Nassau. February is the height of the St. Moritz season—and the Corviglia Ski Club is the place to meet. Some of the group's best-known party-givers— among them Messrs. Onassis and Niarchos—usually stay at the Palace Hotel.

This has given rise to the international set wisecrack: "It's the Greek Grossinger's."

The real Grossinger's, in case anyone has missed the publicity, is a lively, celebrity-packed resort right outside of New York City.

A somewhat quieter group goes to Gstaad to the Winter Palace Hotel. Others travel to Schloss Mittersill in the Austrian Alps near Kitzbühel. And La Colmiane in the French Alps north of Monaco also attracts a fashionable crowd.

Nassau is the other favored winter spot.

"British nobility is a tremendous draw for the international set," a keen-eyed vacationer observes.

Many members of this group own cottages at the exclusive club resorts. Others stay nearby at hotels or clubs. A favorite is the Coral Harbour Club at the tip of New Providence. Only a hundred guests may stay there, and admission is by invitation.

The United States itself is permissible resort country. Many spend at least a little time each year in Palm Beach, Colorado Springs, and White Sulphur Springs. As is the way with this group, a number of Palm Beach aficionados were shaken when the Duke and Duchess of Windsor passed it up one season and went to Tucson instead.

Some follow the racing calendar, traveling around the United States, to London, to Paris, and to Ireland, wherever the horses are running.

"It is the thing to alternate between London and Paris in June," a member of the set told me. "The most *wonderful* parties are given in Paris!"

In July the move is on to the Riviera. Many time their arrivals so as not to miss the opening gala of the International Summer Sporting Club at Monte Carlo. Mr. Onassis is in his element as a party-giver on the Riviera.

Key members of the set have villas and/or yachts of their own. Those who have not yet achieved villa rank go to the Carlton in Cannes, the Hôtel du Cap in Cap d'Antibes, or the Hôtel de Paris in Monte Carlo. Much of their time, to be sure, is spent on board the yachts of their friends.

In August they pack up again and move on to Rome and Venice.

Italy is the scene of some of the most lavish—and at times scandal-producing—parties.

When the set returns to America, members meet again at balls to aid exiled White Russians and Hungarian victims of oppression and at benefits for charities in France, Italy, and Greece.

The parties and resorting are carried out on such a lavish scale that they overshadow many other activities of the international set. Some of the major art collectors of today belong to this group. Mr. Goulandris, for example, spent $297,000 for Gauguin's "Still Life with Oranges." Mr. Niarchos recently lent his art collection to the Knoedler Art Galleries in New York for a showing. Included were the works of Van Gogh, Degas, Toulouse-Lautrec, and many other noted artists.

Somehow the art collecting, business activities, and old-line family connections do not counterbalance the general impression. The public views these people as playboys on a world scale. They are frequently confused with café society.

I find that nothing angers members of the international set more. "Why, *anyone* can belong to café society," they say scornfully.

And they are quite right. It does not even take a lot of money. Members are not required to maintain luxurious homes in New York, Venice, and the Riviera. They do not need to travel to St. Moritz, Palm Beach, and Monte Carlo in season. The women are not expected to wear "name" jewels and designer clothes—although it helps if they do. And café socialites do not pay off social obligations by giving frequent parties for several hundred people with dash. All that is needed is enough money to go night clubbing several times a week.

Today even that requirement can be circumvented. Businessmen and their wives often go the café circuit on one another's expense accounts.

As for a girl, she does not need to have any money of her own. She simply has to be attractive enough to get a date with a man who can afford to take her night clubbing. No one but the most innocent is surprised to find former models, manicurists, hat-check girls, receptionists, chorus girls, and waitresses bearing some of society's biggest names. How did they meet the scions of the old families? It often happened in the cafés.

Café society is no longer society at all. But members are apt to be a little wistful about this, remembering the days when it consisted of the younger high society set. Old-timers tell me that it was started before World War I by an inner-circle group influenced by dancers Irene and Vernon Castle. Bored by the staid social lives of their parents, they slipped off to the clubs to dance the turkey trot, bunny hug, and Castle Walk. The term "café society" was coined in those halcyon days by Maury Paul, the original Cholly Knickerbocker.

Society stayed in the cafés right through the 1930's. But since then it has become déclassé. I found a study done in 1937 by *Fortune* magazine. It pointed out that about one third of café society members were not in the *Social Register*. By today it would be the height of exaggeration to say that one third of its members are *in* the *Register*.

Those who still go to the clubs are attracted by the presence there of celebrities of the movies, television, the stage, and sports. Many of these well-known personalities have infiltrated the cafés in order to gain publicity and to hobnob with socialites.

"Society rings the cowbell that attracts celebrities to a restaurant or club," Marianne Strong, the press agent for the Stork Club, tells me.

Conversely, the presence of theatrical personalities brings in socialites. It also is a magnet for out-of-towners, couples on dates, and businessmen on expense accounts.

The press agents of the top clubs are so well aware of the attracting powers of socialites and celebrities that they make every effort to ensnare key members, Yetta Golove, public-relations woman for the Harwyn, told me. They go through the *Social Register* sending out post cards to families who might go to late night spots. The debutante lists published in the newspapers are also carefully studied and selected names are used in mailings. Cards are sent to stage and screen celebrities, urging their patronage.

This practice is a continuous one. As new names appear on any of the lists, they are considered. And the others get reminders.

Post cards go out regularly, bearing a message that there is dancing at the club, or that it is open until the wee hours.

"It doesn't matter what the cards say," declares Miss Golove. "Their purpose is to remind people of your existence."

Everyone wants to be near celebrities. When Princess Grace and Prince Rainier were in New York, they visited the Harwyn. For months afterward, Miss Golove reports, the table post cards filled out by guests and mailed by the club contain such statements as: "I am sitting right next to Princess Grace." They ignore the sad fact that by then Princess Grace is thousands of miles away in Monaco. The folks back home will not know that anyway.

The old axiom that position is everything in life applies to café society. The position, of course, is that of the table assigned by the all-powerful headwaiter.

"I always know where to look for the celebrities and big society people," one night-club habitué said to me. "They are always placed at certain tables."

I am often told an anecdote about a well-known socialite, who once refused to let a friend bring along an extra luncheon guest. The presence of an additional person would have meant that she could not be given her regular table and she would have lost face. (The name of the lady involved changes from time to time, by the way; the story, however, does not.)

Location is taken with such seriousness that I observe that society's magazine *The Diplomat* had to run a report on just where the best tables are. This is what they found: At the Twenty-One Club, the best upstairs tables are those in the foyer at the top of the stairs. The banquettes along the walls of the first room are ranked in descending order from Table One on the right as one enters. Anyone put in the little rooms to the left or in the third room simply does not rate at all. Downstairs, the favored spots are in the front room: the two tables against the left wall and the first one on the right. The nearest right-hand table is known as "Benchley's corner," in honor of the late Robert Benchley, one of its most famous and regular habitués.

At Le Pavillon the best tables are in the busy foyer leading into the main room. Those placed in the barroom or the back of the room have no social distinction at all. The personal attention of owner Henri Soule is considered the final seal of approval.

At El Morocco the key location is the first table on the right by the headwaiter's desk. The banquettes along the right-hand wall are also good. Personal friends of owner John Perona are seated at his big round table. Those on the far side of the dance floor might as well not be there at all, in terms of prestige.

At the Colony restaurant any of the tables at the front of the room are good, with the banquettes on the right especially favored. At the Stork Club any table at all in the Cub Room will do. Those in the know look at Table Fifty in the first corner or at the tables near the door.

The rulers of café society are the society columnists. All they need to do is mention a person often enough—and, lo, he becomes a member of the set.

Igor Cassini is the current Cholly Knickerbocker, the name that has come to symbolize the society columnist. His influence is augmented by the fact that once a year he runs a list of New York debutantes. A succession of talented reporters have helped him to gather the news for his column. Mary Elizabeth (Liz) Smith is his current assistant.

Charles Ventura has a wide readership, although he tends to neglect the cafés a bit in favor of the international and resort set. In recent months "Society Today," the New York *World Telegram and Sun's* column by Knickerbocker-graduate Joseph X. Dever and Charles Van Rennselaer, has been winning advocates. Socialites say that it is "surprisingly" accurate. (The choice of the quoted word is theirs.) Another well-known column is Nancy Randolph's "Chic Chat" in the New York *Daily News.* "Suzy," the New York *Mirror's* society column, is now done by Aileen Mehle.

It is the thing for old-line society to look down on the columnists and assert that they are "wrong...wrong...wrong." But I was quite unable to find one who did not read them avidly. Knickerbocker has the widest readership among this group.

"The problem of writing a daily column has created vast numbers of members for café society," a former columnist reveals.

Nobody knows the trouble the columnist has in filling the space allotted to him—nobody knows, but the press agent, that is. To get some idea of how easy it is for a publicist to have a client mentioned, here is an item recently placed in one of the leading columns: A popular debutante had been wearing her hair shoulder length. She cut it off short. Her mother disapproved. But her boy friend, a well-known (to column readers) playboy, liked it.

And a popular story when press agents get together is about the days when the activities of oil man Roy Crocker and railroad tycoon Tony Lamb were followed by all the columnists. The wild oats being sown by Lamb's daughter, Angela, were described in columns for months. Need I add that Crocker and Lamb were simply creations of a press agent's vivid imagination? Their function was to provide column mentions for the restaurants and night clubs he was handling.

The columnists themselves regularly visit El Morocco, the Stork Club, and others, trying to pick up news. The captains and maîtres d'hôtel are primary sources of information. They hear all, know all, and usually tell all. If a socialite or celebrity is in one of these clubs incognito—possibly wearing a black wig, which is a popular maneuver nowadays—a captain's keen eye will almost surely spot her. News about engagements or their opposites, divorces, are often leaked from the moment of decision.

Almost anyone who really does spend time in the clubs will eventually be rewarded with a mention, then a line, and then an anecdote in the columns. At that point he has his membership badge in the club.

Café society is basically a New York product, but I find that it does exist to a certain extent in any city big enough to have a supper club or even a hotel with room for dining and dancing. Wherever there are celebrities, this type of social life will appear. Personalities have to go somewhere to be seen and photographed. California, with its movie colony, therefore, has, if anything, a more active night life than New York.

But even in cities where supper clubs are unimportant or nonexistent, there is a group that occupies the same social position as the café set in New York. In some parts of the West it has come to be called "barbecue society," and is made up of people rich enough to give lavish parties. This group has money but has won no entree into society.

Joining in café society is sometimes mistakenly believed to be a way to break into real society. This can happen only to girls—and not very often. A young woman can use the opportunity to meet and ultimately marry a scion of an old family. She can even be made into a glamour debutante (not to be confused with the debutante daughters of the inner circle). But the road to the Junior Assemblies and the *Social Register* in most cases detours around the Stork or El Morocco.

Café society is a way of life. Those in it enjoy it for the pleasure of the moment and the publicity of tomorrow—not for the hope of social advancement.

CHAPTER XIV

Negro Society in America

THE fact that Negro high society exists at all frequently comes as a surprise to whites. Its activities are not reported in non-Negro newspapers. And yet I find that 1,000 Negro girls are debutantes each year. They are presented to society at lavish balls held in cities in every section of the country. Old Guard social leaders, exclusive social clubs, philanthropic groups, charity balls, and debutante cotillions are characteristic of Negro society as well as white.

Contrary to popular belief, achievement is not the only way for people of this race to win social position. There is an aristocracy based on birth, a group that corresponds to white society's "400."

Who belongs to this inner circle? I have made up a brief directory of the best-known families:

The Syphax family of Washington, D.C., is one of the oldest. Members can trace their history all the way back to Martha Washington, wife of the first President. They tell that her grandson, George Washington Parke Custis, fell in love with a Negro slave named Arianna Carter, who was serving as his grandmother's maid. The girl bore young Custis a daughter, Maria, who was brought up on the family estate at Arlington. Maria later married Charles Syphax, a slave who worked as a dining-room servant. Both of them were freed and given a seventeen-acre plot on the estate. The large Syphax family descends from their two daughters and eight sons.

The Fishers, too, have a long heritage. Their forebears were white relatives of Napoleon Bonaparte and citizens of Martinique. This family includes O. Hodge Fisher, the architect, who is married to singer Marian Anderson; Leon Fisher, the industrial chemist, who was the husband of the late Doris Wells, a Texas oil heiress; and the Reverend George A. Fisher II, Episcopal minister of Raleigh.

Descendants of the five daughters of Victor Rochon, last of Louisiana's Creole state representatives, are prominent around New Orleans. They bear the names of Dibble, Taylor, Robinson, Brooks, Craig, Boutte, Cater, Kennedy, Stanton, and Quick.

The Tanner family stems from Richard Tanner, who ran away with a tribe of Indians in order to escape slavery. One of the best-known members of this family is the artist Henry O. Tanner, who won the Gold Medal of France for his painting, "The Raising of Lazarus," which is in the Luxembourg Museum. Others include Mrs. Hallie Dillon Johnson, who established the nurses' school and hospital at Tuskegee, and Mrs. Maudelle B. Bousfield, first Negro principal in the school system of Chicago.

The Tanners take their position very seriously. I have been told that one member, Mrs. Sadie Tanner Mossell Alexander of Philadelphia, used to say sadly, "Frivolity and slothfulness were cardinal sins in our family. I can't remember hearing my grandfather laugh."

The Dammonds of New York are descended from Ellen Craft, a heroine of slave days, and claim a connection with Thomas Jefferson. They like to tell the dramatic tale of Ellen Craft's escape from slavery in Georgia. Fair-skinned Ellen disguised herself as a white man going North for medical treatment, accompanied by his/her manservant, William, who happened to be the real Ellen's husband. They traveled to Boston in first-class accommodations and got there in time to take part in the Faneuil Hall mass meeting against slavery.

The Delany family is prominent both in Raleigh and New York City. In Baltimore the Lane family has a 120-year history. In Philadelphia the Stricklands are well known. Society families in Chicago include the Daileys, the Doyles, and the Paines; in Boston, the Halls; in Washington, the Wests and Curtises as well as the Syphaxes; in Columbia, South Carolina, the Speeds.

Members of these inner-circle families are active in the professions.

As one lawyer explains: They are among the few people of their race who were able to obtain the benefits of a good education—even in pre-integration days—and so could rise in their chosen fields.

In this connection I remember an anecdote I heard about Mrs. Henry Delany, Sr., widow of the first Negro to serve as a bishop of the Episcopal Church in the United States. She is the mother of a judge, a lawyer, a doctor, two dentists, a mortician, a motel owner, and three teachers. When complimented on the accomplishments of her children, she commented wryly: "Well, it's no more than they should have done."

Actually, anyone belonging to this Old Guard has tremendous prestige, regardless of his professional position. There are a number of impoverished aristocrats whose high social standing is not affected in the least by their lack of funds.

Until recently this small group was all there was of high society. Today, the base has broadened. The improved economic and social status of the Negro has made it possible for a fairly large group to concern itself with the forms of an organized society life.

"There is only one way for newcomers to break into the inner circle: through successful careers in the professions," I was told by a prominent businesswoman. "You don't stand much of a chance of marrying your way in. The old-line families are extremely clannish and tend to intermarry."

The person who rises in business will rise socially as well, she pointed out. This is not so simple as it sounds, because it is still very difficult for a Negro to reach the top of his career.

Professional standing is essential in being accepted to membership in the leading men's and women's clubs. And these rule Negro society. They serve as social arbiters. They present the debutantes; members are on key committees for social and philanthropic affairs; their recommendations count heavily in getting children into private schools; many put promising youngsters through college.

I have drawn up a list of the top-ranking men's social clubs: the Royal Coterie of Snakes, Chicago; the Me-De-So Club, Baltimore; the Original Illinois Club, New Orleans; the Comus Club, New York and Brooklyn; the Bachelor-Benedicts, Washington, D.C.; the Strikers, Mobile, Alabama; and the Cotillion Club, Detroit.

These clubs were originally formed by a small group of men in the same profession—usually doctors, dentists, pharmacists, and lawyers. Sons and close friends of members are eligible for membership. They must be proposed, seconded, and passed by the group before being accepted.

A national men's organization with great prestige is the Guardsmen. This group has chapters all along the eastern seaboard from Boston to Atlanta. Members usually belong to leading clubs in their own cities as well. And they are, almost without exception, wealthy and successful men.

This is a purely social club, meeting just to have fun. I have sometimes heard it criticized for this, as almost all Negro organizations work for something—improved education for Negroes, desegregation, and the like. But members of the Guardsmen point out that as individuals they are all active in causes. Most hold $500 lifetime memberships in the National Association for the Advancement of Colored People.

Each chapter takes a turn at playing host to all the others for a weekend's entertainment. The Connecticut group recently leased an entire resort for a weekend. Most years the Guardsmen take a cruise together to Bermuda, Havana, or the Dominican Republic.

The top-ranking women's clubs also have great power in Negro society. One of the best known is the Links, a national organization with 89 chapters. The name, by the way, means the link of friendship.

"And we fondly call our husbands connecting links," says one member.

Founded in Philadelphia in 1946, the club's membership has already expanded to 1,600.

Those belonging to the Links perform the same types of charitable activities as do Junior Leaguers. Members do volunteer work in medical centers, mend toys for needy children, give birthday parties for the aged, adopt poor families at Christmas and Easter, serve as civil-defense plane spotters, form child-guidance and counseling services, and raise funds for scholarships and many other causes.

"Our common goal is that of lending a helping hand to humanity," Norvleate Downing, chairman of public relations for the Links explained to me.

The Girl Friends is also a large and influential women's organization. It is one of the oldest of its type, started in New York City in 1927 by sixteen friends. Today there are twenty-one chapters in as many cities. The group is active in community service.

The Gay Northeasterners is a small and exclusive club, known for its beautiful balls. It was started by the wife of Brigadier General Benjamin Davis and several of her girlhood friends. The original members come from Connecticut and New York.

There are some very small women's clubs with top social standing, too. The Memphis Dinner Club, for example, has only eight members. The Smart Set Club of Houston, founded in 1944, by wives of five of the city's leading doctors and dentists, has expanded to *twelve*.

A number of organizations for both men and women are also influential. Prominent among these is the Jack and Jill of America. Members must be parents. This group runs a club for children, called the Jack and Jill Juniors.

One of the most highly regarded Negro organizations in the country is the Philadelphia Cotillion Society. Despite the name, this has nothing to do with debutantes. It was started in 1949 to raise funds for Mercy Douglas Hospital. Since then it has developed a cultural foundation for the Negro as well. It supports the Dra-Mu Opera Company, which is a showcase for young opera singers, and has started Heritage House where art exhibitions, jazz workshops, and lecture series on the creative arts are held.

Once a year a cotillion—which in this case means a big extravaganza—offers Negro performers an opportunity to demonstrate what they can do.

Only those who make contributions to Heritage House or the Cotillion Society's charity of the year receive invitations to the affair, which is held in Philadelphia's Convention Hall.

In addition to these huge organizations, several smaller clubs for men and women have considerable prestige, at least locally. The Altruist Club of Roanoke, Virginia, has been described to me as an excellent example of these. Its total membership is only thirty couples.

Many prominent Negroes also belong to a number of purely philanthropic organizations. They support and attend benefits. It is customary for the society families who are active in the charities to hold exclusive private parties after the balls.

Some of the biggest affairs are given by the Guilds of the National Urban League and by the Urban Aides. Younger girls belong to the National Junior League, a social-service organization with many chapters.

Members of old-line families work for such long-established charities as the Utopia Neighborhood Club in New York.

One of the best publicized of the philanthropies is the Doll League, which has chapters in Los Angeles and New York. The League runs an annual ball at which admission is by doll. The toys are distributed at Christmastime to needy children in hospitals.

In the big cities such as New York, Chicago, and Los Angeles, membership in yet another type of club—the organizations of people from somewhere else—can affect social standing. These include the Sons and Daughters of Georgia, North Carolina, and Texas; and the Societies of Barbadians, West Indians, Trinidadians, and Jamaicans. The prestige of each varies with the caliber of the membership in any given city. In New York, for example, the West Indians are an extremely important group, made up of professionals and men and women with large landholdings in the Indies.

Belonging to a professional organization also brings a measure of prestige—although not so much as does social-club membership. Many men and women are in both types. Highest ranking are the National Medical Society, National Dental Society, Business and Professional Women, and societies of pharmacists, real-estate brokers, funeral directors, and insurance companies.

"Insurance is one of the most profitable Negro businesses, and some of the top families are in this field," an insurance broker reports. "Undertaking establishments are frequently attached to insurance companies, particularly in the South. So both of these professions have considerable status."

The problem of rising in any profession is greatly intensified by the difficulty of obtaining a good education.

"A Negro child must be exceptional in I.Q. and appearance (or have famous parents) to be accepted in a top-ranking school," a successful doctor said to me ruefully.

I went up to the Urban League of Greater New York to discuss this matter with officials there. They showed me a letter they had received from a leading school advisory service. They had asked which white schools would be likely to accept qualified Negro students. I looked over the list sent them in return and spotted the names of many of the top private schools in the country. Among them were Deerfield Academy, Groton, Loomis, Phillips Exeter, St. Mark's, St. Paul's, Choate, Hotchkiss, Phillips Academy (Andover), Pomfret, the Hill, Lawrenceville, Putney, Abbot, and Westover.

The catch, however, is that so few Negro children are accepted. In the League office I saw a letter sent in 1954 by one of the nation's best-known prep schools (it is on the list mentioned above), reporting that there were three Negroes in the entire school. This was in pre-integration days, but the percentage taken in these high society schools has not risen markedly. It is still too small to solve the educational problems of the Negro.

"And many parents do not wish their children to face the psychological pressure that goes with being the only ones of their race in a given school," a spokesman for the League commented.

"We do accept Negroes," the principal of one of New York's most fashionable girls' private schools told me.

"How it is then that there is not a single one in the school?" I asked.

"Well, only four Negroes have applied in the last three years," she replied. "We accepted two of them, but both decided to go elsewhere."

Their parents did not wish them to be a conspicuous minority. They preferred an all-Negro private school. Unfortunately, there are very few of these. On the elementary-school level some are run in connection with churches. Others are privately owned. One of the best known in the New York area is the Junior Academy of

Brooklyn, which takes students from nursery school through junior high.

"To gain admittance, students must be recommended either by the parent of a child in the school or by a church or one of the recognized organizations, such as Jack and Jill of America or the Business and Professional Women," Mrs. Dorothy M. Bostic, who founded the Academy in the late 1940's, said to me. "We have a waiting list for the earlier grades. Most of our students are the children of professionals."

Tuition in the primary grades is $75.00 a month. But by the fourth grade it is reduced to between $68.00 and $70.00, because the parents have to buy so many books and extra clothing for gym. The school can now accommodate fewer than two hundred students, but will expand when a new building is completed.

The Little Brown Schoolhouse in the Bronx takes two hundred children from the first through the eighth grades, at a tuition of $460 a year.

"Children are recommended by parents of students, by staff members, churches, or the Urban League," Mrs. Helen Meade, director, informed me. "They come from a diversity of backgrounds. Only about 3 per cent are the children of professionals and 5 per cent of white-collar workers."

Psychological and I.Q. tests are given to all the children. Those with emotional difficulties are not rejected. A psychologist gives guidance where needed.

An afternoon program of arts and crafts and games is offered to all the children. As extras, foreign languages, riding, fencing, swimming, and piano lessons are available. There is also a summer camp run in cooperation with the government of Bermuda. The school has been granted the use of an island off the coast of Bermuda during the month of July and students from the Little Brown Schoolhouse can fly over and spend that period there together with Bermudian children. The cost is $300. In August a number of the Bermudian youngsters come to the United States to spend that month at the school's camp at Roxbury, New York.

Another well-known elementary school in New York City is the

Modern School at 539 West 152nd Street. Mildred Johnson is director.

But what comes after elementary school? That is a real problem. Even well-informed parents are not certain of how to find a fine Negro boarding school.

"When parents ask me to recommend a good Negro high school, I don't know what to say," states Mrs. Meade sadly. "I hesitate to recommend a school that is not white administered, because I know it will lack the funds to function well. The problem with Negro education is that most of the schools have to be so underpriced that they cannot give good schooling or even good care."

My informants were able to give me only the following short list of recognized Negro boarding schools:

Palmer Memorial Institute, Sedalia, North Carolina. This is a co-educational school with high academic standing. Students come from all over the country and from Bermuda, Cuba, Liberia, and the British West Indies as well. Most are the children of professionals. Palmer starts with junior high school. It stresses college preparatory courses and a large proportion of the students go on to higher education. The school was founded in 1901. Dr. Charles W. Eliot, president of Harvard University, was first chairman of the board of trustees. Charges for the year are $815.

St. Emma Military Academy, Rock Castle, Virginia. This school has a good military rating, and students come from many states. Boys are taken for the high-school grades only. In addition to the military, St. Emma also offers a complete and practical course in agriculture. Its 1,700-acre campus contains rich farm land. A trade school prepares students for work as auto mechanics, cabinetmakers, and the like. Room and board cost $300, tuition $100, and uniforms $220.

St. Francis de Sales, Rock Castle, Virginia. This is a girls' school for students of high-school age. It is conducted by the Sisters of the Blessed Sacrament and is affiliated with Catholic University of America, Washington, D.C. Each day is begun with holy mass. St. Francis offers college preparatory, business, and general courses. Music instruction is available at $60.00 a year. The cadets from nearby St. Emma Academy join in social activities. The two schools have joint commencement exercises. Room, board, tuition, and general fees are $560, plus $50.00 for uniforms.

St. Frances Academy, 501 East Chase Street, Baltimore, Maryland. This girls' boarding and day school is run by the Oblate Sisters of Providence, a religious community of colored nuns established in Baltimore in 1829. It starts with the ninth grade and offers both a college preparatory and a general course. Charges are $570, with uniforms extra.

By college age the opportunities for good schooling increase. Negroes are taken by almost all the leading white colleges. Again, of course, acceptance is limited to small numbers of outstanding students. But there are also a great many Negro colleges throughout the country. The best known of these is Howard University in Washington, D.C. Founded in 1867, this school graduates about 650 men and women each year. In addition to its excellent scholastic rating, Howard has the highest social rating in Negro society. Other prestige colleges include Fisk University, Nashville, Tennessee; the Atlanta University System, with Morehouse College for men and Spelman College for women, Atlanta, Georgia; Shaw University, Raleigh, North Carolina; Bethune-Cookman College, Daytona Beach, Florida; Hampton Institute, Hampton, Virginia; Morgan College, Baltimore, Maryland; Tuskegee Normal and Industrial Institute, Tuskegee, Alabama; Wilberforce College, Wilberforce, Ohio; and Lincoln University, Lincoln University, Pennsylvania.

As education is essential to social as well as professional advancement, membership in the college fraternities and sororities counts for a great deal.

Alpha Phi Alpha is the biggest Negro college fraternity and has the most prestige. It was started in the early 1900's by eight students at Cornell University, Ithaca, New York. Since then its membership has grown to 25,000. Included are thirty-seven college presidents, eight judges, and five bishops. I am told that more than half the members in the Philadelphia and Greater New York chapters are doctors, dentists, and pharmacists.

The big college sororities, Alpha Kappa Alpha and Delta Sigma Theta, also have considerable social standing. Both of them were founded at Howard University. Delta has 247 chapters. It has a headquarters building in Chicago. There are graduate houses in Washington, D.C., and Birmingham, Alabama, and undergraduate houses on the campuses of the universities of Illinois, Kansas, and Ohio. This sorority has been cited by the American Library Association for its bookmobile and library project.

AKA, which was started in 1908, now has 25,000 members. It has undergraduate chapters in 105 colleges and universities and graduate chapters in 170 cities.

"AKA has given more than $100,000 to N.A.A.C.P. and has contributed more than $350,000 to scholarships," states one of the members proudly.

Education is the decisive factor in a Negro's future, so scholarships are awarded by almost every organization. The Negro Elks, Shriners, and Masons, for example, hold huge affairs at which there are talent contests. The winning Miss Elk or Miss Shrine Temple receives a scholarship. A great many of the debutante balls, too, are given as benefits for education funds.

This brings me to the debut setup. Until fairly recently coming-out parties were for daughters of inner-circle families only. Today a growing number of mass debutante balls give opportunities to many newcomers. In the New York area alone at least six group debut balls are now held each year.

The long pre-debut buildup explained in other chapters is not a part of Negro society life. Subdebutante affairs, for example, are not customary. The nearest thing to them are the parties given by the Jack and Jill Juniors and the "Sweet Sixteen" parties held by many wealthy parents. Socialites maintain that there is less need for an organized subdebutante life, as girls of sixteen are eligible to be debutantes. The eighteen-year age requirement of white society is not carried over.

The influential organizations described earlier rule debutante life. The social clubs, professional associations, fraternities, and sororities give cotillions and determine which girls will be presented. The prestige of the sponsoring group determines the ranking of the ball and of the debutante. The affairs given by the social clubs have the highest status.

"Maneuvering to assure inclusion of a female relative on one of these lists rivals the intrigue of foreign diplomats seeking American financial aid," wrote Gerri Major, associate editor of *Ebony* magazine. "Guest lists, too, are limited; an invitation is a royal command thankfully acknowledged."

About twenty girls are presented each year by the elite Royal Coterie of Snakes in Chicago. The Me-De-So Club of Baltimore selects about fourteen girls a year, the Cotillion Club of Detroit, thirty. The Esquire Club of Cincinnati gives a noted debutante ball, and young women eagerly seek invitations to the cotillions given by the Bachelor-Benedicts of Washington and the Strikers of Mobile, Alabama.

Many individual chapters of the Links and Girl Friends give debut balls with high social standing. The cotillion given by the Los Angeles Links is viewed as the top event of the season. About twenty-five girls are presented each year. The party is held in either the Hotel Statler or the Beverly Hilton, and is always a benefit for Negro causes.

A friend in Washington, D.C., reports that this chapter of the Girl Friends arranges an annual cotillion at which about twenty girls come out. This practice was started in 1957. Although the Girl Friends is the over-all sponsor, other local organizations are invited to present their debutantes at the ball. Each debutante may be brought out by a different club.

More young women are presented in New Orleans than anywhere else. Nonetheless, it is very hard for a girl to become a recognized debutante there. New Orleans society is cliquish and does not welcome newcomers. Members of the inner circle live in the Gentilly section of the city and belong to the top social clubs. There are a great many of these, and each presents the daughters of its members at a ball given during the Mardi Gras.

The Original Illinois Club has the greatest prestige. It is the oldest Negro carnival organization of men to launch debutantes, and its ball is the most sought after. The Young Men's '20's ranks second. Other clubs for men and women include the Original Mikado Club, the Wanderers, Original Les Equinois, and the Mignonettes. I was sent a program of a recent Mardi Gras. It stated that 112 Negro organizations hold balls during the carnival season.

At most of them a king and queen are chosen and debutantes make their bows.

In addition, the Creole Association holds a fiesta at which a mademoiselle and a queen are selected from girls who are descendants of New Orleans' old Creole families.

In other parts of the country small local social groups often give lavish balls. Typical of these are the cotillions held by the exclusive Altruist Club of Roanoke, Virginia, Les Treize of Jacksonville, Florida, and the Smart Set Club of Houston, Texas.

Many chapters of the sororities, AKA, Delta, Sigma Gamma Rho, and Phi Delta Kappa (national sorority of teachers), give debutante balls.

Some of the largest cotillions are put on by the professional organizations. A member of the Brooklyn-New York Business and Professional Women estimates the cost of a recent ball at $50,000. Held in the Grand Ballroom of Brooklyn's Hotel St. George, it was attended by 2,500 guests. The 33 debutantes were aged from sixteen to eighteen. Three of them were awarded $500 scholarships.

How are girls selected for presentation?

They are chosen by the organization giving the ball. To come out at a ranking social-club cotillion, a young woman must be the daughter of a member or of one of his close friends. Each debutante has to be sponsored by someone belonging to the club. She must also be passed by a screening committee.

Most of the girls who are presented at these top affairs come from the old families, or are the children of wealthy and successful parents. These are the people who have close connections with the prestige clubs.

But it is characteristic of Negro society that a girl can be a debutante even if she does not come from a rich or well-known family. This is most likely to happen at those balls given by sororities, fraternities, or professional organizations. Men and women in these groups like to encourage bright and promising youngsters. If a member knows such a child or is introduced to one by friends, her schoolteachers or principal, he may decide to act as her sponsor. The debutantes presented at the Brooklyn-New York

Professional Women's ball, for example, are selected on the basis of "good character, school grades, civic interests."

There are actually cotillions at which no fee at all is charged to the debutante. Her sponsor pays the bills, even buying the girl her gown, gloves, and flowers.

The cost of admission to the major balls varies tremendously. Some ask as little as $2.50 a person. At most affairs the sponsors are expected to take tables. As a rule, supper is not served; there are just setups for liquor.

A number of organizations hire promoters to manage the ball for them on a minimum guarantee-commission basis. The cotillion involved in such cases is almost always a benefit. The debutantes are charged a fee of between $20.00 and $40.00 to help cover the cost of invitations, bouquets, photographs, rehearsals, and pre- and post-ball parties. In addition, their parents are responsible for blocks of ball tickets and are expected to take tables or boxes. One of the most successful of such benefits is put on for the White Plains Community Center by Mrs. Lillian S. Hunter. A recent ball netted $11,000.

No matter who organizes the ball, the pattern is very much the same. A socialite who has attended many cotillions has described to me the way they go: "The ball usually starts with heralds coming out to signal a parade down the dance floor by the National Guard of Honor. This is made up of Negro women of prominence from all over the country. Almost all of the large organizations invite such women to their balls. After the ladies march across the floor, they are seated in a special place of honor. The sponsors then come out, each with a debutante on his arm. At some balls the father accompanies them, too. The presentation ceremony follows. After each girl has been announced and has curtsied, she joins her escort for the formal cotillion figures. The ball then gets under way with dancing and entertainment. As a finale there is a grand march of sponsors, Honor Guard, and debutantes."

The hotels favored for debut balls and other Negro social affairs are the Waldorf-Astoria and the Belmont-Plaza in New York and the St. George in Brooklyn. The Willard is the most popular hotel in Washington, D.C., and the Statler-Hilton and Sheraton Park rank next. In Los Angeles, the Statler and Beverly Hilton are usually chosen, and in Chicago the Morrison.

All-Negro bands play for most of the affairs. Count Basie is the favorite—for those who can afford him. Buddy Walker's Society Orchestra plays for many New York functions, as do Andy Kirk, Reuben Phillips, Cy Oliver, and Mercer Ellington (Duke Ellington's son).

Private debuts retain their popularity with the truly wealthy. One socialite estimates typical party costs at from $2,000 to $5,000. And most seasons there are a few parties with guest lists of 800.

Negro society is just coming into its own. The years ahead can hardly fail to bring a tremendous expansion on the upper economic and social levels. There will be more clubs, more debutante balls, more socialite-sponsored charities; there will be more people leading the kind of life until recently restricted to a small inner circle. As professional opportunities increase, so will the emphasis on status.

CHAPTER XV

Men . . . Men . . . Men

WHEN society's crystal-ball gazers get together, they like to puzzle out the names of those who will make the grade tomorrow. And they almost always agree upon one beautiful young woman, a prominent figure in New York's merchandising world.

The last time I was on such a discussion one Old Guard matron shook her head. "If that girl really wants to make it, she's got to get herself the right kind of husband. Society is a man's world."

This raised a storm of objection from the feminists present. It was promptly pointed out that many of Washington's leading hostesses, such as Perle Mesta and Alice Roosevelt Longworth, are widows, that the best-known member of New York's younger set used to throw parties at which her husband (of that time) walked out.

But as I thought over the socialite's statement, I came to the conclusion that she was quite right in her basic assumption. Despite a few exceptions, society is ruled by men. The most influential organizations are male—the krewes of New Orleans, the german clubs of the South, the Idlewild Club, Piedmont Driving Club, St. Cecilia Society, Allegro Club, to name just a few. The members of these are automatically accepted as real society; in addition, they are considered social arbiters. It is taken as a matter of course that they will select and launch the city's leading debutantes. Most of the highest-ranking city social clubs are made, too—such as the Union, Philadelphia, Somerset, Chicago, Pacific Union, Queen City, Eagle

Lake, and Detroit clubs. I can name only a handful of women's clubs with comparable standing—the Colonoy, Acorn, and Chilton.

Even on the party-giving level, most hostesses are backed up by a husband, who lends the support of his presence, money, and social contacts. The young man who walked out on his wife's parties nonetheless gave her the benefit of his great society name. And I have heard a number of socialites complain bitterly that their husbands will not hear of their going in for heavy entertaining— so they cannot do it.

In general, a woman's position in society depends upon her husband. The *Social Register* board is well aware of this, and treats men a bit more gently. I know of one *Register* family whose son married a young woman of undistinguished origin. His name, and hers, too, now, are listed in the book. This is in sharp contrast to what happened to the daughter of another *Register* family. The girl also married an unknown. In this case, though the parents are still listed, the daughter has been removed.

Women understand this intuitively. The current comeback of society is partly a result of today's emphasis on community life—a natural by-product of the growth of the suburbs. With 147,000,000 Americans living in the suburbs, the typical suburban wife is the typical wife of today. Her home, her children, her social life are more important to her than anything else. Her position in the community means a great deal to her. She has both the incentive and the time to work her way up to a higher social level—provided she has a suitable husband.

A solid marriage to a man of substance is more desirable than it has been since the nineteenth century. If a woman is lucky she has it herself; and she certainly wants it for her daughter.

And so the child is encouraged into a debutante role. Her goal in life, though it is seldom admitted, is to catch a good husband.

Only members of traditional society have always faced this fact openly. The original function of the debut was to present a marriageable girl to all the available, socially acceptable men. Today, when girls of twelve or thirteen are either dating or wishing they were, formal society starts the presentation process earlier. From the very first dancing class, through the subdebutante parties, right up to the climax of the debut itself, the future debutante is given one opportunity after another to meet the "right" kind of boys.

Breaking into such high society functions is of tremendous importance for newcomers. After all, if a Drexel son marries a Smith, their grandchildren will be Drexels—and the Smith connection will be forgotten. Now if the Drexel daughter marries a Smith, making her grandchildren Smiths, the Drexel connection will be lost *unless* the husband is determined to rise in society himself. He can if he wants to. So can his son.

"Even without a Drexel or McCormick connection a man can get a pretty high degree of social acceptance—if he just tries a little," a socialite commented to me. "The man in the Brooks Brothers suit, with a prep-school way of talking, can go everywhere—and often does. No one checks into men's backgrounds too closely. Hostesses are anxious to have presentable extra men, debutantes need escorts and stags for their parties. They can't be too choosy. And even after marriage, charity organizations are always pleased if a woman can attend benefits with a presentable husband, instead of just going to meetings and luncheons alone."

All the families who have been added to society's roster recently have one thing in common: A successful man. In city after city I find that most newcomers break into society via business prominence. The executive in a position of industrial power can usually parlay that to a position of social importance. He controls jobs needed by poor scions of old-line families; he can contribute heavily to charities favored by members of real society; he can hire a press agent and social secretary; he can send his children to prep schools; he can live in the high society style, at the correct address, in the approved kind of house, taking the right kind of vacation, going in for hunting, shooting, and yachting.

But why does he want to? I have been asked this question many times since starting this book. Social life is more important to women than to men, I am told. What does an executive care about dancing classes for the children, debutante parties for the daughters, benefit balls?

A man may not care about such things in themselves. But he may care about becoming a member of society, because of what it can mean to him in business, in politics, and psychologically.

The much-heralded rise of the organization has made it hard for a man to achieve status. A generation ago it was not too difficult for an able and ambitious young man to *be* somebody. He could gain recognition as the owner of the local dry-goods store or the manufacturer of his own brand of cough syrup. Everybody knew who he was. Today, even the most talented man is concealed in the organization. Who can name quickly the heads of such major companies as Aluminum Company of America, International Harvester, Armstrong Cork, or General Aniline? For that matter, I have to consult references before naming the inventor of nylon, Terramycin, or television. What comes to mind quickly are the names of the industrial giants behind them—Du Pont, Pfizer, and Radio Corporation of America.

The sad fact is that organization life deprives a man of a feeling of individual importance. To compensate, he looks for satisfactions in his social life—outside of business. He wants the recognition of the community. So far from scorning his wife's efforts to enter society, he seconds her and even encourages her. The revival of society owes a great deal to the organization man and his unfulfilled dreams.

That is a psychological fact. But I find that it is a hard, cold fact that a position in society is helpful in advancing many careers. Take politics. The days when it was a political necessity for a man to point to a log cabin or shirt-sleeves background are long since over. A candidate now is wiser to remind voters of a heritage of wealth and social position, or, at the very least, a millionaire grandfather.

This is true for major or minor political office in big city and small town alike. Not long ago I ran across a thesis written by a Harvard senior named Charles Ball. In Winchester, Massachusetts, he reported, the contest for selectman found a candidate of Italian origin running against a man of old New England stock. During the course of the campaign it became apparent that the blueblood had the backing of the socially prominent citizens and that they would swing him into office. Luckily the Italian realized in time that he had to fight fire with fire. He began to publicize his family coat of arms, received in Naples in 1337. By making the *Mayflower* descendant appear virtually low class and *nouveau,* he was able to nose out his opponent.

John F. Kennedy comes from a prominent Boston family. Henry Cabot Lodge is a Lodge of the Boston family made a nationwide symbol by the famous doggerel. Averell Harriman and John Hay Whitney are both scions of well-known social families. The late John Foster Dulles had a society background. And the Rockefeller fortune has not handicapped the political or social career of his grandchildren.

"In society today," socialites tell me privately, "Rockefeller is the magic name that opens all doors."

This adulation might have ruined a man politically in another era. Today it is helpful. Many voters seem to think that voting for a rich man and social leader by some strange alchemy gives them caste, too.

This realization makes many a would-be politician eager to become a member of society.

In business, too, social standing is extremely helpful. Employers today are psychologically attuned to valuing a man with society connections. I know a junior executive in a manufacturing plant who was promoted over an equally talented rival when his employer discovered that he was married to a former prominent debutante.

Another young executive confides that he is subjected to considerable pressure by his superior to enroll his children in private school, despite the fact that his $12,000-a-year income makes such schooling almost prohibitive.

"My boss likes to think that he has the type of people working for him who send their children to the right schools," he adds ruefully.

And then there is the more obvious professional advantage: The man with a position in society naturally knows people with money and power. These men are valuable to his firm as customers, clients, or backers. Much business today is done on the golf course, at the country club, and over the lunch table. Executives in seemingly non-social industries have found that membership in exclusive clubs is a great business asset.

"When I want to impress a prospective client, I take him to lunch at the River Club," an executive friend said to me. "In my field, most of the businessmen have never even heard of the River Club. But once they get there and see the atmosphere and notice the kind of service, they realize that it's top drawer. Then they go home and talk about it, and discover that lots of the members are society. And it impresses them."

Today top executives and top society are so intimately entwined that it is hard to tell them apart. The Old Guard is largely made up of the industrial tycoons of yesterday; tomorrow's inner circle will contain those of today.

"I often ask myself," a junior executive told me blithely, "'when business success comes, can a position in society be far behind?'"

CHAPTER XVI

Where Do We Go from Here?

"SOMETIMES I wonder where all this will end," a crack society press agent said to me. "Every day I get phone calls from women who long to become society matrons, mothers who want me to get their daughters presented at cotillions, executives who wish to be built up socially as well as industrially, charity organization officials who are eager to start prestige benefits. Sooner or later everyone's going to be in society. And it won't mean anything at all."

She stopped and thought for a moment. Then she added: "At that point, I guess, it will become the thing *not* to be in society."

I think this press agent goes a bit far with her perverse prediction. But I do believe that it will very soon become the thing for the inner circle *not* to take part in some of the activities that have become characteristic of society during the 1940's and 1950's.

The benefit ball balloon will have to burst. It has been blown up past all reasonable proportions already.

I asked one busy socialite friend how many charity balls she attends.

"During the height of the season I go to at least one a week," she replied. "And once or twice a year I get stuck with benefits three days in a row. It's more wearing than it sounds, too. I serve on a number of ball committees, and so I am planning future benefits while attending current ones."

This woman is more active than most, but it is a rare socialite who can slip through a month without a benefit.

Many members of society would put up with this if the balls were fun when they got there. But most have been expanded until they are little more than high-priced brawls. People in the inner circle like to feel that they know everybody at any social gathering they attend. But no one has 1,000 intimate friends. And that is not an unusual guest list for a benefit. Some are even bigger than that. It has reached the point where a dance for 500 or 600 guests is called "exclusive."

"At many balls you can hardly reach the dance floor—or dance when you get there," comments a society woman darkly. "And as for the food—well, even the best hotel kitchen can hardly serve *la haute cuisine* to hundreds and hundreds of people."

As the balls grow bigger, it gets more expensive to put them on. As they increase in number, the charity organizations are forced into competition with one another. They must attract guests by offering magnificent entertainment, breath-taking decorations, and fabulous door prizes. How can they meet the expenses and still get any benefit from the ball? Most philanthropic groups have come up with the same answer: a commercial sponsor. In theory that should make no difference. But in practice the character of an underwritten ball changes. The sponsor subtly, or not so subtly, plugs his product. Advertising and publicity tie-ins begin to appear. Executives of the firm and their business associates expect and must be given positions on committees.

Once commercialism enters, it takes over. Smaller firms gather around to cash in on this lucrative market. A transportation company, for example, frankly told a newspaper reporter that it uses the *Social Register* as a mailing list, urging socialites to transport guests by bus from pre-benefit parties to the ball and back again, cut rate.

Little remains of the gracious life in the charity ball setup.

Some observers of the social scene, therefore, are given to saying that charity balls will soon be on their way out. Again I cannot quite go along with this. The benefits for charities of marginal importance will probably go under. Many of them were organized to take advantage of the benefit craze. Those going the ball circuit will become more selective. But the major balls have by now become too essential to the charities involved to be allowed to die.

"We receive $30,000 every year from our ball," the official of a leading charity declares. "How could we get along without it? And don't tell me that individual contributions would make up the difference. It just doesn't work that way. The rich people who help us contribute what they can, in addition to attending the ball. And a great many others who would never send a check by mail will come to a party. As for the commercial sponsor, he would not give us the money he spends underwriting the ball. He would simply find another way of spending his advertising and publicity dollars."

This official did not even mention the hidden advantages of holding a ball. For one thing, the publicity brings the beneficiary to the attention of wealthy people. For another, newcomers using charity work as a means of social advancement support those organizations which have a prestige benefit. They contribute both money and hard work.

Quite aside from the charities, executives in many industries would be very reluctant to let the balls go. Take fashion. The benefits have caused a revival of formal dress. They have turned a marginal market for many couturiers into a big one. And the hotels, caterers, florists, dance bands, decorators, stationers, and other firms which service the balls have come to depend upon them for a considerable portion of their income.

The charity ball has become big business, and tremendous efforts will be made to keep it alive.

But I think that even the greatest effort will not succeed in holding the high society group. In time it will become correct for members of the inner circle *not* to go. Some have always limited benefit going to those few Old Guard charities supported by their families and most intimate friends. In a few years most will be doing that.

The balls will then be left to people with money but without the highest society connections. This may kill off some charity balls, as society names have been used as the drawing card to pull in rising socialites. But it is possible that celebrities, political figures, and diplomats will serve as substitutes.

The inner circle will not stop partying. But there will be a reaction to bigness and a swing back to exclusiveness. The number of subscription dances will probably increase. In Philadelphia the private subscription dance has always been a feature of high society life. But in a city such as New York there are surprisingly few. I think there will be more groups on the order of the current New York Assemblies, Leap Year Assembly, Dancers, and the October, Christmas, and April balls. These dances operate on a club basis. A committee invites couples or bachelors and postdebutantes to subscribe. The number of guests a member may bring is strictly limited. In the case of the New York Assemblies, for example, each couple may ask one extra man. The move away from the big balls will naturally lead socialites to form their own groups.

Some of the charity organizations may see the handwriting on the wall in time and salvage the social aspects of the benefit ball by changing it to a debutante cotillion. Members of the inner circle are beginning to complain that there are too many of these already. But they are likely to bring out their daughters at an affair given by a charity they support. And rising socialites can be counted on to flock to any of these ventures.

The number of cotillions given in this country has also grown to the point where the Old Guard is beginning to be more selective. As time passes, they will cling even more closely to private debuts and the Assemblies, St. Cecilia, and Idlewild type of group presentation. But there are not quite enough of these. Members of real society—their children, anyway—are not immune to the national excitement about mass debuts, and yet they wish to remain exclusive. And so some of the hereditary organizations may follow the example of the Society of Mayflower Descendants and the St. Nicholas Society and present daughters of members at their annual dinners.

Despite the tremendous number of debutante cotillions today, I do not see even the slightest sign of a falling off. The saturation point has not yet been reached. Many would-be debutantes are still unable to find room at the existing balls. The number of country-club cotillions will continue to increase. Such coming-out parties are a natural expression of the growing suburban desire for an organized traditional society setup.

Many local chapters of the Junior League will probably copy their sister groups in New York, Stamford, and Baltimore in giving balls for "provisional members of debutante age." And service leagues will follow suit.

In both city and suburb a raft of associations and clubs, which heretofore have given daughters of members short shrift, will take to presenting them as debutantes. Some professional organizations will begin launching debutantes. The American Institute of Architects is already doing just that.

And the future will surely bring even more group presentations. Some will be started by enterprising mothers as solutions to a pressing problem; others by hardheaded businessmen and women as money-making ventures.

Many of these new debutante cotillions will be more glamorous and exotic than any of the past. Foreign balls are likely to become more of a part of American debutante life. It is only good common sense for foreign governments to encourage such affairs as a way of attracting moneyed tourists. Travel agencies, air lines, and steamship companies will naturally give them a publicity boost. I have already described the Versailles Ball, started in 1958. The following year, a London-American Debutante Ball was inaugurated. And in the summer of 1960 American debutante balls were held in both Rome and Vienna for the first time. As I glance over the names of the committees for the Rome Ball I note that the affair is supported by both old and new society.

When I started this book, I was asked many times if I planned to include the "society of accomplishment." This term, originated by Igor Cassini, is used to describe men and women who have done something to merit social approval, instead of (or in addition to) being born into a family with an old name.

These people are in my book; they are at the very heart of it. Some members of the "society of accomplishment" feel overshadowed by the heavily publicized celebrities in the group. They point out that the public at large believes the set to be made up only of movie stars, baseball players, and television personalities. Those men and women who have advanced in industry and in the arts through their own efforts want a different type of social approval.

And they often look back to the dreams and ambitions of their youth. There was always a "first family" in town, looked up to by everyone, leading a vaguely understood life of charity works, exclusive clubs, and debutante balls. When success comes, many people see it in these high society terms. They want to make theirs a "first family." Some of them, as I have shown, succeed.

In coming years I think that the base of society will continue to broaden. Acceptance by high society will remain the status goal of successful men and women for many years to come. The Old Guard will, of course, go right on resisting newcomers. They would like to keep the status quo (of 1890, if that were possible). Society will expand most, therefore, on the level just outside the inner circle. People who advance to that point will lead a life all but indistinguishable from that of the Old Guard. And a few families will slip inside the wall from time to time.

It will not be easy for them, but many will make the effort.

"I may never be fully accepted," a wealthy, self-made executive confided in me. "But my children will be. By the time they've grown up, no one will even remember what a struggle it was!"

The Guidebook

A DIRECTORY OF THE RIGHT SCHOOLS

THE NATION'S DEBUTANTE BALLS

ASSOCIATION OF THE
JUNIOR LEAGUES OF AMERICA, INC.

A Directory of the Right Schools

THIS directory lists the schools which members of society accept as the "right" schools. I have compiled it on the basis of interviews with socialites from major cities, with social secretaries, and with school advisory services. I also studied society pages of newspapers from all over the United States to confirm my findings.

Some of the outstanding schools in the country will not be found on this list. A school can be excellent as far as scholastic rating goes, and still not be attended by members of society. And that is the prerequisite for inclusion in this guide.

I wrote to the schools themselves to obtain facts and figures. Tuition, room, and board charges are the most recent available—in most cases 1959.

The directory is organized in four sections: junior boarding schools, girls' schools, coeducational schools, and boys' schools. Each section is arranged first by states and then by cities, in alphabetical order.

JUNIOR BOARDING SCHOOLS

MASSACHUSETTS

Bement School, Deerfield

This coeducational school takes boarders from the ages of six through fourteen. Day students are accepted, too, from nursery school age on. Children are prepared for (and are accepted by) such noted schools as Andover, Deerfield, Foxcroft, Masters, Phillips Exeter, and Emma Willard. As for sports, skiing is stressed, and students in the higher grades take a five-day mountaineering trip every year. Tuition, room, and board cost $2,100. Katharine F. Bartlett and Mary Harriman Drexler are co-directors.

Eaglebrook School, Deerfield

This boys' school goes from the fourth grade through the ninth. Graduates favor Lawrenceville, Andover, the Hill and Deerfield. Skiing is popular here, too. Tuition, room, and board: $2,200.

Fay School, Southborough

Established in 1866, this is the oldest of the pre-prep schools. Boys are prepared for St. Paul's, St. Marks, Deerfield and other top schools. Riding is a popular sport. Boarding students pay $2,300, with about $300 for extras. A number of day students are accepted too, and tuition for them is $875. A good number of scholarships are awarded.

Fessenden School, West Newton

Students at this boys' school range in age from eight to fourteen. There are about fifteen boys in the three lowest grades. Younger boys have their own cubicles in dormitories (a popular prep school practice). Graduates go on to St. Paul's, Choate, Andover, Proctor, and other prep schools. Emphasizing athletics, the school has its own golf course. Cost is $2,100 for full-time boarding students, $2,000 for those who live in only five days a week. Day students are accepted as well. Tuition for them rises from $550 in the third grade to a high of $900. Two full and fifteen partial scholarships are offered. There is a summer day school as well.

Dana Hall School, Wellesley

This is the separate junior school connected with the well-known Dana Hall School. It is for girls between the ages of eleven and thirteen. The majority of the "graduates" go on to the senior school. Tuition, room, and board cost $1,975. Most students, however, attend by the day, paying a tuition charge of $875.

New York

Malcolm Gordon, Garrison

Boys are prepared for Andover, Episcopal High, the Hill, Kent, St. Marks, Groton, and others. Hockey is stressed in athletics. Tuition, room, and board: $2,000. David C. Gordon, son of the founder, is headmaster.

GIRLS' SCHOOLS

Alabama

Brooke Hill School, Birmingham

This is a small day school for about 200 girls from the age of ten through high school. Most go on to Hollins, Smith, Sweet Briar, Sophie Newcomb, and the southern state universities. Tuition ranges from $475 to $512, depending on the grade.

California

Anna Head School, Berkeley

Graduates of this well-known day school are admitted to the University of California without entrance examinations. Girls can go from first grade all the way through high school. Tuition rises from $500 in the lower grades to $650 in the higher. But sisters of students get a discount. About fifteen boarding students are accepted, at a charge of $1,900.

The Bishop's School, La Jolla

Bishop's takes 240 boarding and day students from the seventh grade on. An Episcopal school, it was established in 1909 by the first Bishop of Los Angeles, with the financial aid of Ellen and Virginia Scripps. The La Jolla climate, which averages sixty-eight degrees both winter and summer, is stressed in the catalog. A students' committee for social service raises funds for charities. One foreign student attends Bishop's each year. Going the other way, arrangements are made to have a number of the American students live abroad with foreign families in the summer. Tuition, $800; plus room and board, it comes to $2,200. One full and 21 partial scholarships are offered.

Marlborough School, Los Angeles

Marlborough is the big society school of the area and future debutantes are conspicuous in the student body. Girls range in age from eleven to eighteen. The school, founded in 1889, is Episcopal by tradition, although members of other faiths are accepted. Tuition: $850 (in 1958).

Katharine Branson School, Ross

This is usually described as a San Francisco school, although it is located eighteen miles outside of the city. The students go into San Francisco to take advantage of the symphony, theater, and other cultural activities there. Katharine Branson has an excellent scholastic reputation. The gifted student is encouraged to do work enabling her to enter advanced courses in college. Graduates go on to the big eastern colleges as well as those nearer home. The 80-odd boarding and 68 day students range in age from twelve to eighteen. Boarding students pay $2,500; day students, $850.

CONNECTICUT

Miss Porter's School, Farmington

When the word "finishing school" is mentioned, most people think of Miss Porter's. It was founded for just that purpose in 1843 by Miss Sarah Porter. She "finished" twenty girls at $200 a year, with such extra charges as $50.00 for piano lessons and $5.00 for laundry. For nearly a hundred years no effort was made to prepare girls for college. They were prepared for debuts instead. And Farmington was known as the "Country Club." Today that has changed, and a good education can be had at Miss Porter's. College preparatory subjects are required and most graduates go on to college. Music and domestic science remain as electives. The school is directed now by Mr. and Mrs. Hollis S. French. Mr. French, a former teacher at St. Mark's School, came to Miss Porter's in 1954.

Miss Porter's enrolls 220 girls between the ages of fourteen and eighteen. Alumnae are called "Ancients." Tuition, room, and board: $2,500. Riding adds $160 to the yearly bill. Those who keep a horse pay $80.00 a month for its upkeep. There are 15 partial scholarships.

Rosemary Hall, Greenwich

This is another extremely fashionable school for girls between the ages of twelve and eighteen. It was founded in 1890. Riding is the sport most emphasized. Graduates go on to the top women's colleges—Wellesley, Smith, Vassar. The school takes 100 day students, charging them $1,000 plus $300 in specified extras. An equal number of boarding students are enrolled, paying $2,700 plus $300. Alice E. McBee is headmistress.

Kent School, Kent

In the autumn of 1960 this famous boys' school will admit girls for the first time. "It should be clearly understood that the project does not make Kent coeducational," says the catalogue.

An annex will be built on a 600-acre farm five miles away from the boys' campus. For two years there will be no mixed classes. Thereafter some honors courses will be coed. The girls' annex will have its own faculty, which will be half women. In 1960 fifty high-school freshmen and fifty sophomores will be admitted. One new class will be admitted each year until the full four-year high school is completed, with a total enrollment of two hundred.

Kent's famous "self-help" program, which enables the school to base tuition on a family's ability to pay, will be applied to the girls. They will get up at 6:05 A.M., make their beds, clean the dormitories and classrooms, wash the dishes, and mow lawns.

Kent's rector and headmaster, Reverend John O. Patterson, backed the plan of allowing girls to enter the school. "Men have to work effectively with women," he told *Time* magazine. "Women are people as much as men."

Westover School, Middlebury

Westover is yet another of Connecticut's socially prominent girls' boarding schools. More liberal than most of its kind, it stresses community service. Rose Dyson, the director of admissions, has been quoted as saying: "These are the girls who will have the time and funds to serve their community, and we want them to realize their obligations as soon as possible."

In addition to sewing and knitting for the poor, the girls do hospital work, visit institutions for blind, deaf, or crippled children, and raise funds for charities by waiting on table and putting on plays.

A religious school, there is daily chapel service. Westover takes 175 girls, from the age of fourteen on. Tuition, room, and board run to $2,650. Outlay for uniforms is $250 in the first year. From then on, one new day and one new evening uniform a year are required.

The Ethel Walker School, Simsbury

This is one of the "rightest" of the right schools, and debutantes are numerous. Riding, hockey, and tennis are all stressed. There is an indoor riding ring. A stable of horses is maintained, and girls can board their own horses. Charge for a stall is $85.00 a month.

The 167 girls range in age from thirteen to eighteen. In most cases four girls share a room. Charges are high, with tuition, room, and board billed at $3,000 plus $400 for uniforms and $250 for riding. Fifteen partial scholarships are given. Isabel Ferguson is the new headmistress.

DISTRICT OF COLUMBIA (Washington, D.C.)

Mount Vernon Seminary, 2100 Foxhall Road

This conservative school stresses social service and community responsibility. It has both boarders and day scholars, starting with the age of thirteen. Tuition comes to $850; boarding students pay $2,700. Mount Vernon Junior College, one of the socially favored junior colleges, is the senior part of this school. Tuition is the same as in the seminary.

ILLINOIS

Roycemore School, Evanston

Also conservative in its teaching methods, this day school takes girls from the age of three and a half, and goes all the way through high school. Boys are accepted in the nursery school only. There are 170 girls in the school and 20 boys. Tuition rises from $400 in the nursery school to $950 by senior year in high school.

IOWA

St. Katharine's School, Davenport

An Episcopal Church school, St. Katharine's was established by the trustees of Griswold College in 1884. By far the largest number of its students are in the elementary school grades. Enrollment totals 140 girls. Although some boarding students are accepted from the age of eight on, St. Katharine's is primarily a day school. Tuition rises progressively from $200 in nursery school to $700 from tenth grade on. Adding room and board brings the bill to $1,800.

LOUISIANA

Louise S. McGehee School, New Orleans

This is a progressive day school—but one that is attended by girls from many of the old families. It is located in the Garden District of the city. About 250 girls from the fifth grade on are enrolled. More than half of the graduates go on to New Orleans' own Sophie Newcomb College. Randolph-Macon and Hollins are also favored. Tuition: $510 to $610.

MARYLAND

The Bryn Mawr School, Baltimore

Originally this was a prep school for Bryn Mawr College, but now graduates go on to any of the big colleges. It is a country day school, enrolling 565 girls from the ages of four to eighteen. Tuition ranges from $475 in the first grade to $750 from fifth grade on.

Garrison Forest School, Garrison

This socially approved school is located in hunting country, twelve miles north of Baltimore. Riding is, naturally, a most popular sport. Students who ride well enough may hunt with the elite Green Spring Valley Hunt. There is an annual horse show, as well as a "little show" for beginners. A service league prepares the girls for community responsibility. Uniforms are worn

Only two off-campus weekends a year are allowed. The 170 day students range in age from ten to eighteen, and the 120 boarding students from thirteen to eighteen. Tuition for the day students mounts from $600 to $725. Boarding students pay $2,600, plus $250 for riding lessons. Jean Gilmor Marshall and Nancy Jenkins Offult are headmistresses.

Oldfields School, Glencoe

Oldfields is a very small school with an intimate family atmosphere. It was started in 1867 by Mrs. John Sears McCulloch, an intrepid woman with an invalid husband and eight children.

Enrollment is limited to eighty girls of high-school age. The student-teacher ratio is eight to one. The school maintains its own stables. Qualified riders may hunt with the society-favored Elkridge-Harford Hunt Club. Tuition, room, and board cost $2,800. There are three partial scholarships. Duncan McCulloch, Jr., is headmaster.

The Duchess of Windsor, a noted graduate, describes the school in detail in her autobiography:

"'Gentleness and courtesy are expected of the girls at all times,' was posted on the door of every room in the dormitory. Even the two basketball teams were called 'Gentleness' and 'Courtesy.'"

The Duchess played guard for "Gentleness." The rules of the school were strict, she recalls. The girls were not allowed to write to boys or to get letters from them. Only two weekends home a year were allowed. Similar weekend rules still exist at many of the girls' schools.

St. Timothy's School, Stevenson

"St. Tim's," as it is called, is one of society's favorite schools. Founded in 1882, the school over the years has taught some of society's big names. The Duchess of Windsor states in her book that in her day most of the girls in her set went either to St. Tim's or Oldfields. This is still true.

It has a campus of breath-taking beauty—220 acres of rolling fields and woods. Riding is a most popular sport.

Miss Ella R. Watkins, headmistress, describes the school as in "the middle range of being strict." Freshmen and sophomores are allowed two weekends off campus a year; juniors may take three, and seniors four. But in general the discipline is much more relaxed than it used to be—at St. Tim's and at most schools. Routine rules are maintained through an honor system. Uniforms still are worn.

The school takes about 120 girls of high-school age. Tuition, room, and board are $2,700 plus $200 for uniforms.

MASSACHUSETTS

Abbot Academy, Andover

This old school, established in 1829, is located twenty-three miles north of Boston. Many daughters, granddaughters, and great-granddaughters of alumnae are now enrolled. The school takes 180 boarding and 45 day students, ranging in age from thirteen to eighteen. Music instruction is excellent; professionals teach skiing and skating. Cost is $2,250 for boarding students, $800 for day students. There are 31 partial scholarships. Mary Hinckley Crane is principal.

The Winsor School, Boston

Parents of Boston's future debutantes favor this day school for girls between the ages of ten and eighteen. It has an enrollment of 325. In teaching, this school used to be described as rigid, but by today it has considerably modified its method. Most graduates move on to Radcliffe, Smith, and Vassar. Tuition rises from $800 to $950.

Beaver Country Day School, Chestnut Hill

Beaver is one of the most famous of the old progressive schools. It was founded after World War I by a group of liberal-minded parents who wanted a progressive school near Boston. They asked Eugene Randolph Smith, who had developed the Park School in Baltimore, to establish a school in Chestnut Hill. Over the years Beaver has continued to be a leader in progressive education. A social-welfare committee encourages the students to take their place in the community. The school enrolls 420 girls from eight to nineteen years of age. Tuition goes from $650 in fourth grade to $950 by the ninth. There is also a summer day camp, costing $204.

Brimmer and May School, Chestnut Hill

This school, formed by the merger of the Brimmer and May schools, is extremely popular with Boston's debutante set. It is a country day school for girls from nursery school through high school. Boys are admitted to the first grades, but very few attend. Tuition rises from $325 to $800. A number of scholarships are available. There is also an outdoor summer school. A summer day camp, costing $200, is run by the school.

Concord Academy, Concord

The enrollment at this well-known school has doubled in the last ten years, and it now takes 220 students from sixth grade on. The admissions office claims that it turns away two out of every three applicants. Smith and Radcliffe are favored by graduates. Tuition, room, and board cost $2,850; tuition for day students is $1,100. Mrs. Livingston Hall is headmistress.

Walnut Hill School, Natick

This old (1893) boarding and day school was originally founded to prepare girls for Wellesley. Now, though, graduates go on to many other colleges as well. Walnut Hill takes only 140 boarders and 40 day students, ranging in age from thirteen to eighteen. Tuition, room, and board come to $2,100; tuition alone is $825.

Miss Hall's School, Pittsfield

The 70-acre campus is situated on the banks of the Housatonic River in the Berkshire Hills. A woodland park and a pond used for skating are on the grounds. Professional instruction in skiing is offered. The curriculum makes special provision for individual research projects for gifted students. There is an active community-service program. Committees of students work with the hospitals, the Coolidge Home for Crippled Children, the Visiting Nurse Association, United Community Fund, and Girls' Club. Both boarding and day students—about 150 in all—range in age from thirteen to eighteen. Tuition is $975; plus room and board, it comes to $3,000. Elizabeth M. Fitch is headmistress.

Dana Hall Schools, Wellesley

Known for art and music instruction, this school attracts students from many states and from some foreign countries as well. Riding is a popular sport, and there is both an indoor and an outdoor riding ring. Tuition is $950 for day students. Boarding students pay $2,500. A maximum monthly allowance of $25.00 is suggested. Twelve scholarships are offered.

This section of the school is for girls of high-school age. As has been noted in the section on junior boarding schools, there is also a separate Junior School for girls between the ages of eleven and thirteen.

At the other end of the educational scale is Pine Manor Junior College, which is also a division of the Dana Hall Schools. Students at this socially-favored junior college live in small houses, each taking between ten and twenty girls. In two of the houses only French is spoken, and there are French and Spanish dining rooms. Music, art, drama, dance, child education, and riding are stressed.

MICHIGAN

Kingswood School, Cranbrook, Bloomfield Hills

This is the girls' school in the Cranbrook school system which also includes the Cranbrook School for boys and Brookside School, a coed elementary school. All of them are run by the Cranbrook Foundation. George G. Booth, multimillionaire newspaper publisher and patron of the arts, financed the creation of the Foundation in 1926. It is named after the Booth ancestral home in England. Cranbrook includes the three schools: the Christ Church, Cranbrook; the Cranbrook Academy of Art, and the Cranbrook Institute of Science. Four of the Cranbrook institutions (excluding Brookside and Christ Church) were designed by Eliel Saarinen, the world-famous architect. Saarinen was awarded the gold medal of the New York Architectural League for his work.

All three schools are able to use the facilities of the Art and Science Institutes. They are affiliated with the Episcopal Church but are non-sectarian. Kingswood has 195 day students, ranging in age from eleven to eighteen, and eighty-five boarders in the over-thirteen age bracket. The cost is $1,100 to day students; $2,300 to boarding students. Fifteen partial scholarships are offered. There is also a summer day camp, costing $100.

MISSOURI

Mary Institute, St. Louis

This excellent country day school has a nationwide reputation. Gifted children are given special attention and may take an accelerated course. An outdoor theater encourages students with dramatic inclinations.

Graduates go on to such top eastern colleges as Smith, Vassar, and Wellesley. Ronald Beasley, the headmaster, was formerly in charge of the history department at Groton. There are more than 550 girls ranging in age from four to eighteen. The tuition rises from $475 to $850. There are twenty-one full scholarships and nine partial ones. A summer session is offered to the older girls at a cost of $150.

NEW JERSEY

Kent Place School, Summit

This school takes 310 day and 50 boarding students on its semirural 27-acre campus. Day students start at kindergarten age, boarders at eleven. Riding is a popular sport. Tuition rises from $450 in first grade to $975 by eleventh. Boarding students are charged $2,350.

NEW YORK

The Berkeley Institute, 181 Lincoln Place, Brooklyn

This well-known day school, founded in 1886, draws many of its students from the old Brooklyn families. Although generally considered a girls' school, Berkeley is coeducational for the first six grades. It provides a classic, conservative curriculum, preparing students for the big eastern colleges. Enrollment totals 120 boys and 270 girls. Tuition mounts from $380 to $775. There are four full and 36 partial scholarships. Helen Burtt Mason is headmistress.

Packer Collegiate Institute, 170 Joralemon Street, Brooklyn

Packer's solid reputation in Brooklyn dates back to 1845. This "girls'" school also accepts boys for the first few grades. Girls can continue through high school and through junior college as well. There are more than 480 students in the elementary and high school, about 65 in the junior college. Tuition begins at $425 and goes to $800. Paul David Shafer is head.

The Masters School, Dobbs Ferry

Often called "Dobbs," this school has a 94-acre campus in a pleasant suburb near New York City. The enrollment consists of 220 boarding students and 90 day students. Graduates go on to such fashionable junior colleges as Briarcliff or Bradford or to the big women's colleges. Tuition for day students is $1,250; plus room and board, costs come to $2,750 (1958). Elizabeth Brooke Cochran is head.

The Brearley School, 610 East Eighty-third Street, New York City

Known throughout the East for its high scholastic standards, Brearley offers many opportunities to the gifted child. It is particularly suitable for the bright child who is stimulated by competition. Although many students do make debuts, Brearley is the one of New York's fashionable day schools most frequently recommended to families not planning to have a daughter travel the debutante road.

A student body of 560 girls goes from kindergarten through high school. Graduates go on to the top women's colleges: Bryn Mawr, Radcliffe, Smith, etc. There is no boarding department, but the school does sometimes arrange for out-of-town girls to board with private families. Tuition starts at $650 for kindergarten and rises progressively to $1,150 by seventh grade. Jean Fair Mitchell is head.

The Chapin School, 100 East End Avenue, New York City

Chapin is still described in one handbook as a school that provides a "liberal education as well as training in the social graces." Its student body includes many of society's "big names." A large number of debutantes have Chapin diplomas. Students start in the first grade and can continue through high school. Enrollment totals 440. Uniforms are required. Graduates frequently move on to Smith, Wheaton, Radcliffe, and other big women's colleges: Tuition: $600 to $1,100.

Convent of the Sacred Heart, 1 East Ninety-first Street, New York City

This is one of the many convents of the Sacred Heart throughout the country. It enrolls 240 girls, aged from five to eighteen. Tuition goes from $300 to $600. Reverend Mother Margaret Shea is the Superior. Another of these well-known convent schools is at Noroton, Connecticut.

Dalton Schools, 108 East Eighty-ninth Street, New York City

Dalton is a famous progressive day school—one of the few of its genre to attract a society clientele. Dalton is coed from nursery school until high school. From then on it is just for girls. The student body is made up of 370 girls and 210 boys. Tuition climbs from $600 to $1,100.

Miss Hewitt's Classes, 45 East Seventy-fifth Street, New York City

This fashionable day school is favored by many wealthy New Yorkers. Emphasis is on art and music. The enrollment consists of 205 day students from nursery school through high school. There are also 20 boarders. Graduates go on to the junior colleges, such as Sweet Briar and Briarcliff, or to the big women's schools. Tuition for day students mounts from $450 in nursery school to $1,150 from seventh grade on. Boarders add $1,400 to tuition charges for a five-day week and $1,700 for a full week. Mrs. Lowell R. Comfort is the head.

The Lenox School, 170 East Seventieth Street, New York City

This small school takes 185 day students from the ages of six to eighteen. Tuition ranges from $600 to $1,150. Dr. Cecily Cannan Selby, formerly on the faculty at M.I.T. and Cornell Medical College, has just been made head. She replaces Miss Olivia Green, who was headmistress for thirty of the forty-three years the school has been in existence.

The Nightingale-Bamford School, 20 East Ninetieth Street, New York City

Nightingale-Bamford developed from private classes started by Frances N. Nightingale in 1906. Enrollment now totals 284. The girls range in age from five to eighteen. Tuition starts at $550 and goes to $1,150. Edna Hill Robillard is headmistress.

The Spence School, 22 East Ninety-first Street, New York City

The school was started in 1892 by Miss Clara Spence. The finishing-school reputation clung to it for many years. It now does prepare girls for college. All of its graduates go on to college, or at least junior college. A school with a most pleasant atmosphere, Spence tries to teach manners as well as the standard curriculum. Although Miss Barbara Colbron, the head, maintains that not more than half of the girls are debutantes, most New Yorkers view Spence as a debutante school. The enrollment is 315. Girls go from kindergarten through high school. Tuition begins at $550 and rises to $1,150. There are three full and 26 partial scholarships.

Marymount Secondary School, Tarrytown

This is one of the many Marymount schools. Sister schools can be found in New York City, New York; Arlington, and Richmond, Virginia; Los Angeles, Santa Barbara, and Palos Verdes, California; and in Quebec, Rome, Paris, London, Barcelona, and Colombia. The schools are under the direction of the Religious of the Sacred Heart of Mary. This school takes 130 boarding students and 70 day students from the ages of eleven to eighteen. There is also a lower school for children from kindergarten through the sixth grade. Tuition costs $650; tuition, room, and board come to $1,700.

Emma Willard School, Troy

In 1814, Emma Willard, a pioneer in women's education, founded this now-famous boarding school. Science courses, the equal or superior of those then being taught in the men's colleges, were offered from the start. The school has always been known for its high academic standards, and is viewed as a top-notch college preparatory school. Graduates go on to Vassar, Mount Holyoke, Wells, and other big women's colleges. Riding is the popular sport, and good riders may hunt with the Old Chatham Hunt. There is an active social-service program aiding the community and raising funds for national and international relief projects. Enrollment totals 290 boarding and 40 day students of high-school age. Tuition, room, and board come to $2,700. Day students pay $600. Anne Wellington is headmistress.

North Carolina

Salem Academy, Winston-Salem

This school derives from the Salem Female Academy founded in 1772. It added a boarding department in 1802. The school shares some facilities with Salem College but is a separate entity. There are 94 boarding students and 30 day students of high-school age. Graduates go on to the leading southern colleges, such as Hollins, Duke, and Randolph-Macon, and to some eastern schools as well. One handbook comments that the school attracts "daughters of the more forward-looking families of the South." Tuition is $700; adding room and board brings charges to $1,650.

Ohio

The following two schools were selected as "the" schools by a leading debutante:

Hathaway Brown School, Cleveland

Located in Cleveland's fashionable Shaker Heights, this school is tops socially as well as academically. It takes 430 day students from the ages of four to eighteen, and 40 boarding students of high school age. Most of the boarders have their own rooms. Uniforms are required. Graduates tend to go East to college. Tuition for day students rises from $525 in first grade to $800 from ninth grade on; boarders pay $2,300. Anne Cutter Coburn is the head.

Laurel School, Cleveland

Laurel is also in Shaker Heights. It had its beginnings in a group organized by Miss Jennie Prentice in her own home in 1896. It now takes 425 girls from nursery school through high school. The high school also has 45 boarding students. Boys are admitted to the nursery school and kindergarten only. Tuition ranges from $350 to $750. Boarding students pay $2,000.

OKLAHOMA

Holland Hall School, Tulsa

This school was established in 1922 when Tulsa's wealthy families began to clamor for a good school to prepare their daughters for college. Originally a boarding school, it became a day school in 1950. Graduates go on to such colleges as Mills, Wellesley, Swarthmore, and Briarcliff. Girls attend from the age of four right through high school. Boys are admitted to the earliest grades only (up to the age of eleven). Tuition: $300 to $600.

PENNSYLVANIA

The Baldwin School, Bryn Mawr

Baldwin was founded in 1888 to prepare girls for Bryn Mawr. By now, though, graduates go on to any of the big colleges. Academic standards are high. Students go in to nearby Philadelphia for concerts and other cultural events. Chapel is required. A service league gives the girls an understanding of social problems.

Uniforms are required during school hours. Off-campus weekends are limited to three a year. Baldwin's enrollment totals 148 boarding students and 378 day students. The day students can go from kindergarten straight through high school; boarding students must be at least thirteen years old. Tuition rises from $360 in kindergarten to $885 by tenth grade. Adding room and board brings charges to $2,215 for the first two years; $2,250 thereafter. The school advises parents to limit spending money to $6.00 a month for younger girls, $10.00 to $15.00 for older girls. Rosamond Cross is headmistress.

The Shipley School, Bryn Mawr

This fashionable sixty-five-year-old school has many Main Line family names on its enrollment list. It, too, offers kindergarten through high school to day students, and has 390 students in that division. Boarding school starts at the age of fourteen, and there are over one hundred boarding students. Graduating classes number about sixty. Being near to Philadelphia, students can take advantage of its cultural opportunities. They can also attend some lectures at Bryn Mawr College, which is just across the road. Tuition starts at $450 in nursery school and rises to $930 by sixth grade. Plus room and board, charges come to $2,750. There are three full and 29 partial scholarships. Margaret Bailey Speer is headmistress.

The Agnes Irwin School, Wynnewood

A country day school for girls between the ages of four and eighteen, Agnes Irwin is located in one of Philadelphia's most fashionable suburbs. Such names as Biddle, Dorrance, and Strawbridge are to be found on the board of directors. Founded in 1869, Agnes Irwin is a conservative school. It prepares students for art school and junior colleges as well as college. Enrollment totals 380. Uniforms are required from fourth grade on. Tuition starts at $500 and mounts to $950. There are 27 partial scholarships. Three scholarships are given to daughters of alumnae. Mrs. Grier Bartol is headmistress.

SOUTH CAROLINA

Ashley Hall, Charleston

This popular southern school, headed by Caroline Pardue, prepares girls for southern colleges and for some of the big eastern schools as well. It uses one of the beautiful old (1816) houses for which Charleston is famous. The fountain-filled gardens are spacious and lovely. Riding is a popular sport. Girls learn fashion designing and sewing under the direction of Mrs. J. Trapier Jersey. There is an annual fashion show at which each girl taking the course models three outfits she has made herself. Chapel services are held daily, and church attendance is required (church to be selected by parents).

Primarily a day school, it has 340 day students ranging in age from six to eighteen. There is also a boarding department for girls from twelve to eighteen, in which 90 girls are enrolled. Tuition rises from $375 to $475. Boarders pay $1,700.

TEXAS

The Hockaday School, Dallas

Hockaday is one of the country's high-ranking girls' schools. It was established in 1813 by Miss Ela Hockaday at the request of a group of parents who wanted to have their daughters prepared for the eastern colleges. It is due to move soon to a new 100-acre campus north of Dallas. A new school costing $3,000,000 will be built. At that time, school authorities claim, teaching of foreign languages will be started in the primary grades and there will be greater emphasis on art, music, and drama.

There are nearly 380 day students, starting with the first grade, and 120 boarders. Tuition climbs from $600 in first grade to $950 in high school. Room and board add $1,650 to the tuition rate. Dr. Bernard D. Shea is headmaster.

Radford School for Girls, El Paso

This well-known day and boarding school is situated at an elevation of 3,722 feet in a mountain pass on the outskirts of El Paso. The school catalogue apprises parents of the climate—331 days a year of sunshine. School work is planned to allow students two hours off during the sunniest part of the day. In addition, many classes are held in an outdoor patio. Camping and riding are popular student activities. The school is noted for its excellent instruction in foreign languages. There are 180 day students, from five-and-a-half years of age on up, and 70 boarders aged eight or over. Heavily endowed by Mr.

and Mrs. George Radford, the school is able to charge one of the lowest tuition rates in the country. Tuition costs $250 in first grade, $325 in high school. Boarders pay $1,250.

St. Mary's Hall, San Antonio

St. Mary's is one of the oldest girls' schools in Texas, which does not make it old by eastern standards. It was founded in 1879 by Bishop R. W. B. Elliott, and the religious influence is still strong. Students take advantage of San Antonio cultural events. Outdoor swimming and riding are popular sports. An annual school horse show is held. Uniforms are worn from third grade on. For everyday this consists of a dark blue or white skirt, a white middy with black tie, and saddle shoes with dark blue or white socks. For special occasions the uniform is white with purple tie and cap.

Day students are between six and eighteen years old and pay tuition of $450 in the lower grades, $650 in the upper. Boarding students are accepted from the age of ten. They pay $1,900. Two out-of-school weekends a semester are allowed. The school suggests that parents deposit $450 to cover expenses.

VIRGINIA

St. Agnes Episcopal School, Alexandria

This boarding and day school is popular with service and State Department families. There are more than 350 day students, from five to eighteen years old, paying between $350 (first grade) and $600 (high school). There are also 30 boarding students starting with the age of eleven, paying $1,700 for seven days a week; $1,550 for five. Boys are admitted to kindergarten and the first two grades. Then most of them go on to St. Stephen's School.

Chatham Hall, Chatham

Chatham Hall is one of society's favorite schools, with girls coming from 30 states. As the student body is small—only 165 boarding and 10 day students—applications are made years in advance. The school claims a long waiting list. Chatham Hall has developed from a small southern finishing school, but today most graduates do go on to such schools as Smith and Vassar. It is situated on 350 acres in the Piedmont section of Virginia. And, as might be expected, riding is a major activity. The school has its own stable, with 28 horses. Riders participate in Virginia horse shows.

Tuition, room, and board are $2,400, with riding an almost essential extra at $100 a semester. Parents are urged to limit allowances from $8.00 to $12.00 a month. The Reverend William W. Yardley is rector of this Episcopal church school.

The Madeira School, Greenway

Although it is actually located in Greenway, Virginia, across the river from Washington, D.C., this school is usually described as a Washington school. It is often called "Miss Madeira's," a throwback to the days of its founder. Its student body contains the cream of the future debutante crop. Miss Allegra Maynard, the director, claims that the school can take only one out of every four applicants.

Madeira has a boarding department with 150 students and a country day school with 75. Girls range in age from fourteen to eighteen. As at many of the fashionable girls' schools, riding is a most popular sport, even though it adds an extra $350 to the bill. Boarding students pay $3,000; day students, $850. There are seven full and nine partial scholarships.

The school is conservative in its teaching methods and many graduates go on to Vassar, Smith, and Wellesley.

Foxcroft School, Middleburg

Viewed as the most exclusive boarding school in the country, socialites will do almost anything to get in. The school's claim that four out of five applicants are turned away is never disputed. Only 122 girls in all are admitted.

"It's for the very, very rich," comments one society matron, who is only very rich.

Ability to ride is almost an entrance requirement. The students themselves own 20 out of the 40 horses in the school's stables. Each owner pays $95.00 a month for the animal's upkeep. It only seemed natural for Foxcroft to reopen its dormitories in the summer of 1957 to accommodate the 10 teams in the national rally of United States Pony Clubs.

A Foxcroft trademark is the twice-a-week close-order military drill. This practice was started during World War II and has become a school tradition. All students belong to the Foxcroft Corps.

In an effort to arouse a sense of social responsibility, this former finishing school has its girls do volunteer work in a baby clinic.

Rules are strict, with an elaborate demerits system. Even seniors are allowed only three regular weekends away from school.

Foxcroft has been run for more than forty years by Charlotte H. Noland, usually called "Miss Charlotte." Today she leaves the scholastic side of the school to its academic head, Van Santvoord Merle-Smith, Jr. He is one of an increasing number of men heading the top girls' schools. Although some graduates do go on to the high-caliber women's colleges, there is a strong tendency for girls to attend such junior colleges as Briarcliff and Sweet Briar. Students range in age from thirteen to eighteen. Tuition, room, and board cost $2,900 plus $150 for specified extras. There are one full and twelve partial scholarships.

The Collegiate School, Richmond

Collegiate is usually discussed as a girls' school, despite the fact that boys are admitted to the first eight grades. Although it was formerly owned by the Presbyterian League, Collegiate is now non-sectarian. Residents of Richmond describe it as a liberal school, and say it shows less religious prejudice than is common in the South. Graduates often go on to such schools as Hollins or Sweet Briar. Tuition ranges from $350 to $575. Catherine S. Flippen is headmistress.

St. Catherine's School, Richmond

This is Richmond's most fashionable school, attended by many future debutantes. It is an Episcopal school, and religion is emphasized. A service league is active in community, national, and international causes. This is one of the many private schools that teach sewing. Riding is, of course, the popular sport.

Day students start at the age of five; boarding students at thirteen. Tuition goes from $325 to $625; boarders pay $1,800.

Stuart Hall, Staunton

Stuart Hall is a popular society school with a long southern tradition. It was founded in 1843 as the Virginia Female Institute. The name was later changed in honor of Mrs. J. E. B. Stuart. The widow of the famed Confederate general was principal for nineteen years. Students like to point out that General Robert E. Lee was once a member of the board of trustees. There is a Granddaughters' Club, made up of descendants of alumnae.

Fine arts are stressed in the curriculum. A service league works in cooperation with the Red Cross. Stuart Hall is an Episcopal school.

There are 145 boarding students, ranging in age from thirteen to nineteen, and 15 day students. Charges amount to $1,600 ($450 for day students). Daughters of clergymen get a $200 discount. The student with the highest academic average in the school receives a scholarship, and a number of other scholarships are given as well. Martha Dabney Jones is headmistress.

WASHINGTON

Annie Wright Seminary, Tacoma

The school is named after the daughter of Charles B. Wright, president of the Northern Pacific Railroad, who was its first benefactor. The Wright family still contributes heavily to the school, particularly in the person of Mrs. Thomas P. Harney of Philadelphia.

Annie Wright Seminary is located on a ten-acre campus overlooking Puget Sound. The girls can go skiing on Mt. Rainier. Home economics is stressed. Both day and boarding students are taken from first grade through high school. Uniforms are required. Tuition, room, and board are $2,100 for the six lower grades, $2,200 thereafter. Tuition for day students rises from $300 to $650.

WISCONSIN

Milwaukee-Downer Seminary, Milwaukee

This old (1848) school has an enrollment of 250 day students, ranging in age from four to nineteen, and 60 boarders of high-school age. Boys are admitted to the nursery school. Tuition ranges from $275 to $725. Boarding students pay $1,850. There are 14 full and 16 partial scholarships. Elizabeth Anderson is headmistress.

COEDUCATIONAL SCHOOLS

ARIZONA

Orme School, Quarter Circle V-Bar Ranch, Mayer

This is the best known of the West's ranch schools, and students come from all over the country. It is a real working cattle ranch—40,000 acres—located at an altitude of 3,800 feet, seventy-five miles north of Phoenix. The idea of the school was developed by Mr. and Mrs. Charles H. Orme, Jr., for their own children. Their son is now the managing director. Each student has a horse assigned to him. All do chores, handle livestock, learn to rope calves. Mr. Orme assures parents that, nonetheless, the children acquire "refinements important in any gracious, cultured home." Jeans and shirts are virtually a uniform, although girls must wear skirts for dinner. The school enrolls 78 boys and 52 girls from the fifth grade on. Cost is $2,250. Extras include $80.00 a semester for horse feed. There is also a summer camp, attended by 150 children, which costs $625.

DELAWARE

Tower Hill School, Wilmington

The endowment of this day school totals $1,608,000—not altogether surprising to those who note that Pierre S. du Pont, III, is president of the trustees. Tower Hill takes 550 boys and girls from the ages of four to nineteen. Tuition rises progressively from $375 in nursery school to $775 from ninth grade on. About 9 per cent of the students get scholarship help.

FLORIDA

Graham-Eckes School, Palm Beach

Students from many states attend this school in Florida's famous resort. Enrollment is fifty girls and fifty boys, aged from twelve to twenty. Boys and girls have separate campuses but do the classwork together. Tuition, room, and board: $2,600.

Palm Beach Private School, Palm Beach

This day school is patronized by wealthy resort families. Although students are accepted from the ages of three to eighteen, most go elsewhere to high school. The student body is made up of about 130 boys and the same number of girls at a tuition charge of $400 to $950, depending on the grade.

ILLINOIS

The Latin School of Chicago, Chicago

The Latin School has an excellent reputation. It was formed in 1953 by the merger of the old Chicago Latin School for Boys and the Girls Latin School of Chicago. It takes 250 boys and the same number of girls from nursery school through high school. Tuition charges mount from $375 to $900. There are 11 full and 23 partial scholarships.

Lake Forest Country Day School, Lake Forest

This school was formed in 1958 by the merger of the Lake Forest Day School and the Bell School. It is now headed by Appleton A. Mason, Jr., formerly headmaster of Bell. In one of Chicago's most fashionable suburbs, the school takes students from nursery school through the age of fifteen, and prepares them for the big eastern boarding schools. The enrollment now totals 210 boys and 220 girls. Tuition: $300–$750.

North Shore Country Day School, Winnetka

Located in Chicago's most highly social suburb, this school is attended by children from the city's North Shore and attracts a group from outside the state as well. It takes coeducation with a grain of salt. Boys and girls start together at the age of four, are separated during early adolescence, and are then brought back together in the highest grades. There is also a boarding department for boys of high-school age. A few of them board on campus with faculty families. The school is owned by the parents. Tuition rises from $400 to $1,050. The boarding-school rate is $1,950. Nathaniel S. French is headmaster.

Francis W. Parker School, Chicago

This well-known progressive day school was founded in 1899 by educator Francis W. Parker. He was aided by Anita McCormick Blaine. The school stressed science from kindergarten on long before it was standard to do so. The arts are also emphasized from the earliest grades. Programs are geared to the individual needs and talents of the students rather than to a rigid curriculum. The student body is made up of about 250 boys and 250 girls from the ages of four through seventeen. Tuition mounts from $550 in the first grade to $1,050. The scholarship program is exceptionally liberal.

MASSACHUSETTS

Milton Academy, Milton

This famous and socially favored boarding and day school was founded in 1798. It is located ten miles from Boston, and about half the student body comes from there. The elementary school has its own quarters and is for local children. The boarding department takes boys from the ages of twelve to eighteen and girls from fourteen to eighteen. The school's policy on weekends home is liberal. Graduates favor Harvard, Yale, and Radcliffe. Tuition in the elementary school varies according to grade from $450 to $850. Tuition in the secondary school is $1,100 to $1,200 for boys, and $1,000 to $1,100 for the girls. For boarding students, the charges are $2,400 for boys and $2,600 for girls.

MICHIGAN

Brookside School, Cranbrook, Bloomfield Hills

This is the elementary day school in the Cranbrook setup described earlier (under Girls' Schools). It takes boys and girls up to the age of twelve. Then most of the girls go on to Kingswood, the boys to Cranbrook. Tuition rises from $400 to $700.

NEW YORK

Green Vale School, Glen Head, Long Island

Although I have resisted listing most of the private schools in the New York suburbs (most serve only one or two small communities), I find that I cannot exclude Green Vale. For one thing, its location on Long Island's Gold Coast means that it draws its student body from suburbs occupied by families belonging to the Old Guard of New York. For another, it was Gloria Vanderbilt's school during the spectacular child-custody suit of the 1930's. The publicity it got then has left such an indelible impression that people keep asking me what I know about the school. Green Vale is coeducational for kindergarten and elementary school. Above the fourth-grade level, the boys are in a separate unit. The first year of high school, the highest grade offered, is for girls only. The enrollment totals more than four hundred students. Tuition starts at $525 and rises to $950. All the graduates go on to such prep schools as St. Paul's, Andover, Choate, Madeira, and St. Timothy's. Archibald R. Hoxton is head.

NORTH CAROLINA

Asheville Country Day School, Asheville

Boys and girls from the ages of five to sixteen are prepared for the big prep schools. Graduates go on to Shipley, Baldwin, Abbot, etc. Tuition starts at $350 in first grade and rises to $550 by the ninth. There are three full and ten partial scholarships. Marshall M. Abell is headmaster.

PENNSYLVANIA

Germantown Friends School, Philadelphia

Most of the Friends' schools have high scholastic ratings but are not society schools. This is perhaps the one exception—a result of the Quaker influence on Philadelphia high society. Students go from kindergarten (tuition, $350) all the way through high school ($750).

Sewickley Academy, Sewickley

This is another well-known pre-prep day school, taking boys and girls from the ages of four to fifteen. Virtually all its graduates go on to such top prep schools as Madeira, the Hill, Choate, Hotchkiss, Chatham Hall, Andover. Sewickley is conservative in teaching method. Tuition starts at $315 and goes up to $790.

VERMONT

The Putney School, Putney

This is a liberal and progressive school that emphasizes individual projects. Grades are not given. Putney owns one thousand acres of land, including a farm where many boys and girls work. Students may rent or keep a horse at school at a charge of $300. Sometimes two youngsters share a horse. The student body of the high school numbers ninety-nine boys and eighty-seven girls. Graduates favor Harvard and Radcliffe. The charge for boarders is $2,500; for day students it is $1,200. More than 30 per cent of the students get scholarship aid. Putney has an elementary day school called the Little School. An eight-week summer work camp is available for one hundred children of high-school age. The school also conducts an eight-week trip to Cape Breton Island, Nova Scotia, where it owns a 225-acre farm. Summer trips abroad are sponsored as well.

WISCONSIN

Wayland Academy, Beaver Dam

Wayland is located two hours from Chicago and five from Minneapolis and St. Paul, so students come from these areas as well as from Wisconsin. It takes 230 boarders and 50 day students, aged twelve to nineteen. Wayland is a Baptist school, founded in 1885, and church attendance is compulsory. In 1955 there was extensive reconstruction. Tuition costs $450 for day students; plus room and board it totals $1,800. With an endowment of $800,000, the school is able to offer 60 partial scholarships. Jobs paying $200 to $300 are available for students who need them.

BOYS' SCHOOLS

CALIFORNIA

The Cate School, Carpinteria

This school was formerly known as the Santa Barbara School. It is very small, limiting enrollment to ninety-two students, aged thirteen to eighteen. Cate uses nearby beaches for swimming, surfing, and sailing. The Junior Rifle Club belongs to the National Rifle Association. Each boy takes part in a weekly work program. Charges are $2,200. Francis Parkman, Jr., the head, was formerly assistant dean of Harvard.

Webb School of California, Claremont

This small well-known school takes only 140 boarding students and 30 day students between the ages of twelve and nineteen. It was founded by Thompson and Vivian Webb of the family long known in the South as educators. The school's rifle club is affiliated with the National Rifle Association. Fossil hunting is the absorbing interest of a group of students. Each summer a number of them take a five-week camping trip to the fossil beds of South Dakota, Wyoming, Nebraska, and Utah. Graduates of Webb go on to both California and Eastern Ivy League colleges. Charges to boarding students are $2,350. There are 32 partial scholarships.

The Thacher School, Casa de Piedra Ranch, Ojai

A boarding school for boys between the ages of thirteen and eighteen, Thacher is known for its way of combining the outdoor life with studies. Boys clean their own rooms, wait on table, and maintain the building and grounds by taking turns at "work days" every other week. Almost every boy has his own horse. In the winter, skiing is a popular sport. Groups take annual boat trips to Santa Cruz. A number of graduates do go on to Yale and other Ivy League colleges, but most attend California schools. Enrollment totals 113. Tuition, room, and board come to $2,400, plus extra charges of $250 to $400. Newton Kimball Chase is headmaster.

COLORADO

The Fountain Valley School, Colorado Springs

Boys come from 20 states to attend Fountain Valley. The location allows riding, skiing, mountain excursions, and swimming in an outdoor pool. A handbook points out that it was founded to "teach social consciousness in boys." But academic standards are high, and graduates go on to the big colleges. Day students are accepted in the seventh and eighth grades at a tuition rate of $1,050. In high school almost all are boarders. Charges amount to $2,400.

CONNECTICUT

Kent School, Kent

The much-copied Kent self-help plan was developed here by the founder, Reverend Frederick H. Sill. Boys clean their own rooms, wait on table, and do chores around the place. This is said to save the school $100,000 a year in maintenance costs and makes it possible for the tuition to be based on the individual family's ability to pay.

"Parents make an annual contribution to the school's budget," says the catalogue. "Extra fees run $150."

The student body is made up of 300 boys ranging in age from thirteen to eighteen. New students are not accepted beyond the ninth grade. The school is Episcopal. Boys are prepared for Princeton, Yale, and other Ivy League colleges. A girls' annex is being started, which amazes old grads. From the date of its founding in 1906 until 1940 no dances were held on campus, and girls were hardly ever seen there.

The Hotchkiss School, Lakeville

One of the top prep schools in the country, Hotchkiss was founded by Maria H. Hotchkiss, widow of the inventor of the machine gun. In its early days its head, Dr. Huber Gray Buehler, used to say: "There is only one rule in this school, 'Be a gentleman.' " This is still said to be a school aim. Skiing, boating, golf, and trapshooting facilities are all available on the 483-acre campus. Enrollment is limited to 350 boys of high-school age. Graduates favor Yale. Tuition, room, and board come to $2,350. Parents are asked to deposit $100 for expenses. There are 43 scholarship funds, providing a large number of partial and a few full scholarships. The Reverend Thomas Huntington Chappell is headmaster.

Pomfret School, Pomfret

This well-known prep school attracts students from as far away as Wyoming and Texas. Boys learn administration by operating their own bank, store, and athletic-equipment service. There is a work program. The shop actually builds much of the equipment used by the school. Skiing is a popular sport. Pomfret offers the four high-school years only. Cost is $2,200 a year. About one-fifth of the boys get scholarships.

The Choate School, Wallingford

This is another of the nation's prestige prep schools, founded in 1896. It takes 530 boarders from the ages of twelve to eighteen, and 20 day scholars. Although this is a non-denominational school, there is daily chapel. Boys must devote one-half hour a day to a work program. In addition to the standard prep-school sports, skeet shooting is taught. And boys can learn forestry. No uniforms are worn, but jackets and ties are required at classes and meals. Cost is $2,600 for boarding students, $900 for day students. Many scholarships are available. The Reverend Seymour St. John is headmaster.

Loomis School, Windsor

Although primarily a boarding school with 235 boarders, Loomis does take more than one hundred day students as well. The age minimum for students is thirteen. Tuition for day students is $500; for boarders, $1,800. Five full scholarships and fifty-four partial ones are offered.

DELAWARE

St. Andrew's School, Middletown

St. Andrew's has an endowment of $13,330,283—a benefaction of Alexis Felix du Pont. As a result, the school is able to scale tuition according to the parents' ability to pay. The charge ranges from $500 to $1,800. But the lower tuition rates are available only to students in the first quarter of the class. There are four full and 102 partial scholarships. St. Andrew's is Episcopal, and is attended by 156 boys aged from twelve to eighteen. Students are prepared for the Ivy League colleges.

ILLINOIS

Lake Forest Academy, Lake Forest

This school, established in 1857, has succeeded in resisting the military-school tendency of prep schools in the area. It is located in a fashionable suburb of Chicago on what was once the estate of J. Ogden Armour. Daily chapel is required. Socially, the boys meet girls from nearby Ferry Hall at dances and other activities. Age requirements are thirteen to eighteen. There are 150 boarding students, paying $2,200, and 40 to 45 day scholars, paying a tuition of $1,175. A summer day camp, costing $225, is maintained for boys of elementary-school age. Harold H. Corbin, Jr., is headmaster.

INDIANA

Culver Military Academy, Culver

Culver is known the country over. The War Department has given the school its highest rating. In 1941 the Academy was made an honor naval training school. Its academic standing is also good. Boys are prepared for more than two hundred colleges. Graduates go on to the University of Michigan, Northwestern, Stanford, and Princeton, in addition to the United States Military and Naval academies. Culver's student body of nearly eight hundred boys, aged twelve to eighteen, comes from thirty-eight states and sixteen countries. Boys are selected on the basis of tests, family background, character, and school record. The Academy is headed by Major General Delmar Taft Spivey, who was formerly commandant of the Air War College, Maxwell Air Force Base. The charges are $1,900 plus $388 for riding.

Uniforms cost $460 in the first year. About 110 students receive scholarships. The Academy runs three summer schools: a woodcraft camp for boys aged nine and a half to fourteen, costing $550 for eight weeks; a naval school for boys of fourteen to eighteen also costing $550; and a horsemanship school for boys of fourteen to eighteen at $600.

MASSACHUSETTS

Phillips Academy, Andover

Usually called "Andover," this is one of the most famous boys' prep schools in the world. Its graduates have a real edge socially as well as academically. Nonetheless, it is somewhat more liberal than most of the other top boys' schools, and has students from varied family backgrounds. With an endowment of $17,000,000, the school is able to give a considerable amount of scholarship assistance. An Andover Fund annually contributes more than $200,000, and 229 students get scholarship aid. As a result, the school is able to claim that "Phillips Academy is open to any qualified boy without regard to the financial position of his parents." Boys must be of high-school age.

Founded in 1778, Andover's early patrons included the Washingtons and Lees of Virginia and the Lowells and Quincys of Massachusetts. Today its 790 students are gathered from 43 states and 19 foreign countries.

Andover is conservative in its teaching methods. Of its 20,000 alumni, about 45 per cent went to Yale and 20 per cent to Harvard. A typical graduating class (1958) of 226 boys attends the following colleges: 53 at Yale, 29 at Harvard, 21 at Princeton, and 19 at Brown. Cost is $1,600 for boarding students, $800 for day (there are only 50 day students). John M. Kemper is the head. Andover has a summer session that serves as a "laboratory for trying out new educational ideas."

Middlesex School, Concord

This select school for 196 boys from seventh grade on is one of society's favorites. The scholastic rating is high. As for sports, hockey, basketball, squash racquets, skiing, and skating are popular. Boys may join the Middlesex Yacht Club or Rifle Club (with parental approval). Most students have individual rooms but eat in a common dining room where they take turns waiting on table. Tuition, room, and board come to $2,200 a year; tuition alone for day students is $850. Additional charges run about $250 a year. Seven competitive scholarships of $1,500 are awarded. Lawrence Terry is headmaster.

Deerfield Academy, Deerfield

Another of the nation's best-known boarding schools, Deerfield was founded in 1797. It is headed by Frank L. Boyden, a recognized leader in education today. He is said to screen applicants carefully in terms of ability. Boys range in age from thirteen to eighteen. Graduates go to any of the Ivy League colleges. Cost to boarding students is $2,300. There are twenty-three full and one hundred partial scholarships.

Groton, Groton

This is *the* prep school for many of the Old Guard. An Episcopal school, it was established in 1884 by Reverend Endicott Peabody. Its board of trustees includes such names as Morgan, Blair, Pratt, Coolidge, and Davison.

Although an advertisement claims that "boys are sought from a wide diversity of background," Groton retains its reputation as a most exclusive school. Only 200 boys in all, between the ages of twelve and nineteen, are accepted as "Grotties." In 1959, fifty-two boys received scholarships.

Society's opinion of the school can be seen in the fact that an invitation to the Groton-St. Mark's dance held in New York each year does wonders in helping a young girl to become a recognized debutante.

Boys sleep in cubicled dormitories. They are expected to clean their own cubicles. Scholarship boys are not given extra chores.

In a typical year about half the graduates go on to Harvard; another quarter are divided between Yale and Princeton. Cost is $2,150. Reverend John Crocker has been head since 1940.

St. Mark's School, Southborough

This is another of society's favorites, and is also Episcopal. An excellent prep school, it attracts boys from all over the country. The student body totals 205 boarding students and 25 day students from the ages of twelve to eighteen. Upper-school boys have rooms of their own; lower-school boys sleep in cubicled dormitories. St. Mark's is known for its "monitor" system of student government, which dates from the school's beginnings nearly one hundred years ago. Under this system six or seven outstanding seniors act as student representatives and oversee the lives of the younger boys. By and large, St. Mark's is paternalistic (as are many of the top boys' boarding schools). Favored sports are swimming at an outdoor pool and ice hockey on an artificial ice rink. In an effort to teach social responsibility, the school operates Brantwood Camp for more than two hundred needy boys from Boston and New York. The camp is completely staffed by St. Mark's students and graduates, and is definitely a part of the school's program. A work plan is maintained. Boys clean their own rooms, wait on table, and help in the maintenance of the school. Tuition, room, and board are $2,180. Day students pay $750. At present 56 boys are receiving scholarship help. Applications for scholarships are made to Ladd MacMillan. William Wyatt Barber, Jr., is headmaster.

Roxbury Latin School, West Roxbury

This fine day school for boys between the ages of twelve and eighteen was established in 1645 as the "Free Schoole in Roxbury." Later, tuition charges were added. Today the charge is $400 for Roxbury boys, $500 for others. There are four full and 12 partial scholarships. Originally Roxbury prepared for Harvard only, and even now nearly half of its graduates go there. It is a small school, taking only 185 boys.

MICHIGAN

Cranbrook School, Bloomfield Hills

Here is the boys' division of the Cranbrook setup described earlier (under Girls' Schools). There are 200 boarders and 170 day students between the ages of twelve and eighteen. Graduates overwhelmingly favor Harvard, with Yale and Cornell next. Charges are $2,300 for boarders and $1,250 for day students. Harry D. Hoey is headmaster. A summer school camp offers both academic courses and military training. Cost is $400.

MINNESOTA

Shattuck School, Faribault

Shattuck is both a military and a church school (Episcopal). It has good academic standing. Students between the ages of thirteen and nineteen come from all over the United States. Tuition, room, and board come to $2,000. Uniforms cost about $235. Three full and 30 partial scholarships are offered. A summer school camp for boys between the ages of nine and eighteen provides tutoring and make-up courses, in addition to sports.

NEW HAMPSHIRE

Proctor Academy, Andover

This small boarding school takes only 130 boys between the ages of fourteen and nineteen. It was founded in 1848 as the coeducational Andover Academy. In 1879 it was renamed. Skiing is a popular winter sport here, as in most schools in this area. Forestry, fishing, and hunting also occupy the students. Sailing is a major extracurricular activity. Eight twelve-foot sailing dinghies and many rowboats are built each year in the school's boat shop. There is a work program for all boys. Cost is $2,200. Sons of Unitarian ministers are given a $1,000 scholarship. Others can get scholarships ranging from $100 to $500. Lyle H. Farrell is headmaster.

St. Paul's School, Concord

St. Paul's is another of the schools favored for scions of society's big-name families. It is very exclusive and about 35 per cent of its student body is made up of sons of alumni. With an endowment of more than $12,000,000, St. Paul's is able to offer 18 full and 73 partial scholarships. The catalogue lists 51 special scholarship funds. The enrollment totals about four hundred fifty boys between the ages of twelve and eighteen.

The first rector, Reverend Henry Augustus Coit, set up the school along the lines of the English public ("private" as Americans use the word) school, and the influence is still there. The classes are known as "forms." The students in this Episcopal school attend Evensong. The boys in the upper forms have separate rooms; the younger boys sleep in cubicles in the dormitories.

The largest group of graduates go on to Harvard, with Yale and Princeton next in that order. Cost is $2,000 plus specified extras of $250. The Reverend Matthew Madison Warren, D.D., is rector.

The Phillips Exeter Academy, Exeter

This world-famous and excellent school is somewhat more liberal in its acceptance policy than the Groton-St. Paul's-St. Mark's group. "Exeter," as it is known, wants boys with ability and takes any really outstanding boy, including a few Negroes. With an endowment of $25,000,000, it is able both to keep charges low ($1,800) and to offer an exceptionally large number of scholarships. In 1958–59, 171 boys received scholarship aid. Of these, 58 were full scholarships.

Exeter is a big school, taking 725 students ranging in age from thirteen to eighteen. About forty day students are also admitted, at a cost of $750.

The school was founded in 1781. It has been described by the late John P. Marquand as "the most beautiful and aesthetically satisfying of all New England schools." It is well equipped, with a 45,000-book library and ten laboratories. Some classes are taught according to the Harkness Plan, which is a prep-school version of the college seminar: Classes are informal and students sit around a table. For sports, Exeter has a swimming pool, artificial rink, twelve playing fields, and twenty-three tennis courts. A summer session costing $600 is offered. Exeter graduates favor Harvard, with smaller numbers going to Yale and Princeton. William G. Saltonstall is headmaster.

NEW JERSEY

Bordentown Military Institute, Bordentown

Students are prepared for college as well as the military life. Graduates go on to many of the big colleges. The school has the United States Army's Honor Rating for its ROTC unit. There is a separate junior school. Tuition, room, and board come to $1,850 plus $325 for uniforms. A small number of day students are also admitted, paying $900 in tuition.

The Lawrenceville School, Lawrenceville

This school is popular with the sons of the rich along the eastern seaboard. It takes more than six hundred boys from the eighth grade through high school. Lawrenceville is one of the oldest boarding schools in this area, founded in 1810. Heavily endowed at $2,705,000, it offers two full and sixty-three partial scholarships. Tuition, however, remains high. Costs to boarders run $3,000, to day students (a minority group) $1,250. The English "house system" is used. This means that every house on the Lawrenceville campus is like a home, with the resident housemaster taking the paternal role. Athletics are run on an interhouse rather than an interclass basis. In teaching, the round-table method of instruction is used where possible. There is an experimental theater. Lawrenceville is non-sectarian. Allan V. Heely is headmaster.

NEW YORK

Polytechnic Preparatory Country Day School, Ninety-second Street and Seventh Avenue, Brooklyn

Founded in 1854, Poly Prep remains Brooklyn society's favorite school for boys. There are 480 students ranging in age from ten to eighteen. Most graduates go on to the Ivy League colleges. Tuition rises from $875 to $925. J. Folwell Scull, Jr., is headmaster.

The Manlius School, Manlius

Manlius is situated eleven miles southeast of Syracuse. It offers a liberal-arts curriculum in addition to the military. Boarding students start at the age of twelve and continue through high school. Day scholars range in age from eleven to fifteen. Boarders pay $1,800 and day students $575.

The Allen-Stevenson School, 132 East Seventy-eighth Street, New York City

This is one of New York's fashionable day schools for boys between the ages of five and fourteen. Virtually all of its student body of close to 200 boys go on to prep school. The school derives from a class of three boys taught by Francis Bellows Allen in 1883. It is basically conservative in its teaching. Tuition ranges from $650 to $950. Henry P. Tiffany, Jr., is head.

The Browning School, 52 East Sixty-second Street, New York City

Enrollment at this very small school is limited to 165 boys from pre-primary through high school. Its prestige is high. A luxury apartment house recently included in its advertisement the enticing fact that it was very near to the school. Tuition rises from $700 in first grade to $1,100 in high school. Charles W. Cook is headmaster.

Buckley School, 120 East Seventy-fourth Street, New York City

Buckley is another pre-prep day school favored by the sons of the well-to-do. The student body totals 320 boys from the ages of six to fourteen. All graduates go on to the leading prep schools. Tuition ranges from $775 to $975. James M. Hubball is head.

Collegiate School, 241 West Seventy-seventh Street, New York City

Collegiate was the first "public" school in New York State. It was founded in 1738 by the West India Company and the Classis of Amsterdam (church governing body), and has been functioning ever since, except for a brief hiatus during the American Revolution when the city was under British occupation. The school is affiliated with the West End Collegiate Dutch Reformed Church and has daily chapel services, but boys of other religions are enrolled, too. Collegiate accepts a number of foreign-born students. It is a day school for boys from nursery all the way through high school. Total enrollment is 345. Collegiate is conservative in teaching methods, stressing a solid, old-fashioned education from the very start. Students work hard. Tuition rises from $750 in first grade to $950 in the high school. Carl W. Andrews is the new headmaster following the retirement of Wilson Parkhill, headmaster for twenty-five years.

St. Bernard's School, 4 East Ninety-eighth Street, New York City

St. Bernard's is very much in favor with New York's society set. It takes 250 boys aged from six to fourteen. At that point they move on to the nation's top prep schools, including Groton, St. Paul's, the Hill, and Deerfield. Tuition rises from $725 to $1,000. R. I. W. Westgate is headmaster.

Trinity School, 139 West Ninety-first Street, New York City

The Society for the Propagation of the Gospel in Foreign Parts founded Trinity in 1709. Religious training is stressed. Students start in first grade and can continue all the way through high school. This is a day school. It is affiliated with the Trinity-Pawling School at Pawling, a boarding school for high-school students. Tuition mounts from $500 in first grade to $800 in high school.

Peekskill Military Academy, Peekskill-on-Hudson

This old (1833) military school is located forty-five miles from New York. Graduates make liberal-arts and engineering colleges, in addition to military.

Boys are taken from the age of ten on. There is a special junior school for seventh-graders and eighth-graders. Day students pay $720. Tuition, room, and board come to $1,850, plus $325 for uniforms.

North Carolina

Asheville School, Asheville

This boarding school for boys between the ages of twelve and nineteen has a student body made up of 150 boys from 30 states. The school is situated on a 300-acre campus, with woods and a lake. Students go on to such colleges as Harvard, Duke and Yale. The cost is $2,200.

Ohio

Hawken School, Cleveland

Located in Lyndhurst, this is one of the two top boys' schools in the area (University is the other). It is a day school and goes all the way from kindergarten through high school. Tuition climbs from $515 to $825. Scholarships are given for financial need only. A summer day camp is maintained on school grounds.

University School, Cleveland

This socially approved school in Shaker Heights holds down its enrollment. From nursery school through sixth grade, it is limited to 120; from seventh through ninth grade, to 160; and from tenth on, to 210. There are 55 boarding students, some of whom live in only for the five-day school week. Graduates overwhelmingly favor Yale, with Williams, Dartmouth, Denison, Princeton, and Washington and Lee next. Tuition rises from $650 in nursery school to $1,050 in ninth grade. The five-day boarding plan costs $2,000.

Pennsylvania

Shady Side Academy, Pittsburgh

There are separate campuses for the three schools that make up the Academy. A junior day school for boys from the age of five is located at 400 South Braddock Avenue; a coed school consisting of sixth, seventh, and eighth grades has a 60-acre campus at 500 Squaw Run Road; and a senior boarding and day school for boys is at 423 Fox Chapel Road. Graduates move on to such schools as Yale, Lehigh, and Harvard. Tuition, room, and board range from $1,800 to $2,000; tuition alone rises from $500 to $1,150.

The Hill School, Pottstown

The Hill is popular with well-to-do and society families. It was founded in 1851 as a "home" school where boys and teachers could live together. The effort is still made to keep that warm atmosphere. There is a special program for gifted boys. Graduates favor Yale and Princeton. With a $1,000,000 endowment, the school gives 14 full and 128 partial scholarships. Tuition, room, and board for the 430 boarding students come to $2,300 each. A few day students are also accepted. Tuition for them is $800. Edward T. Hall is the head.

RHODE ISLAND

Portsmouth Priory School, Portsmouth

This is one of the top Catholic boys' boarding schools. It is situated on Narragansett Bay, only eight miles from Newport. Attendance at daily morning and evening prayers is compulsory. Most graduates go on to Harvard, Georgetown, Yale, and Princeton. The charge is $2,100 for boarding students, $600 for day students.

St. George's School, Newport

Admission to this small—200-student—prep school is so highly desired that three out of four applicants are turned away, according to school officials. Boys come from 21 states and 11 foreign countries. The school is predominantly Episcopal. There is a self-help plan involving waiting on tables and caring for rooms. St. George's maintains Camp Ramleh for needy Rhode Island boys, and students volunteer their services. Charges are $2,200 for boarding students, $750 for day students. Reverend William A. Buell is headmaster.

TENNESSEE

The Webb School, Bell Buckle

Boys come from all over the South to attend this school in the blue-grass section of central Tennessee. It was founded in 1870 by William R. Webb and his brother. William Webb's son established the well-known Webb School of California.

Most graduates go on to southern colleges. Webb takes about 150 boys from the ages of eleven to eighteen at a charge of $1,400.

VIRGINIA

Episcopal High School, Alexandria

This is another of society's favorites. Started in 1839, it prepares boys for the University of Virginia and the Ivy League colleges. Episcopal accepts 250 boys of high-school age. Tuition, room, and board amount to $1,900. Sons of Episcopal clergymen get a 30 per cent discount.

St. Christopher's School, 711 St. Christopher's Road, Richmond

This Episcopal school prepares boys for such schools as the University of Virginia, Washington and Lee, and Princeton. Day students can start at kindergarten age, boarding at twelve. Tuition ranges from $325 to $575; boarders pay $1,600. Robert W. Bugg is head.

Staunton Military Academy, Staunton

Staunton was founded in 1860 by William Kable, who soon went off to the Civil War as a Confederate captain. He returned to direct the school for more than fifty years, and then his son took over.

The academy enrolls six hundred boys from the ages of ten to nineteen. The junior school is separate. Students come from more than thirty states. Graduates go on to the University of Virginia, West Point, and the Ivy League colleges. Tuition, room, and board come to $1,425. Uniforms cost $375 in the first year, $175 from then on. A few day students are accepted at a tuition rate of $700.

Woodberry Forest School, Woodberry Forest

Located in the Piedmont section of Virginia, this is one of the nation's best-known prep schools. Although not a church school, religion is stressed. There is a limited work program. Tuition, room, and board come to $1,875. Day students pay $600. Eleven competitive scholarships are offered, plus twenty grants of $600 to sons of alumni. Joseph M. Mercer is headmaster.

The Nation's Debutante Balls

The following cotillion directory is the result of a spot check I made of cities, suburbs, and small towns. It is not a complete listing of the nation's debutante balls. That could be compiled only by covering every single community in the United States. But each section of the country is represented. And the list does give a clear indication of the widespread popularity of cotillions today.

The balls are listed first by states and then by cities in alphabetical order.

ALABAMA
Debutante Presentation Ball, Mountain Brook Country Club, Birmingham
Redstone Club Ball, Birmingham Country Club, Birmingham

ARKANSAS
Cotillion Club Ball, Texarkana Country Club, Texarkana

CALIFORNIA
Winter Ball (East Bay Ball), Claremont Hotel, Berkeley
Cameo Debutante Ball, Los Angeles
Coronet Debutante Ball, Beverly Hills Hotel, Los Angeles
Las Damas Pan Americanas Debutante Ball, Los Angeles
Las Madrinas Debutante Ball, Biltmore Hotel, Los Angeles
Valley Hunt Club Debutante Ball, Pasadena
Debutante Cotillion, Sheraton Palace Hotel, San Francisco
Debutante Ball of the Music Academy of the West, Coral Casino, Santa Barbara

COLORADO
Denver Symphony Guild's Debutante Ball, Brown Palace Hotel, Denver

CONNECTICUT
Darien-New Canaan Autumn Cotillion, Wee Burn Country Club, Darien
Greenwich Debutante Ball, Greenwich Country Club, Greenwich
New Britain Christmas Cotillion, New Britain
New Haven Assembly, New Haven
Stamford Junior League Debutante Ball, Stamford Yacht Club, Stamford

DISTRICT OF COLUMBIA (Washington, D.C.)
   Debutante Cotillion and Thanksgiving Ball, Shoreham Hotel
   Washington Assembly, Sulgrave Club

FLORIDA
   Debutante Heart Cotillion, Fort Lauderdale
   Presentation Ball, Florida Yacht Club, Jacksonville
   Debutante Ball, Surf Club, Miami
   Goodfellows Charity Ball, Orlando Coliseum, Orlando
   New Year's Eve Debutante Ball, Rosalind Club, Orlando
   Debutante Ball, Bath and Tennis Club, Palm Beach
   Debutante Ball, Coliseum, St. Petersburg
   New Year's Eve Ball, Huntington Hotel, St. Petersburg

GEORGIA
   Halloween Ball, Piedmont Driving Club, Atlanta
   Cotillion and Parents' Debutante Ball, Savannah
   Junior Assembly Debutante Ball, De Soto Hotel, Savannah

ILLINOIS
   Passavant Debutante Cotillion and Christmas Ball, Conrad Hilton Hotel,
      Chicago

KENTUCKY
   Spinsters Cotillion, Louisville Country Club, Louisville

LOUISIANA
   Mardi Gras balls given by the krewes, New Orleans
   Demoiselle Club Ball, Shreveport Country Club, Shreveport

MARYLAND
   Bachelors Cotillon, Lyric Theater, Baltimore
   Junior League Ball, L'Hirondelle Club, Baltimore
   Sweetheart Ball, Friendship International Airport Ballroom, Bel Air

MASSACHUSETTS
   Debutante Assembly, Statler Hotel, Boston
   Debutante Cotillion, Sheraton-Plaza Hotel, Boston
   Debutante Cotillion, Concord
   New Bedford Assembly, New Bedford
   Salem Debutante Assembly, Salem

MISSISSIPPI
   Delta Debutante Ball, Greenville Country Club, Greenville
   Plantation Cotillion, Rosedale

MISSOURI
   Jewel Ball, Nelson Art Gallery, Kansas City
   Veiled Prophet Ball, Kiel Auditorium, St. Louis

NEBRASKA
Ak-Sar-Ben Coronation, Coliseum, Omaha

NEW JERSEY
Englewood Junior League Cotillion, Aldecress Country Club, Demerest
Montclair Cotillion, Montclair
Morristown Assembly, Morristown
Debutante Cotillion for the Valley Hospital, Ridgewood
Short Hills Debutante Ball, Short Hills Club, Short Hills
Summit Cotillion, Canoe Brook Country Club, Short Hills

NEW YORK
New York City and Suburbs
Yuletide Ball, Saint George Hotel, Brooklyn
Forest Hills Gardens Cotillion, Community House, Forest Hills
Garden City Cotillion, Garden City
Holly Ball, Scarsdale Golf Club, Hartsdale
Debutante Assembly and New Year's Ball, Waldorf-Astoria Hotel, New
  York City
Debutante Cotillion and Christmas Ball, Waldorf-Astoria Hotel, New York
  City
Gotham Ball, Plaza Hotel, New York City
Greensleeves Ball, Sheraton-East Hotel, New York City
Grosvenor Ball, Plaza Hotel, New York City
International Ball, Astor Hotel, New York City
Junior Assemblies, Plaza Hotel, New York City
Junior League Ball, Plaza Hotel, New York City
Mayfair Assembly, Pierre Hotel, New York City
Mistletoe Ball, St. Regis Hotel, New York City
Westchester Cotillion, Shenorock Shore Club, Rye
Westchester Country Club Debutante Cotillion, Westchester Country Club,
  Rye
Sleepy Hollow Assembly, Sleepy Hollow Country Club, Scarborough
Tuxedo Autumn Ball, Tuxedo Club, Tuxedo Park

NEW YORK STATE
Snow Ball, Buffalo
Mid-Hudson Cotillion, Poughkeepsie
Symphony Ball, Genesee Valley Club, Rochester

NORTH CAROLINA
Charlotte Debutante Club Ball, Charlotte Country Club, Charlotte
Durham Cotillion and Christmas Ball, Durham
Greensboro Debutante Ball, Greensboro
North Carolina Debutante Ball, Memorial Auditorium, Raleigh
Winston-Salem Debutante Ball, Winston-Salem

OHIO

Cotillion of the Charity Ball, Akron
Assembly Ball, Union Club, Cleveland
Bachelors Cotillion, Sinton Hotel, Cincinnati

OKLAHOMA

Bachelors Ball, Oklahoma City
Beaux Arts Ball, Oklahoma City

PENNSYLVANIA

Lancaster Assembly, Lancaster
June Ball, Bellevue-Stratford Hotel, Philadelphia
Philadelphia Assembly, Bellevue-Stratford Hotel, Philadelphia
Cinderella Debutante Ball, William Penn Hotel, Pittsburgh
June Ball, York

RHODE ISLAND

Debutante Assembly Ball, Providence

SOUTH CAROLINA

St. Cecilia Ball, Hibernian Hall, Charleston
Assembly Ball, Greenville
Debutante Club Ball, Poinsett Hotel, Greenville

TENNESSEE

Cotton Ball, Chattanooga

TEXAS

Bachelors Cotillion, Austin
Order of de Pineda Presentation Ball, Corpus Christi Country Club, Corpus
    Christi
Idlewild Ball, Baker Hotel, Dallas
Terpsichorean Ball, Baker Hotel, Dallas
Assembly Ball, Ridglea Country Club, Fort Worth
Steeplechase Ball, Ridglea Country Club, Fort Worth
Allegro Ball, Houston
Bolero Club Ball, River Oaks Country Club, Houston
Colonial Ball, Laredo
San Antonio German Club Ball, Menger Hotel, San Antonio

VIRGINIA

Southside Virginia Debutante Ball, Danville Auditorium, Danville
Christmas Cotillion of the Hampton Roads German Club, Hampton
Debutante German Ball, Lynchburg
Norfolk German Club Ball, Monticello Hotel, Norfolk
June Debutante Ball, Country Club of Virginia, Richmond
Richmond Christmas German, Commonwealth Club, Richmond
Roanoke Assembly, Roanoke

WASHINGTON
Christmas Ball, Olympic Hotel, Seattle
Spokane Club White Cotillion, Spokane

WEST VIRGINIA
Debutante Presentation Ball, Pritchard Hotel, Huntington

WISCONSIN
Service Club Charity Ball, Milwaukee Auditorium, Milwaukee

Association of the Junior Leagues of America, Inc.

There are Leagues in the following cities:

ALABAMA
Birmingham
Montgomery
Mobile

ARIZONA
Phoenix
Tucson

ARKANSAS
Fort Smith
Little Rock
Texarkana

CALIFORNIA
Fresno
Long Beach
Los Angeles
Oakland
Pasadena
Sacramento
San Diego
San Francisco
Santa Barbara

COLORADO
Colorado Springs
Denver

CONNECTICUT
Bridgeport
Greenwich
Hartford
New Britain
New Haven
Stamford
Waterbury

DELAWARE
Wilmington

DISTRICT OF COLUMBIA
Washington

FLORIDA
Fort Lauderdale
Jacksonville
Miami
Orlando
St. Petersburg
Tallahassee
Tampa

GEORGIA
Atlanta
Augusta
Columbus
Macon
Savannah

HAWAII
Honolulu

IDAHO
Boise

ILLINOIS
Chicago
Evanston
Peoria
Rockford
Springfield

INDIANA
Fort Wayne
Indianapolis
South Bend

IOWA
Cedar Rapids
Des Moines
Sioux City

KANSAS
Kansas City
Topeka
Wichita

KENTUCKY
Lexington
Louisville

LOUISIANA
Baton Rouge
New Orleans
Shreveport

MAINE
Bangor
Portland

MARYLAND
Baltimore

MASSACHUSETTS
Boston
Fall River
Holyoke
Pittsfield
Springfield
Worcester

MICHIGAN
Battle Creek
Birmingham
Detroit
Flint

Grand Rapids
Lansing
Saginaw

MINNESOTA
Duluth
Minneapolis
St. Paul

MISSISSIPPI
Jackson

MISSOURI
Kansas City
St. Joseph
St. Louis

MONTANA
Butte
Great Falls

NEBRASKA
Lincoln
Omaha

NEW JERSEY
Elizabeth
Englewood
Montclair
Morristown
Newark
Oranges—
   Short Hills
Plainfield
Trenton

NEW MEXICO
Albuquerque

NEW YORK
Albany

Binghamton
Bronxville
Brooklyn
Buffalo
Elmira
Kingston
Larchmont
Mount Kisco
Newburgh
New York City
Pelham
Poughkeepsie
Rochester
Scarsdale
Schenectady
Syracuse
Tarrytown
Troy
Utica

NORTH CAROLINA
Asheville
Charlotte
Durham
Greensboro
High Point
Raleigh
Wilmington
Winston-Salem

OHIO
Akron
Canton

Cincinnati
Cleveland
Columbus
Dayton
Toledo
Youngstown

OKLAHOMA
Oklahoma City
Tulsa

OREGON
Portland

PENNSYLVANIA
Bethlehem
Erie
Harrisburg
Lancaster
Philadelphia
Pittsburgh
Reading
Scranton
Wilkes-Barre
Williamsport

RHODE ISLAND
Providence

SOUTH CAROLINA
Charleston
Columbia
Greenville
Spartanburg

TENNESSEE
Chattanooga
Kingsport
Knoxville
Memphis
Nashville

TEXAS
Abilene
Amarillo
Austin
Beaumont
Corpus Christi
Dallas
El Paso
Fort Worth
Galveston
Houston
Lubbock
San Angelo
San Antonio
Tyler
Waco

UTAH
Ogden
Salt Lake City

VIRGINIA
Hampton Roads
Lynchburg
Norfolk
Richmond
Roanoke

WASHINGTON
Seattle
Spokane
Tacoma

WEST VIRGINIA
Charleston
Fairmont
Huntington
Parkersburg
Wheeling

WISCONSIN
Milwaukee
Racine

CANADA
Alberta
Calgary
Edmonton

BRITISH COLUMBIA
Vancouver

MANITOBA
Winnipeg

NOVA SCOTIA
Halifax

ONTARIO
Hamilton
Toronto

QUEBEC
Montreal

MEXICO
Mexico City